PANZERGRENADIER
ACES

The Stackpole Military History Series

**THE AMERICAN
CIVIL WAR**
Cavalry Raids of the Civil War
Ghost, Thunderbolt, and
　Wizard
Pickett's Charge
Witness to Gettysburg

WORLD WAR I
Doughboy War

WORLD WAR II
After D-Day
Armor Battles of the
　Waffen-SS, 1943–45
Armoured Guardsmen
Army of the West
Australian Commandos
The B-24 in China
Backwater War
The Battle of Sicily
Battle of the Bulge, Vol. 1
Battle of the Bulge, Vol. 2
Beyond the Beachhead
Beyond Stalingrad
Blitzkrieg Unleashed
Blossoming Silk against
　the Rising Sun
Bodenplatte
The Brandenburger
　Commandos
The Brigade
Bringing the Thunder
The Canadian Army and the
　Normandy Campaign
Coast Watching in
　World War II
Colossal Cracks
Condor
A Dangerous Assignment
D-Day Bombers
D-Day Deception
D-Day to Berlin
Destination Normandy
Dive Bomber!
A Drop Too Many
Eagles of the Third Reich
The Early Battles of
　Eighth Army
Eastern Front Combat
Exit Rommel
Fist from the Sky
Flying American Combat
　Aircraft of World War II

For Europe
Forging the Thunderbolt
For the Homeland
Fortress France
The German Defeat in the East,
　1944–45
German Order of Battle, Vol. 1
German Order of Battle, Vol. 2
German Order of Battle, Vol. 3
The Germans in Normandy
Germany's Panzer Arm in
　World War II
GI Ingenuity
Goodwood
The Great Ships
Grenadiers
Hitler's Nemesis
Infantry Aces
In the Fire of the Eastern Front
Iron Arm
Iron Knights
Kampfgruppe Peiper at the
　Battle of the Bulge
The Key to the Bulge
Knight's Cross Panzers
Kursk
Luftwaffe Aces
Luftwaffe Fighter Ace
Luftwaffe Fighter-Bombers
　over Britain
Massacre at Tobruk
Mechanized Juggernaut or
　Military Anachronism?
Messerschmitts over Sicily
Michael Wittmann, Vol. 1
Michael Wittmann, Vol. 2
Mountain Warriors
The Nazi Rocketeers
No Holding Back
On the Canal
Operation Mercury
Packs On!
Panzer Aces
Panzer Aces II
Panzer Aces III
Panzer Commanders of the
　Western Front
Panzergrenadier Aces
Panzer Gunner
The Panzer Legions
Panzers in Normandy
Panzers in Winter
The Path to Blitzkrieg
Penalty Strike

Red Road from Stalingrad
Red Star under the Baltic
Retreat to the Reich
Rommel's Desert Commanders
Rommel's Desert War
Rommel's Lieutenants
The Savage Sky
Ship-Busters
The Siegfried Line
A Soldier in the Cockpit
Soviet Blitzkrieg
Stalin's Keys to Victory
Surviving Bataan and Beyond
T-34 in Action
Tank Tactics
Tigers in the Mud
Triumphant Fox
The 12th SS, Vol. 1
The 12th SS, Vol. 2
Twilight of the Gods
Typhoon Attack
The War against Rommel's
　Supply Lines
War in the Aegean
Wolfpack Warriors
Zhukov at the Oder

**THE COLD WAR /
VIETNAM**
Cyclops in the Jungle
Expendable Warriors
Flying American Combat
　Aircraft: The Cold War
Here There Are Tigers
Land with No Sun
MiGs over North Vietnam
Phantom Reflections
Street without Joy
Through the Valley

**WARS OF AFRICA AND
THE MIDDLE EAST**
Never-Ending Conflict
The Rhodesian War

**GENERAL MILITARY
HISTORY**
Carriers in Combat
Cavalry from Hoof to Track
Desert Battles
Guerrilla Warfare
Ranger Dawn
Sieges

PANZERGRENADIER ACES

German Mechanized Infantrymen in World War II

Franz Kurowski

STACKPOLE
BOOKS

Published by
STACKPOLE BOOKS
5067 Ritter Road
Mechanicsburg, PA 17055
www.stackpolebooks.com

Cover design by Tracy Patterson

Printed in the United States of America

10 9 8 7 6 5 4 3 2 I

Library of Congress Cataloging-in-Publication Data

Kurowski, Franz.
  [Grenadiere, Generale, Kameraden. English]
  Panzergrenadier aces : German mechanized infantrymen in World War II / Franz Kurowski.
      p. cm. — (Stackpole military history series)
  Translation of Grenadiere, Generale, Kameraden.
  Includes bibliographical references and index.
  ISBN 978-0-8117-0656-8
  1. Germany. Heer—Armored troops—History—20th century. 2. Germany. Heer—Armored troops—Biography. 3. World War, 1939–1945—Tank warfare. 4. World War, 1939–1945—Biography. 5. World War, 1939–1945—Campaigns. I. Title.
  D757.54.K813 2010
  940.54'13430922—dc22
                            2010006939

Contents

Foreword

My heartfelt greetings to all comrades who have taken this book into their hands. I am glad to see the by-name mention of so many friends and comrades.

In gratitude I look back on all of the grenadiers, *Panzergrenadiere* and fusiliers, however, who are not mentioned in this book and whose selfless sense of duty was responsible for enabling the acts of bravery of those named. It is an honor for me to have been a member of this branch of service.

Horst Niemack[1]

---

1. Translator's Note: *Generalmajor* Horst Niemack was one of the most highly decorated infantry officers of the German Army of World War II, receiving the Swords to the Knight's Cross of the Iron Cross on 4 June 1944. While chiefly famous for his service in the elite *Panzergrenadier-Division "Großdeutschland,"* he went on to command the equally elite *Panzer-Lehr-Division* for the last few months of the war before being severely wounded and evacuated from the front in April 1945. After the war, he went on to serve in the German Army again and rose to the rank of brigadier general. Horst Niemack died on 7 April 1992.

Introduction

Panzergrenadiere

THE DEVELOPMENT OF A NEW WAY OF INFANTRY FIGHTING
The front had stalemated during the last half of the First World War.
Although Germany's opponents attempted to force a war of movement
again—using many new weapons in the process—they did so without
success. Although they had been able to penetrate and even roll up
German lines with the weapon that was regarded as a sensation at the
time—the tank—they never enjoyed a large-scale operational success
because they failed to develop a force of escort infantry that was able
to accompany the tanks in combat.

Horse cavalry formations were able to keep pace with the tanks
and even pass them, as they did at Cambrai, but their operational
employment opportunities were limited in the age of modern defensive
weaponry, such as machine guns.

Based on those facts, the general staffs of all countries were faced
with the requirement to motorize infantry formations. Those initial
attempts signaled the birth of what would become the *Panzergrenadiere,*
the armored infantry.[1]

The tactical and operational doctrine for the employment of the
mechanized infantry called for them to work closely with the armored
force which, combined with the employment of other motorized
elements, such as engineers, anti-armor and antiaircraft, created
a force-multiplying effect that has ever since been referred to as
"combined arms." ✠

---

1. Translator's Note: Although this aspect of the development will be covered in depth
   later on, it is important early on to emphasize that armored infantry did not neces-
   sarily mean that the forces were under armor protection. On the contrary, throughout most of the war, forces labeled as *Panzergrenadier* often only had a small portion of their forces maneuvering on the battlefield in armored personnel carriers
   (*Schützenpanzerwagen* or, abbreviated, *SPW*). Generally, the *Panzergrenadiere* rode to
   battle on trucks and then dismounted for combat operations. In discussions of *Panzergrenadiere,* the modern term for them, mechanized infantry, will be used.

1

After the First World War, Colonel J. F. C. Fuller in England developed new ground-warfare doctrine. It was based on the limited success that the tanks had had and referred to as "naval warfare on land."[2] One of the prerequisites for this revolutionary turn in battle tactics was the incorporation of infantry into the complete motorization of the ground forces.

By making the infantry equally maneuverable with the tanks—Fuller envisioned not only regiments but divisions of motorized forces—armored forces would be capable of making deep penetrations into the enemy's front and the breakthroughs would enable an advance all the way to the divisional, corps and field-army headquarters of the opposing forces.

The tanks, which would form the iron fist, would be escorted in that exploitation by forces representing the other combat arms, especially the infantry and the artillery.

Sir Basil Liddell Hart, the famous military theoretician, expanded on those basic ideas a bit later. In his writing, he referred to the "Mongol flood" of Genghis Khan in 1241 and summarized: "Fully motorized forces need to be capable of performing in a manner that is comparable to that of the fast Mongolian mounted forces."

The English had their first practical experience with this new form of warfare in Iraq in 1923, when General Lindsey crushed a revolt against the English with tanks and motorized escort forces. From that fighting, the British drew the conclusion that rapidly moving armor had to be accompanied by equally rapidly acting infantry.

In England, an armored demonstration formation was created that was presented to the British General Staff in 1927. The demonstration formation was tasked with testing the lessons learned from Iraq.

The experimental formation had a machine-gun battalion as part of it. It was employed on cross-country-capable half-tracked vehicles. The machine-gun battalion may be considered the "godfather" of the British mechanized infantry forces, even if the half-tracked vehicles had no armor on them.

Similar trials were also conducted in the USA, even though the British did away with the experimental armored force in 1928, since

---

2. Translator's Note: All quotations from other languages are reverse-translated in the book, meaning that they are translated directly from the German and may not correspond literally with the passage in its original language for obvious reasons.

it appeared to be too costly to introduce and the British General Staff was still not convinced of the future of armored forces, a shortsightedness that afflicted a number of countries, to include some of the leading lights of the German armed forces at the time. Providing the theoretical construct, to a large extent, was the French concept of armored employment, which soon dominated in almost all of the armies of the world. According to the French experts of the time, the tanks were to be used primarily to support the foot infantry. That doctrine, of course, seriously underestimated the capabilities of armored forces, with similarly serious consequences for many armies, especially the French. The French doctrine, of course, was borne of experiences from the First World War. Unfortunately, the lessons learned by them and the British were the wrong ones.

After the First World War, the German 100,000-man army was prohibited from any sort of motorization. Despite that, the idea of making the infantry more mobile was not abandoned, at least theoretically. Above all, it was Heinz Guderian, young general staff officer, who wrote about theories of maneuver warfare, those of other countries and his own. The core of his doctrine centered around the necessity of having all of the branches supporting the tanks to possess the same maneuverability and speed as the tanks themselves. In addition, he demanded armored protection for the infantry.

Guderian's ideas paved new pathways in the development of armor doctrine, pathways that would be of decisive importance in the later development of mechanized infantry.

But it was not until 1931, when Guderian was the chief of staff of the Inspectorate for Motorized Forces, that the future mechanized infantry came into being, initially purely on a theoretical level. The new motorized forces were considered to be a part of "combined arms" from the very beginning. The motorized forces not only had tanks, they also had *Schützen* or motorized riflemen. The motorized riflemen were to form the basis for the future mechanized infantry.

Motorcycle infantry, or *Kradschützen*, also formed an element of the developing force. Providing reconnaissance capabilities were motorized reconnaissance battalions, whose organizing principles were based around the requirements of combined-arms armored warfare.[3]

Organized as such, the armored divisions were to be employed within the framework of a corps, where they would force a breakthrough as the result of their massed combat power. Once they penetrated the enemy's front, they would advance deep into his rear area and contribute decisively to the elimination of enemy through his operational envelopment and eventually encirclement.

After the initial trials at Munster, three armored divisions were established: the *1. Panzer-Division,* the *2. Panzer-Division* and the *3. Panzer-Division.* Above and beyond the armored fighting vehicles— which were still generally too lightly armed and armored for the demands of modern maneuver warfare—there were no cross-country or armored vehicles at the time that the motorized riflemen could have used.

The formation within the first few armored divisions formed that had the infantry element was the *Schützen-Brigade,* which generally had a *Schützen-Regiment* and a *Kradschützen-Bataillon.* Later on, the motorcycle infantry were seen as division troop elements and the brigade received an additional *Schützen-Regiment.*

The motorized riflemen were transported on four- and six-wheeled vehicles that were capable of carrying half a squad of infantry. The motorcycle infantry had motorcycles with sidecars.

In addition to the three armored divisions, three light divisions (*leichte Divisionen*) were formed, as well as four motorized infantry divisions (*Infanterie-Divisionen [mot]*). While the respective infantry components of those divisions bore differing designations, they all shared the hallmarks of motorized infantry.

Initially, the demand of the armored forces that the infantry be able to accompany the tanks into battle while mounted could not be

---

3. Translator's Note: Of course, all of the divisions had reconnaissance battalions. In addition, the cavalry also developed its own guidelines for motorized reconnaissance, in addition to horse-mounted reconnaissance. Later on, all of the motorized reconnaissance elements came under the doctrinal oversight of the Inspectorate for Armored Forces.

met. There were two reasons for that. On the one hand, it was not possible to start manufacturing armored personnel carriers to any large extent prior to the start of the war (especially since armored vehicles—tanks—assumed priority). Also playing a role was the fact that Guderian had become a formation commander—he started the war as a commanding general—and could no longer wield direct influence on the development of the armored force.

✠

What were the desired physical requirements for the vehicles that would transport the motorized riflemen?

Cross-country maneuverability was seen as a great advantage. Half-tracked vehicles seemed to be the answer, since they offered practically the same mobility as fully tracked vehicles while generally being easier and cheaper to manufacture, especially since there were already prototypes available that were used as prime movers for motorized artillery and antitank guns. The two prime movers weighed one and three tons. The three-ton version formed the basis for a medium armored personnel carrier—what would become the *Sd.Kfz. 251*[4] family of vehicles—and the one-ton prime mover became the *Sd.Kfz. 250*, a light armored personnel carrier. Both were given a light armored superstructure that was open at the top but which provided limited armored protection against shrapnel and small-arms fires from the sides.

Production never kept up with demand, and the vehicles were generally limited to one battalion of the mechanized infantry regiments, with the light *SPW's* also being used for the reconnaissance battalion as well.

✠

It was during the campaign in Poland that the worth of the armored and motorized formations was clearly proven. It should be mentioned, however, that almost all of the riflemen underwent their baptisms of

---

4. Translator's Note: *Sonderkraftfahrzeug* or special-purpose vehicle.

fire dismounted. It was only one company of *Schützen-Regiment 1* of the *1. Panzer-Division* that actually conducted mounted operations in *SPW's*.

With regard to the continued development of the "motorized riflemen" into "mechanized infantry," the campaign in Poland saw a number of important changes in its wake. The *leichte Divisionen* were reorganized and redesignated as *Panzer-Divisionen*. They had been seen as too weak and not up to the demands placed on them, even against the largely non-motorized Polish forces. The single tank battalion was expanded into a regiment with two tank battalions. They generally kept their complement of infantry, however, with the result that their regiments were stronger than those of the original armored divisions.

During the winter of 1939/1940, all of the lessons learned were consolidated and evaluated. Training continued to emphasize "combined arms." *SPW's* were modified to carry mortars and also to fire them while still mounted in the vehicle. The firepower of the rifle companies had proven to be too weak, with the result that the number of machine guns was doubled in each company. As a result of those changes, a motorized rifle company generally had 18 light machine guns, 2 heavy machine guns and 3 medium mortars. Each *Schützen-Brigade* also received a self-propelled infantry gun company whose vehicles mounted 15-centimeter infantry guns. In some cases, *SPW's* were also outfitted with 3.7-centimeter antitank guns, in addition to a variety of other weapons systems.

These changes in firepower manifested themselves to good advantage during the campaign in the West. The tanks grew to rely on rapid assistance from motorized infantry elements, since they were often at a disadvantage without them. It was thanks to motorized rifle support that the breakthroughs in the Ardennes, the crossing of the Meuse and the forcing of the enemy defenses along the Sedan were successful. Once the motorized rifle forces screened the long flanks of the divisions, the tanks were able to rapidly advance into the enemy's rear areas.

Despite the many improvements, most of the motorized infantry forces still fought their engagements dismounted. They rode to battle, but had to continue the fight on the ground once there. That meant they were oftentimes unable to maintain the offensive tempo of the tanks. Worse, once they got to the point of penetration, they frequently had to break renewed enemy resistance that flared up after the tanks had passed. On the other hand, if the tanks slowed down, then they usually lost their primary advantages—speed and the element of surprise.

As a consequence, the senior command determined from the lessons learned in the West that the losses among the motorized infantry had been too high as a consequence of a lack of mechanization. And, furthermore, the coordination with the tanks, despite continuing efforts, had still been too inadequate. Training needed continued emphasis and the number of armored vehicles needed to be increased, which was no mean task when the industrial base still did not produce enough armored vehicles and the economy was still not on a "total war" footing.

The continued division of effort in the management of the motorized infantry forces—the infantry school at Döberitz, the cavalry school at Krampnitz and the armor school at Wünsdorf—had also proven disadvantageous. Consequently, the responsibility for the training, equipping and organization of the motorized riflemen eventually became a responsibility of the armored forces.

In the end, the German Army High Command also decided to increase the number of armored formations. Once again, there were a number of organizational changes, which frequently led to a diminution of the existing armored and motorized division firepower and strength, since the new divisions could not be assembled out of "thin air." The number of tanks in the tank divisions was generally reduced by half. To make up for that deficit, however, most of the armored divisions received a second motorized rifle regiment, since only one was identified as not being enough.

During the initial months of Operation "Barbarossa," as the first year of fighting in the Soviet Union was called, it was the momentum of the armored forces that helped bring about the astonishing successes of the German armed forces.

Once again, valuable lessons were learned for the conduct of mounted infantry operations. The *SPW's* were up-gunned with the addition of machine guns, often front and rear, and additional ones were outfitted with armor-defeating weapons, such as the 3.7-centimeter antitank guns, which, in themselves, were upgraded through the remainder of the war to larger and larger calibers. With the increasing numbers of *SPW's*, it was possible for the mechanized infantry to keep pace and communicate much better with the tanks. Standing *Kampfgruppen*—battle groups—were often formed consisting of the division's tank regiment and the *SPW*-equipped battalion of the infantry regiment. As enemy resistance increased and the employment of hand-held and effective anti-armor weaponry became more prevalent, the mechanized riflemen became increasingly indispensible.

However, whenever the terrain became difficult or there were tremendous downpours, the half-tracked vehicles of the mechanized infantry also had their problems. That said, they were in no way comparable to the difficulties encountered in similar situations by the motorcycles and trucks. The "mud period" of Russia even proved difficult to fully tracked vehicles, such as tanks, and oftentimes all vehicular movement came to a standstill.

During the winter of 1941/1942, many of the crews of the tanks and the mechanized infantry also had to dismount from their vehicles when German logistics could not keep pace with the operational tempo. Most commanders attempted to shield those forces—especially highly trained tank crews—from ground employment, but it frequently could not be avoided. Those vehicles that remained operational were often held back by the division as a ready reserve against the winter-hardened and equipped Soviet forces.

Until the spring of 1942, mechanized operations practically ceased to exist. In anticipation of the summer offensive of 1942, vehicles, parts and equipment started to filter back to the divisions, with the result that the armored divisions were all able to report at least one complete mechanized battalion that year. On 5 July 1942, the numerous designations that were often used for the motorized and mechanized infantry forces were eliminated when orders required all of the formations to be designated as *Panzergrenadier*. Of course, the redesignation did nothing to change the actual composition of the formations except in instances were force-structure changes had already been programmed. Among the other changes was the introduction of a "unified" branch color—meadow green or *wiesengrün*—for the mechanized infantry forces of the armored divisions but, in actual fact, the regiments continued to use an often bewildering array of branch colors until the end of the war, including white (*weiß*), golden yellow (*goldgelb*) and pink (*rosa*).

Fighting with the tanks, the mechanized infantry were able to achieve great success during the summer offensive of 1942. They worked hand-in-glove with the tanks and were a great help in fending off enemy tank hunter/killer teams. Because they were not "buttoned up" in combat operations, they also had greater opportunity to observe—albeit in a very dangerous way—and engage enemy antitank guns or identify them to their larger armored brothers-in-arms. Whenever infantry pockets of resistance were encountered, they were an effective foil, since the tanks were often defenseless against well-camouflaged and well-positioned infantrymen.

Because of their constant employment at the hot spots of the battlefield, it should not be considered unusual that many enlisted *Panzergrenadiere* received high awards for bravery and small-unit tactical decision making that was successful to the outcome of an engagement.

Despite the successes of the armored forces, there were still many deficiencies and shortfalls. For the mechanized infantry, the armor of the *SPW* proved too weak against the increasingly lethal countermeasures of the enemy. There were still not enough *SPW's* to meet even the self-imposed organizational limits. Of course, the loss of an *SPW* on the battlefield also meant the loss of a squad of infantry, if only temporarily. Since the "ground" strength of the mechanized infantry was always considerably less than that of a conventional infantry battalion, losses of personnel within mechanized infantry battalions were proportionately worse.

The only immediate answer to such concerns on the battlefield was to place continued emphasis on cooperation and coordination between the tanks and the *SPW's*. In addition to eliminating enemy armored vehicles, the tanks also had to eliminate pockets of resistance that were heavily armed or improved. For their part, the mechanized infantry had to protect their comrades from enemy hunter/killer teams, especially in built-up areas or wooded terrain. Although not doctrinally intended to do so, the mechanized infantry could also be employed in removing obstacles and clearing minefields, especially when engineer forces were not on hand or were insufficient.

At this point in the war, the mechanized infantry began to fight more and more from its motorized "mounts." The *SPW*, in and of itself, became a sort of weapon and, in conjunction with fast and flexible decision making, success was often at hand. The mechanized infantry tended not to dismount, unless the conditions required it and it was no longer possible to go around the enemy. The armored force had found a complementary weapon of decisive importance and the tankers considered the *Panzergrenadiere* to be equal brothers-in-arms.

In order to increase the firepower of the mechanized infantry, those formations started to be issued the *MG 42* in 1942. The machine gun, whose sustained rate of fire was 1,500 rounds a minute, was often referred to as a "bone saw" among the lower ranks, the *Landser*. Thanks to its high rate of fire and reliability, the newly introduced machine guns were well received by the forces in the field and helped beef up thin German lines and pockets of resistance with incomparable firepower.

Employment fundamentals continued to be refined:

> Prerequisite for the command and control of mechanized infantry was an expansive, anticipatory thinking, ability to make rapid decisions and the capability of transforming the decision into brief radio traffic. Additional means of communication were directional signals by means of tracer or pyrotechnics, hand-and-arm and flag signals, and personal conversation, as often as possible, between commanders and subordinate leaders before and during the engagement. It was the birth of combat communications.[5]

With the increasing heavy armament of the *Panzergrenadiere*—heavier and more antitank and infantry weaponry were added to the tables of organization and equipment—the battalions were able to take on more and more missions, including combat reconnaissance, screen broad sectors, execute separate attacks against the enemy's flanks and rear, perform flank guard and other security missions and function as advance guards. Not that the battalions and regiments had not been

---

5. Author's Note: See Oskar Munzel, *Gepanzerte Truppen*. Hereafter referred to as Munzel.

tasked with such requirements before, it was just that with increasing firepower they were in a better position to successfully execute them.

In the winter of 1942/1943, the mechanized infantry were often forced to fight dismounted again, as the front stalemated and positional warfare set in.

☨

In the spring of 1943, changes occurred that furthered the status of the development and organization of the *Panzergrenadiere. Generaloberst* Heinz Guderian had become the inspector general of the *Panzertruppe* after his forced "retirement" in December 1941 for refusing to follow the *Führer's* orders to the letter outside of Moscow. His stated objective was to increase the combat power of the armored and mechanized infantry divisions while, at the same time, sparing materiel and personnel. Based on the most recent after-action reports and lessons learned form the front, he started to reorganize the *Panzergrenadier* regiments. All of the subordinate elements of the regiments increased their firepower. Based on the restructuring, the mechanized infantry companies (*SPW*) had the following firepower:

- 30 light machine guns, with three each on each squad vehicle (mounted on the front of the fighting compartment on a swing arm).
- 4 heavy machine guns on two *SPW's*, which were consolidated into a heavy machine-gun section.
- 2 medium 8.1-centimeter mortars, also consolidated into a mortar section.
- 3 3.7-centimeter antitank guns, distributed among the three platoon leader vehicles.
- 2 short-barrel 7.5-centimer cannon, consolidated into a cannon section.

In addition, at the regimental level, there was also a platoon of flamethrower vehicles, which had a devastating effect out to 60 meters. All of the weapons in the *SPW* companies were capable of being fired from the vehicle. That decisively increased engagement speeds. All of the weapons were also capable of being dismounted, as well.

In addition, energetic efforts were made to expedite and increase the production of *SPW's*. *SPW's* were being increasingly used by all of the branches of the services, with more than 20 versions ultimately being produced for the artillery, the engineers, air defense, medics and signals.

Effective 1 April 1943, the entire mechanized force also underwent a redesignation, from *schnelle Truppen* (Fast Forces) to *Panzertruppen* (Armored Forces). At that point, all of the *Panzergrenadier* elements belonged to the *Panzertruppe*.

Just as pressing to the inspector general, however, was training that incorporated the latest lessons learned on the battlefield. Manuals, circulars, training aids and other training materials were rewritten, overhauled or newly written from scratch, including many intended directly for the soldier in the field that made use of comic-book style illustrations and doggerel to drive home the main teaching points.

In addition to the basic training for all of the soldiers, schools were established for company, battalion and regimental command that concentrated on the doctrine and tactics of the *Panzergrenadiere*. The officers were familiarized with the equipment, in addition to receiving theoretical instruction. Eventually, the home of cavalry at Krampnitz also saw the addition of a *Panzergrenadier* schoolhouse.

While all of this was going on, the German fortunes of war continued to take a turn for the worse. After the catastrophe of Stalingrad, the Germans had to concede an operational defeat at Kursk in July 1943. The enemy had not been idle in the meantime, and his tactics, doctrine, organization and equipment had also been improved. In the end, the enemy defenses proved to be too well prepared for any assault, despite the massive employment of much of the *Panzertruppe* in the epic battle. Despite the efforts to improve the striking power of the *Panzertruppe*, most of the *Panzergrenadier* still continued to arrive on the battlefield on trucks. The *SPW*-mounted soldiers were still few and far between.

Offensive warfare, except in the cases of narrowly defined local attacks and the increasingly rare operational-level attack, was becoming a thing of the past. The tanks and the mechanized infantry were being increasingly used as mobile reserves in the defense and as "fire brigades" for sealing off penetrations and straightening out threatened sectors of the front.

In the West, the virtual Allied air supremacy forced the Germans to generally move only at night in formation and then to only commit forces on the ground in piecemeal fashion or when weather conditions prohibited Allied aerial activity. In some cases, carpet-bombing attacks were conducted against German armored formations, the most famous of which was against the *Panzer-Lehr-Division*, the only formation in the German armed forces where both of its *Panzergrenadier* regiments were completely equipped with *SPW's*. The 1,000-bomber raid virtually eliminated the division as an effective fighting force for the rest of the Normandy campaign.

When the Soviets launched their summer offensive of 1944—Operation "Bagration"—an entire army group was rendered combat ineffective. While the losses in men, materiel and terrain were enormous, they might have been much greater had it not been for the employment of the few armored formations available to slow down and eventually stop the Soviet juggernaut. Those successes did not come without a price, however, and most of the armored forces employed in that sector of the front were bled white, frequently requiring reconstitution.

The last great operational offensive of the German forces in the West occurred in the Ardennes offensive, the so-called "Battle of the Bulge," in December 1944 and January 1945. Once again, large numbers of armored forces—both Army and *SS*—were concentrated and employed *en masse*. Despite the advantage of surprise and initially overcast weather conditions that prevented the Allied air forces from operating, the forces were employed totally unsuited for the massed employment of armor. Consequently, the only chance for success was a sudden blow that managed to break through to the open terrain to the west within a day or two. The Germans never managed to achieve that and the fighting turned into a small-unit slugfest that further decimated forces the Germans could ill afford to spare.

A similar fate befell the German forces in the East, when operations were conducted in the spring of 1945 to free encircled Budapest and maintain the strategically important access to Hungarian oil.

Tactical and operational doctrine continued to be refined, and a number of changes were introduced and contemplated towards the end of the war, including the organization of mixed battle groups—*Kampfgruppen*—on a permanent basis. None of this helped in the end phase of the war, though, and despite increased production of weapons, vehicles and equipment, the Germans frequently had difficulty keeping just the combat vehicles moving due to fuel shortages.

Perhaps even more disadvantageous was the loss of irreplaceable officers and noncommissioned officers after the many years of war. At the time, the official lifespan of commanders and leaders was calculated as follows:

Battalion commander – 30 days
Company commander – 21 days
Platoon leaders – 7 days

Despite the high losses—or, perhaps, partly because of them—the number of decorations for bravery were overrepresented among the mechanized infantry forces. Out of the 169 Oak Leaves to the Knight's Cross of the Iron Cross that were awarded in 1945, 94 went to *Panzergrenadiere* and *Grenadiere.*

We shall allow retired *Generalmajor* Oskar Munzel to have the last word in this summary introduction:

> Looking back, one can say that the members of the newly created mechanized infantry force, which had developed a type of fighting that was heretofore unknown in foreign armies and had employed it successfully, may look back with justifiable pride on their accomplishments.
>
> Their success was closely connected to that of the *Panzerwaffe,* and they had wrested a separate and honorable place for themselves among the armored forces of the German military of that time.[6]

---

6. Author's Note: Munzel.

A good view of an *Sd.Kfz. 251 Ausf. C* armored half-track with a full complement of *Panzergrenadiere*. The two *MG 34s* generated considerable covering firepower in infantry engagements.

An *Sd.Kfz. 250/1* light armored personnel carrier. Used primarily as a reconnaissance vehicle with *Panzer* and *Panzergrenadier* divisions. Also occasionally used as a command vehicle.

An *Sd.Kfz. 251/9* mounting a 7.5-cm L/24 and used as a support vehicle for an armored infantry company. This vehicle was quite effective in its intended role. The unofficial name for this vehicle was *Stummel* (stump).

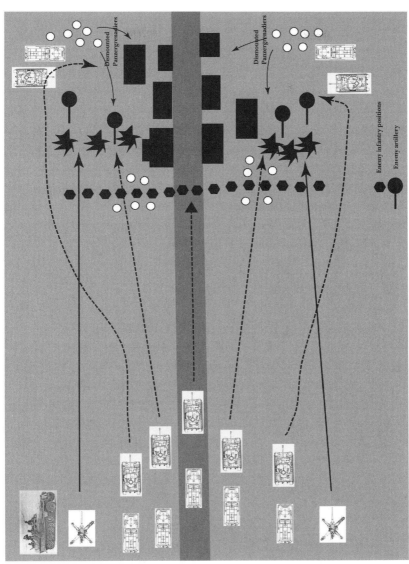

Dismounted
Panzergrenadiers

Dismounted
Panzergrenadiers

Enemy infantry positions

Enemy artillery

1. Artillery and tank gun fire supresses enemy artillery. 2. Tanks and armored personnal carriers (APCs) attack both frontally and from the flanks. 3. Dismounted *Panzergrenadiers*, covered by tanks, attack enemy infantry and artillery positions from the flanks and rear while also protecting the tanks from tank hunter teams.

Helmut Beukemann

CHAPTER 1

Generalleutnant
Helmuth Beukemann

FRONTLINE SOLDIER AND COMMANDER
IN TWO WORLD WARS

Helmuth Beukemann was born in Hamburg on 9 May 1894, the son of the director of the local bureau of statistics. He attended college-preparatory courses at the *Wilhelms-Gymnasium*, receiving his diploma there. In the spring of 1914, he entered *Infanterie-Regiment 165* in Quedlingburg as a *Fahnenjunker*, an officer candidate.

Assigned to the *Ludendorff-Brigade*, he participated in the *coup de main* on Lüttich (Liége), receiving the Iron Cross, 2nd Class. In October 1914, he received his commission as a *Leutnant*, with the date of rank being made retroactive to 19 February 1913. He participated in all of the fighting of his regiment in France. On 23 May 1916, he received the Iron Cross, 1st Class, for the successful conduct of a patrol.

During the fighting of 1918, Beukemann, who had just been promoted to *Oberleutnant*, also received the Knight's Cross of the Imperial House Order of the Hohenzollerns, with Swords. By the end of the war, he was the regimental adjutant. Following the war, he was accepted into the *Reichswehr*. He was stationed in Quedlinburg for two decades. Until 1926, he was a platoon leader in the *8.(MG)/Infanterie-Regiment 12*, followed by a tour as the company commander of the 6th Company and then another company command tour in his former 8th Company (Machine Gun). He was promoted to *Hauptmann* on 1 February 1928.

After serving as a company commander for eight years, *Hauptmann* Beukemann was transferred to Munich on 1 October 1934 to serve as a tactics instructor at the military academy there. Two months later, he was promoted to *Major*. On 1 October 1937, while still serving at the academy, he was promoted to *Oberstleutnant*. On 10 November 1938,

he returned to troop service, being designated as the commander of
the *I./Infanterie-Regiment 89* (*12. Infanterie-Division*) in Schwerin.

In July of 1939, the division was transported by sea to Königsberg[1]
in East Prussia. The division took part in the campaign in Poland as
part of the *I. Armee-Korps*, which was allocated to the *1. Armee*. His
division's route led from Tannenberg across the Narew and the Bug to
the fighting east of Warsaw.

In the course of the fighting, he later earned clasps to both of
his Iron Crosses, signifying the second award of the same medals in
the Second World War. He was already demonstrating cleverness and
decisiveness in the early fighting, and he was selected for regimental
command, which he assumed over *Infanterie-Regiment 382* (*164.
Infanterie-Division*) on 13 January 1940. At the start of the war in the
West in 1940, the regiment had been stationed at the Königsbrück
Training Area, where it provided instructional and demonstration
forces for battalion command courses. During the campaign in
the West, the division was allocated to the *12. Armee* and moved to
occupation duties in Reims following the fighting. It was there that
Beukemann was promoted to *Oberst* on 1 September 1940.

Beukemann's regiment remained on occupation duty in France
until the end of the year, initially at Reims, then along the Channel
coast and, finally, in the Vosges Mountains, where it received some
mountain training. At the beginning of January 1941, the division was
moved to Romania and into the area south of Bucharest. It then went
to Giorgiu to prepare for crossing the Danube into Bulgaria.

The Germans had been moving forces into the Balkans, because
the increased massing of British forces in the Near East, on Crete and,
finally, on the Greek mainland posed a threat to the German southern
flank. Also of importance was the protection of the Rumanian oil fields,
which were so vital for Germany, and a bolstering of the Axis power of
Italy, whose misadventures in Albania and along the Greek border had
reached catastrophic proportions. Another important reason was that
preparations for the war with the Soviet Union were already underway
in the respective high commands of the German Armed Forces. The
initiation of a war there also meant that this southern area needed to
be protected. Finally, operations in that theater would help to divert

---

1. Translator's Note: German territory confiscated by the Soviet Union after the war,
   renamed Kaliningrad and transformed into a restricted military district.

British forces from North Africa, where German and Italian forces were also conducting operations.

At the beginning of March, the division crossed the Danube, a movement that was allowed by the Bulgarians. At the crossing point, the river was more than 1,000 meters wide. The crossing posed special problems to the commanders of the division, including *Oberst* Beukemann, but they were able to be mastered.

The movement over the deeply snowed-in Schipka Pass and to the Bulgarian-Greek border was also a test for the young grenadiers of the regiment. The division sector ran from south of Plovdiz (Philippopel) to the crests of the Rhodope Range which, in some cases, reached peaks of 2,000 meters. For the first time, the horse-drawn limbers of the divisional artillery had to master high mountains. In some cases, the caissons were pulled by water buffalo!

The forward-most element of the division was Beukemann's *Infanterie-Regiment 382*. Once the regiment reached its assigned sector along the border, Beukemann immediately started scouting and reconnaissance, personally participating in the patrols. The Greek frontier fortifications—the Metaxas Line—posed a seemingly impregnable barrier.

At first light on 6 April, offensive operations started. The Greek frontier outposts were overrun by the *II./Infanterie-Regiment 382* of *Oberstleutnant* Geißler. The regiment had to cross seven destroyed bridges, numerous obstacles and a gigantic cliff demolition before Geißler's advance guard reached Ehinos, some 20 kilometers distant.

At that point, the soldiers started to receive heavy fire. Beukemann, who was with the advance guard, could see the muzzle flashes from the numerous bunkers located on Hill 785.

Leutnant Dr. Mandel, the regimental liaison officer, reported counted at least 20 active bunkers. Then came an ominous report: "Bogged down in front of large road obstacle covered by the enemy!"

"Hold everyone up! Have them take cover! I want the 3rd Battalion to envelop!" Beukemann ordered. He knew that a frontal attack would have caused unnecessary casualties. He then joined the 3rd Battalion, which had been in the second march serial. He ordered *Major* Fett, the acting battalion commander, to prepare to envelop to the east.

Beukemann concluded his preparations by stating: "We will not attack until the anti-tank and anti-aircraft guns and elements of the divisional artillery have closed up."

A short while later, he went back to the 1st Battalion, which was bringing up the rear. He ordered the battalion to leave the march route. He directed it to march along the mountain paths across the range, shooting past Ehinos and then advancing on Xanthi from that area.

Beukemann, who then rejoined the main body of the regiment near Ehino, figured that the 1st Battalion would be all that was needed to take Xanthi. After it succeeded in doing that, he wanted it to proceed west towards the coastal plains and take the crossings over the Nestos at Toxote. The regiment would close up later.

Of course, the overall plan could only be realized if Beukemann's remaining two battalions succeeded in taking the cliff positions on Hill 785 and clearing a path to their objectives.

The anti-tank and anti-aircraft guns, as well as the divisional artillery, were personally briefed by Beukemann as they arrived. Assault engineers also showed up. They were attached to Beukemann's forces, and he directed them on their attack objectives.

The heavy weapons then opened up on the positions in the cliffs, which had revealed themselves through their muzzle flashes. The powerful 8.8-centimeter guns took out four bunkers. Once the enemy positions had been softened up, Beukemann's men attacked, with the regimental commander in the lead. In bitter bunker fighting, the men advanced, meter by meter. The engineers attacked and neutralized pockets of resistance. The enemy command-and-control bunkers were identified and destroyed through concentric fires. Shortly before dark, the divisional artillery took out the enemy's main defensive positions by means of several direct hits.

Half of the enemy's defensive positions had been taken and it had already turned dark when a radio message was received from the 1st Battalion: "1st has reached Xanthi; city in our hands."

Beukemann ordered an emissary to be sent to the remaining enemy fortifications. An officer volunteered. He advanced waving a white flag and was led to the Greek colonel in charge. The German officer outlined to him the hopelessness of the Greek situation and requested that the Greeks honorably surrender.

The Greek colonel had already heard that Xanthi—his higher headquarters—was in German hands, and so he accepted the German offer.

When it turned light, *Oberst* Beukemann saw the white flags of surrender being pushed out of the remaining bunker embrasures. A short while later, the soldiers exited without arms. It was not until then that Beukemann realized the extent of the mountain fortifications—a main bunker at a higher elevation and three redoubts farther forward. More than 600 Greek soldiers had set up defensively among the 70 fighting positions and individual dugouts, some of which had been blasted into the cliffs. All of the positions were interconnected through tunnels and communications trenches. Speed was of the essence and Beukemann issued his orders rapidly: "2nd Battalion moves out immediately! Advance in the direction of Stavroupolis along the Nestos. The 3rd Battalion assembles and moves along the main road to Xanthi."

Moving by motorcycle, Beukemann and Mandel headed towards the Nestos, where the 1st Battalion had bogged down. When he was unable to move any more by motorcycle, Beukemann commandeered a horse and rode the rest of the way. He reached his battalion, which was bogged down along the river, taking heavy fires from the far bank.

Beukemann discovered the enemy had already blown up all of the bridges. Furthermore, there were enemy field fortifications on the far bank that would have made any river-crossing attempt a bloodbath. Beukemann directed artillery to be brought forward as soon as possible. Once there, they started to engage the fortifications over open sites. The enemy then pulled back, apparently not willing to wait for the artillery to take out the bunkers, one by one.

By then, Saloniki had fallen and, on the morning of 10 April 1941, the Greek Army High Command for Eastern Macedonia surrendered unconditionally.

The quick surrender was partially due to the rapid advance of Beukemann's *Infanterie-Regiment 382*, which had overrun the most important enemy bastions and turned the enemy out of its defenses. For his personal example during those operations, his decisiveness in critical situations and the importance of the success of his regiment, Beukemann was awarded the Knight's Cross to the Iron Cross on 14

May 1941. But before he received the highest German wartime award, Beukemann's regiment accomplished one more major feat of arms.

After the Greek surrender on the mainland, *Infanterie-Regiment 382* was entrusted with coastal defense in the area from Alexandroupolis to Porto Lago (southeast of Xanthi). Every time that Beukemann looked out from his tent, he could see the "Mountain of the Gods" on the island of Samothraki. The view inspired him to recommend an extraordinary operation to his division commander, *Generalleutnant* Josef Folttmann: he wanted to take the island, 60 kilometers away and supposedly occupied by the enemy, in a surprise raid by a company of men. Folttmann finally approved the operation after several requests by his most successful regimental commander.

At first light on 19 April, five fishing cutters filled with men of the *2./Infanterie-Regiment 382* of *Oberleutnant* Scott and the regimental commander, headed out to sea from Porto Lago. They reached the island and landed, whereupon they were greeted by fires from Greek policemen. Once the Germans were ashore, the Greek police disappeared, and the local populace greeted the Germans enthusiastically. There was no contact with British forces on the island. Emboldened by his success there, Beukemann began inquiring about the British forces on the island of Lemnos.

Beukemann knew that the island had been important during the First World War, since it was the site of a joint British-French headquarters, and forces had been launched from there for the ill-fated Gallipoli operation. Beukemann discovered from the local fishermen that there was a lonely "smuggler's bay," where his forces could land unobserved by the British forces on the island.

The chief naval officer for the Aegean Sea provided Beukemann with a naval navigator, *Korvettenkapitän* Frijus-Plessen, and 10 motor launches. *Kampfgruppen*[2] were formed. Antitank guns and heavy machine guns were brought on board the launches in such a fashion that

---

2. Translator's Note: Battle groups. Battle groups were *ad hoc* elements formed to accomplish a specific mission. They usually consisted of a core group (infantry or armor) and were supplemented by other arms, such as reconnaissance, artillery, engineers and air defense.

they could be fired from the boats. In addition, the division provided engineer assault craft and combat engineers under *Oberleutnant* Otto. It also made arrangements for Beukemann's 2nd Battalion and a battery of divisional artillery to be loaded on a commercial ship in the harbor of Kavalla, for transportation to the island and arrival on the scheduled morning of the landing, 25 April. Once there, the battalion command was to be briefed by the regimental commander on his mission, based on the situation at the time.

The movement of the 1st Battalion to Lemnos on the launches went according to plan. *Oberst* Beukemann and his naval navigator were aboard the first boat, the *Thrakia.* Joining the *Thrakia*, which was armed with an antitank gun and three heavy machines guns, were three other launches, all of which formed the advance guard. The advance guard forces came from the 4th Company of *Hauptmann* Tribukait.

The landing force was able to get into Purnia Bay without incident. But once there, Greek outposts opened fire, all at once. Beukemann ordered the engineer assault craft to launch. The assault craft then raced through the waters of the bay towards the Greek positions. Heavy machine guns opened fire. Lances of flame shoot through the darkness from the German boats. One after the other, the Greek outposts were eliminated.

The landing craft then headed ashore, moving slowly until they bottomed out. *Oberst* Beukemann collected his men around him: "Attack Windmill Hill!"

The grenadiers started their attack from the march. The Greek company positioned on the hill attempted in vain to hold up the attack. After half an hour, the hilltop was in German hands. From there, Beukemann was able to observe the Aegean and Mudros, the island's main harbor.

"Over there, *Herr Oberst!*" Mandel pointed out to his regimental commander. They could see the Greek freighter *Delos*, which had the 2nd Battalion on board. Radio the battalion: "Cruise around the bay and await further orders."

The message was transmitted. It was obvious Beukemann did not need the extra men where he was.

Beukemann turned to *Hauptmann* Tribukait: "Take Mudros with a reinforced company." I will attack Kastron[3] with the main body of the battalion. We will initially go with you in the direction of Mudros."

The heavy infantry weapons they had brought with them supported the company attacking Mudros. After pockets of resistance had been eliminated, the town was taken around 1000 hours. A short while later, Beukemann ordered all vehicles in the town to be confiscated. He informed Tribukait to immediately send a radio message to the 2nd Battalion. It was to dock at Mudros and disembark.

A captured truck took Beukemann in the direction of Kastron. The main body of the battalion moved in the direction of the city, which was reached around 1100 hours and taken in the face of weak Greek resistance. Later on, Beukemann discovered that the British had left the island the day before. That same morning, he had a radio message transmitted to *Generalleutnant* Folttmann: "Lemnos in our hands!"

In the course of the operation, the regiment had lost only one man: *Gefreiter* Brauer, a motorcycle messenger, who was ambushed by the Greeks.

A Greek admiral, a naval captain and 314 soldiers were taken prisoner. Large quantities of weapons and ammunition were captured, as were 150 maritime vessels of all types. For the capture of Lemnos, *Oberst* Beukemann was given a certificate of appreciation from the commander in chief of the army. *Oberst* Beukemann was entrusted with the military administration of the island, and a good-natured relationship was soon developed with the island's inhabitants.

The occupation went smoothly with the exception of a single incident at sea that claimed four lives. The incident occurred on 12 May 1941. Every day, a boat travelled between the island and the mainland. On that day, it was occupied by *Oberleutnant* Schott and seven soldiers. The boat was about three kilometers out to sea when it was sunk by a torpedo from a British submarine. When the British boat surfaced, a few of the men swimming in the open sea were shot by the British crew.

That evening, *Oberst* Beukemann went out to the spot to commemorate the unfortunate men who had been killed in contravention of all of the rules of warfare. They decided to erect a

---

3. Translator's Note: Kastron is the capital of the island and is located on the west side.

memorial to the fallen, which still stands to this day and can be seen in the photo section of this book.

At the beginning of August 1941, the regiment was loaded on the *Arkadia* and shipped to Saloniki under the protection of Italian torpedo boats. Beukemann was installed as the local military commander there, and his regiment was committed against Greek partisans. The partisans had blocked the Saloniki–Sofia roads on several occasions and ambushed individual vehicles. The safety of the forces there and the local populace were soon assured.

At the beginning of 1942, the division received orders to relieve the *5. Gebirgs-Division* on Crete. The forces of the division were moved to Athens by train; on 18 January, *Infanterie-Regiment 382* continued on to Crete by ship. Forty nautical miles from the island, the ships were attacked by British submarines. The *City di Livorna*, was hit buy two torpedoes and sank within eight minutes. The regimental headquarters and its commander were on board.

Despite the short period of time, the Italian torpedo boat, the *Lupo*, whose commander had been awarded the Iron Cross, 1st Class, was able to rescue almost all of the men, who had been on board the stricken ship. Despite the danger posed by explosions, the *Lupo* ran alongside the ship, rescued soldiers and fished the shipwrecked out of the waters. At the same time, in accordance with its orders, the convoy continued steaming ahead to avoid being a target for other submarine attacks. Out of the 400 soldiers on board, only 8 were killed in that incident.

Once on Crete, the regiment was entrusted with the defense of the center section of the island. The division was redesignated for its new mission: *Festungs-Division Kreta.*[4] *Oberst* Beukemann had his headquarters in Rethymnon. The time spent on the island was fairly pleasant for *Oberst* Beukemann and his men. He visited the gravesites of the antiquities and climbed the Ida. It was a deceptive calm, however, since the *Panzer-Armee Afrika* was engaged in heavy fighting only a few hundred kilometers to the south. The war was also raging in Russia, while Beukemann and the rest of the division were saddled with rear-area duties.

A number of officers and enlisted personnel had already requested transfers to frontline units, when orders arrived on 20 June 1942

4. Translator's Note: Fortress Division "Crete."

ordering the division to make preparations for shipment to Africa. It was to be moved by air. The first *Kampfgruppe* planned for deployment was the reinforced *Infanterie-Regiment 382*. With the attachment of a battalion from *Artillerie-Regiment 200*, the divisional artillery, and *Pionier-Bataillon 220*, the divisional engineers, and a 2-centimeter *Flak* battalion, the entire force consisted of nearly 7,000 men. Based on that headcount, the transport by the *Luftwaffe* had to take place without field messes or vehicles. The mountain artillery pieces could be field disassembled and the infantry guns were forced aboard the aircraft— but none of them had their prime movers.

The movement started at the beginning of July. Thirty-five *Ju 52's* were employed on the first day of the lift. They returned that same day to Crete to make a second sortie. Once on the ground, *Oberst* Beukemann received ordered relayed from *Generalfeldmarschall* Rommel that when the soldiers had landed they were to make their way immediately to the front at El Alamein, some 600 kilometers farther to the west. He was to use all vehicles that were headed that way to transport his men. There were no dedicated assets available to move the men forward. Beukemann left a "go-getter" behind to organize things, while he made his way to the front to find Rommel.

The first vehicle, an Italian truck, got him as far as Bardia. A second one took him from there through Sollum as far as Sidi Barani. Beukemann went to the German airfield there and convinced the airfield commander to fly him to Fuka. Once there, a *Luftwaffe* officer made a staff car available to him, with which he reached Rommel's command post some 48 hours after having arrived in theater. The command post was located in the coastal region in the vicinity of Sidi el Rahman, just a few kilometers from the front.

"Good to see you, Beukemann!" Rommel said, receiving the *Kampfgruppe* commander. "I'm happy to be getting such a large group of reinforcements. We need them!"

Rommel then had Beukemann briefed on the critical situation at the front. There had been heavy fighting since the beginning of July and the enemy's deep penetrations had to be sealed off and cleared up by employment of the field army's reserves and even, on occasion, employment of the escort forces guarding the senior command post.

"Beukemann," Rommel closed, "you are to see to it that all arriving soldiers are formed into *Kampfgruppen* immediately, without regard for their former units of assignment. They are to be brought to the front immediately. You are to take over command of the sector where the Italian *Sabratha* Division is employed and where the enemy has achieved a penetration. You are to prevent a breakthrough!"

Beukemann was given a number of difficult missions right from the start, and his newly arriving forces were faced with a unique "march" to the front.

Beukemann's soldiers basically hitchhiked to the battlefield, riding on top of ammunition crates and fuel drums. Despite the gravity and difficulty of the situation, small groups of men competed to see who could arrive at the front first. It was a testament to the character and leadership of Beukemann that such things occurred.

Near the field army's command post, the soldiers were assembled as they arrived and formed into *Kampfgruppen*. Five days after the last of his forces had landed in Africa, Beukemann reported back to Rommel: "I wish to report to the *Herr Generalfeldmarschall* that all of my forces are on hand and being employed."

"Thank you, Beukemann!" Rommel replied. "That must be a unique accomplishment, and you and your men are to be complimented!"

Rommel was not far off in his assessment. There was no similar achievement in the annals of the desert war. The story was essentially lost in the wake of the dramatic events that were soon to occur at El Alamein.

Within a few days of being inserted into the front, Beukemann's forces underwent British barrage fire. While the men were awaiting the attack that was expected to follow, a German tank battalion commander appeared at Beukemann's headquarters. The battalion commander had voluntarily shown up on his own initiative: "*Herr Oberst*, we stand ready to be employed with 25 tanks behind your command post!" It was the type of comradeship that went without saying in the desert theater of war. The enemy attack was turned back.

Rommel appeared nearly every day in Beukemann's sector. It was obvious that he was trying to form an impression of his new forces. Typical of Rommel, the inspection often went out to the farthest outposts. It did not take too long before the men of the newly redesignated *Panzergrenadier-Regiment 382* recognized Rommel firsthand.

Beukemann later recalled that he never received a single written order while he was working under Rommel. Every order was personally delivered by the commander in chief. One time, when Beukemann was complaining in the field army command post that his forces still lacked adequate vehicular transportation, Rommel grabbed him by the arm and led him outside.

"Take a look over there, Beukemann!" Rommel said, pointing to the horizon in the east, where an enemy column could be seen moving in the rear area. "If you want to be motorized, then you need to look over there. You're not going to get any vehicles from me."

There were almost daily breakthrough attempts along the German-Italian lines, generally directed against the Italians. In bitterly fought immediate counterattacks, *Kampfgruppe Beukemann* helped seal off and clean out enemy penetrations on the sectors of the *Sabratha*, *Trieste* and *Trento* Divisions.

By then, the rest of the division had followed Beukemann's forces into the desert. In honor of its new mission, it was redesignated as the *164. leichte Afrika-Division*. When the division commander took ill and could no longer command, Beukemann assumed acting command of the forces. It was his first stab at division command, and it occurred in the midst of a crisis situation. Despite that, Beukemann passed his leadership baptism of fire with flying colors. During the same period, he was awarded the Italian Medal for Bravery. On more than one occasion, his men had saved an Italian division from almost certain destruction.

At the end of August, Beukemann was summoned to the field army's command post. Rommel informed him that he had been assigned to the unassigned officer manpower pool in anticipation of assuming command of a division in some hot spot along the Eastern Front. "I'm sorry to see you leave, Beukemann," Rommel said, "but this will give you a better chance to advance."

Full of mixed emotions, Beukemann took leave of the division he had served in for so long. It was especially hard for him to leave his old regiment. He departed Africa from the airfield at Tobruk, stopping at Crete, Athens and Brindisi, before landing in the homeland. He reported to the Army Personnel Office in Berlin and discovered that he had been earmarked to command the *75. Infanterie-Division,* which was involved in heavy fighting in the Woronesch area. It was a command he was to hold from 15 September 1942 until 10 July 1944.

✠

After an incident-free flight to the Eastern Front, *Oberst* Beukemann reported in to the commander in chief of the *2. Armee, Generaloberst* von Salmuth. The men knew each other from the time that Salmuth had been a battalion commander in *Infanterie-Regiment 12.*

Beukemann was informed that his new division had been involved in fighting for the industrial city of Woronesch for several days. The Germans had created a large bridgehead there as part of their summer offensive, and the Soviets were trying every means available to them to take it back, having already attacked there four times. Salmuth wanted the city taken, and he entrusted Beukemann with the task.

In order to ensure unified command, *Oberst* Beukemann was also given command over elements of the *75. Infanterie-Division,* whose commander had been summoned back to the Don to establish a blocking position along the west bank. In addition, two infantry regiments from neighboring divisions were also attached to his command. In all, Beukemann had eight infantry regiments reporting to him. In direct support of the division was also the corps artillery of the *VII. Armee-Korps.* To the right of the division was the Hungarian 2nd Army, with the Italian Alpine Corps farther to the south. South of them were Rumanian forces. To the north were forces of the *XIII. Armee-Korps.*

Beukemann quickly became acquainted with his division, especially since there were comrades there whom he knew from *Infanterie-Regiment 89* in the Polish campaign. With all the forces at his disposal, Beukemann worked out an attack plan that was approved by the corps and the field army. Beukemann's forces assaulted and took the southern part of the city, after receiving support from howling salvoes of rockets. Although still "new" as a division commander, he demonstrated that he had what it took to lead a large formation in the field. In his efforts, he was ably supported by his operations officer, *Oberstleutnant* Groll, and his logistics officer, *Major Freiherr* von Ketelhodt.

It turned quieter over the next few months, and the higher headquarters were busily planning for the evacuation of the bridgehead, which had started to become untenable. During that time, Beukemann was promoted to *Generalmajor* (1 November 1942).

In January 1943, the battle for Stalingrad reached its apex. The Soviet preparations for a general offensive along their Briansk, Woronesch and Southwest Fronts became evident. The Woronesch bridgehead started to be evacuated. Initially, depots and rear-area services were sent back.

In the second half of January, the Soviet offensive was launched. Shortly after it started, the Hungarian and Italian forces to the south had been smashed. Shortly after that, the Soviets launched attacks against the *XIII. Armee-Korps* to the north. Those efforts paid off in the form of a breakthrough. The Soviets intended to encircle and destroy the *2. Armee* by means of a pincers movement.

From 23 to 25 January, the positions in the bridgehead that had not yet been attacked were evacuated without enemy contact. Nonetheless, the Soviets had already advanced far along the deep flanks of the *75. Infanterie-Division* and the other divisions of the corps. By the end of January, the *VII. Armee-Korps* was encircled. There were nine German divisions in the pocket, along with the remnants of the Hungarian IV Corps. For the breakout attempt, the division received what was left of the *340. Infanterie-Division* and the *377. Infanterie-Division*, as well as elements from the *57. Infanterie-Division* and the *323. Infanterie-Division*. Beukemann's reinforced division formed the center group of the breakout effort being planned by the *2. Armee*. The northern group was commanded by *Generalleutnant* Siebert (*57. Infanterie-Division*) and the southern group by *Generalleutnant* Gollwitzer (*88. Infanterie-Division*).

The northern group was directed to breakout across the Tim River. The southern group was to move west from Stary Oskol. Both groups had the benefit of a road network. In contrast, the center group had to establish its own path through terrain bereft of a road network. The area had a deep snow cover and temperatures often sunk to -30 (-22 Fahrenheit). There were extreme shortages of fuel, rations and ammunition.

Consequently, Beukemann ordered the destruction of all vehicles, with the exception of field ambulances. To set the example, he had his staff car blown up first, and the general marched back with his foot soldiers. On 6 February 1943, the center group was completely encircled in the area of Jastrbowka.

The general decided the only way out was to conduct a breakout attack to the southwest in an effort to join up with the forces of the southern group under Gollwitzer.

After and during preparatory fires by all of the available artillery, Beukemann's grenadiers moved out to attack. As they moved forward, the shells continued to howl overhead towards the enemy's positions. The men worked their way forward by leaps and bounds, the general and the battalion and regimental commanders all up front with their men. They were a true band of brothers, sworn to help one another in their combined efforts to break out.

The enemy started his defensive fires. Salvoes of rockets spread carpets of death and destruction. The *Ratschbumm*—the feared Soviet 7.62-centimeter field gun—fired into the attack groups. A Soviet mortar brigade joined in, and the German attack, which had started with such promise, bogged down.

After it turned dark, the Soviets sent an emissary to *Generalmajor* Beukemann. The general listened to the Soviet demands for capitulation and turned them down. After the emissary had disappeared, Beukemann summoned his commanders: "Gentlemen, the Soviets expect us to attack at the same spot tomorrow morning. They will focus all of their defensive efforts there. We are going to break off our attack there, regroup and assault westward instead. There has to be a gap in their lines somewhere there."

Beukemann's calculations proved correct. The grenadiers marched west through the heavy snow squalls that had commenced in the meantime. There was only a thin enemy outpost line facing them, which was quickly swept away after the first assault. The division, which the corps and the field army had given up for lost, surfaced at Manturowo.

The subsequent withdrawal through Obojan, Sudscha and Sumy, constantly forced Beukemann to make independent decisions of great import. Despite all the difficulties, he succeeded in getting the formations entrusted to him back to Sumy, despite the pursuing enemy. There, he set up another defense, and the Soviets, who had expected the total destruction of the German units as the culmination point of their operation, were stopped.

There were two Knight's Cross recipients out of the dramatic and successful withdrawal operation: *Oberstleutnant* Hermann Siggel, the commander of *Grenadier-Regiment 172*, and *Oberleutnant* Schneider, a young and dynamic company-grade officer. Siggel went on to become the 552nd recipient of the Oak Leaves to the Knight's Cross about 2 months later.

For his efforts, *Generalmajor* Beukemann received the German Cross in Gold on 20 January 1944. He was promoted to *Generalleutnant* on 1 May 1943.

✠

During Operation "Zitadelle" in July 1943, Beukemann's division was involved in the efforts to pin Soviet forces to prevent their being employed against the German main effort. It was not intended to deploy the division in the main attack until the armored forces had broken through. Of course, the breakthrough never happened, and the division soon found itself on the defensive and in a general withdrawal. The division fought its way back to the Dnjepr, withdrawing through Romny and Priluki. By then, the division had been allocated to *Generaloberst* Hoth's *4. Panzer-Armee*, where it established a new main line of resistance along the west bank of the river at Kiev.

The Soviets launched another major offensive there in November. The Soviet pincers, thrusting past the Ukrainian capital to both the north and south, joined up to the west. For the second time, the division found itself encircled. This time, *Generalleutnant* Beukemann led his forces out to the south in bitter fighting. What was left of the division eventually linked up with the German front in the vicinity of Bejala Cerkow.

The division then wound up in the Tscherkassy Pocket in January and February 1944, where it was encircled for the third time. Despite massive efforts to relieve the encircled forces, the German armor was unable to break all the way through and the troops had to attempt to break out. The grenadiers again faced seemingly impossible odds.

After several attempts, the men succeeded in making it through to the awaiting forces, along with other elements of the embattled corps. Once again, *Generalleutnant* Beukemann was an example to his men, leading personally from the front.

The fighting continued in deep snow and unimaginable conditions. In the course of the subsequent withdrawals, the division found itself in the "wandering pocket" of *Generaloberst* Hube, thus marking the fourth time it had been encircled. Eventually, the pocket rejoined the German lines, where it then contributed a great deal in stopping of the Soviet offensive at Czernowitz–Tarnopol.

✠

In the middle of July 1944, Beukemann, who had been in almost uninterrupted combat duty since the start of the war, was transferred to the unassigned general officer manpower pool of the German Army. Six weeks later, he assumed command of a rear-area division headquarters in Prague, where he then experienced the revolt of the Czechs in May 1945. It was thanks to his caring leadership that most of the forces entrusted to his command at the time, as well as thousands of ethnic Germans and refugees, made it to Pilsen, where they were able to enter the American zone. It was there that *Generalleutnant* Beukemann also entered captivity.

After spending time at POW camps in Regensburg, Riedenburg, Dachau, Neu-Ulm and Garmisch, he was released in 27 June 1947. He returned to the Hamburg area as a retiree. He passed away on 13 July 1981.

Horst Niemack.

The memorial for *Grenadier-Regiment 382* on the Greek island of Lemnos

A *Panzergrenadier* tank hunter waiting for enemy armor with a deadly Teller mine model 42 that carried 5 kilos (11 pounds) of explosive charge. Note the helmet's camouflage cover.

Rudolf Brasche

CHAPTER 2

Feldwebel Rudolf Brasche

PANZERGRENADIER IN THE EAST AND THE WEST

The extended ridgeline, which became visible at first light, formed the southern limit of Kamjenka Valley. The *13. Panzer-Division* had been in position there since 1 December 1942.

As members of the Headquarters Company of *Panzergrenadier-Regiment 93*, three *Obergefreite* of a machine-gun section occupied their defensive position. The senior machine gunner was *Obergefreiter* Rudolf Brasche; his assistants were *Obergefreiter* Richard Gambietz and *Obergefreiter* Wilhelm Grunge. It was a machine-gun action that would go down in the pages of military history.

✠

"Something looks fishy, Rudi!" Gambietz pointed to the wall of the brickworks, along whose edge the headquarters Company of *Hauptmann* Kumm had established itself. The Russians were still thought to be in the brickworks proper.

The remaining companies of the regiment, which had positions in the main line of resistance along the Mius at Pokrowskoje, adjoined farther to the east.

"I hope we'll stay here, Richard," Brasche replied in a relaxed tone. "This is just the right spot for wintering over after an 80-kilometer retreat. It must be warm over there in the brickworks."

"We could fire up one of the ovens," the huge East Prussian added.

All three of the men had been detailed to support the engineer platoon, which had established positions behind the clay bricks, which had been piled up into makeshift walls. The thermometer registered -22 degrees (-7.6 degrees Fahrenheit).

"Feldwebel Wegener's coming," *Unteroffizier* Laupert informed his squad. Grunge added: "With four men from the company headquarters' section!"

The squad leaders were summoned. When *Unteroffizier* Laupert returned, he had a telling grin on his face. He said: "Gentlemen, I always wanted to see a brickworks from the inside . . ."

"Does that mean . . . ?"

"That means that we are going into the brickworks to check out whether there are still Russians on the premises. If the buildings belong to us as a flank position, then we will be right up next to the Mius on the left. Besides, the main line of resistance will match the rolling terrain from there."

Unteroffizier Laupert briefed his squad. When it started to turn dark on the first day of December 1942, the men headed out. With his machine gun at the hip, Brasche snuck forward behind an outbuilding towards the southern part of the brickworks. The snow crunched under the men's boots. Brasche could hear the labored breathing of the men behind him. Shortly thereafter, the drying shed was in front of them. Remnants of bricks were crushed beneath Brasche's boots, with reddish dust forming into small clouds. His heart was beating like crazy; he could feel his pulse racing in this neck.

There was a rattling in front. The three men of the machine-gun section froze in place. A narrow shadow approached them: a cat! It jumped off to the side with a meow signaling complaint and then disappeared.

"Let's go!" Laupert whispered. By then, he had made his way forward and took over the lead: "Follow me!"

They went around a pile of bricks and saw the oven at the end of the outbuilding. A whispered command was issued, and they went to ground, whereupon they crawled back to the mountain of bricks. Laupert and Brasche had seen figures in front of them, practically mummy-like in their appearance due to the layers of clothing, after one of the "mummies" had struck a match.

Laupert ordered the machine gun to take up a position. He ordered Kneisel and his machine gun to set up farther to the right.

Both machine guns went into position as ordered. A little farther to the right, one of the brick walls that had been artfully assembled suddenly collapsed. A German cursed, and the Red Army men grabbed their weapons. Additional Soviets spilled out of the opening to the firing pit.

Kneisel's machine gun began to hammer away. Bursts from the 72-round drums of the Soviet submachine guns replied. Rounds tore apart wood and brick. Brasche squeezed off a burst. Suddenly, a white-hot lance of flame appeared to head straight towards him.

The *Obergefreiter* rolled to the right and was able to get behind a mound of bricks with his machine gun in time. Dust rose; there was crashing and banging. Pulling the machine gun behind him by the stock, he reached a side entrance with his comrades. Pressing themselves close to the ground, they climbed into it.

The enemy fires from the firing pit grew ever more intense. Kneisel's machine gun could be heard between the enemy bursts.

Brasche informed his assistant machine gunners they were going to go around the enemy.

In the distance, where the neighboring platoon had "rearranged" the original brick wall, there was the sound of hand grenades exploding—German and Soviet.

The three men of the machine-gun section groped their way to the end of the hall. They wanted to turn in towards the firing pit when they heard the soft clatter of felt boots, which was making its way over to them from the chimney and the administration building. They threw themselves on the ground, and Brasche took aim at the spot where the newly arriving enemy had to appear. As if on cue, the enemy arrived. Calls echoed through the darkness; orders were shouted.

Brasche fired, swinging the barrel from left to right. The sounds of the moving men stopped, and figures collapsed to the ground. Hand grenades came sailing through the air towards the men and exploded with an ear-deafening roar next to them.

"Take cover!" Brasche shouted mechanically to his comrades.

A few moments later, the Soviets continued their assault in an effort to relieve their comrades at the firing pit.

Brasche's machine gun rattled again. Gambietz fed in another belt. Grunge was firing from a captured submachine gun. A hand grenade smacked into the snow in front of them. Brasche's hand shot forward, grabbed the agent of death and sent it hurling back to the enemy.

It blew up about two meters from the men, practically causing Grunge to go deaf. But the shrapnel shot harmlessly above him. One piece thudded against his helmet.

"Hand grenades!" Gambietz called out as he started to arm one. A few seconds later, the first one was hurtling towards the enemy.

"Let's go!" Brasche ordered. They jumped up and ran along the path that had been trampled in the snow. Walls of snow flanked them. They then approached the firing pit from another direction. As they ran, they saw a string of tracers from a slow-firing Maxim that was headed towards the mountain of bricks. Bursts of Soviet submachine-gun fire pelted towards them and they threw themselves down into the snow.

Brasche slipped forward a bit farther, until he had the gunner of the Maxim in his sights. He squeezed the trigger. The burst of fire arced its way over to the enemy; the stock jerked in rhythm to the firing, until the rattling suddenly stopped.

"Extractor broken!" Brasche yelled to his comrade.

Grunge ran through the entire magazine of his submachine gun. A couple of Red Army men, who had been in the process of tossing hand grenades, collapsed to the ground. Gambietz fired after the others who were headed in the direction of the firing pit.

Unteroffizier Laupert came running up. The machine-gun section followed him to some sort of opening in the walls of the firing pit. Laupert ripped off his helmet, placed it on the barrel of his submachine gun and moved it in front of the opening. A burst of fire flung the helmet to the side. The men then tossed hand grenades into the firing pit. When they exploded, the enemy resistance was broken.

Wounded Soviets came out. They were unarmed. *Feldwebel* Wegener appeared. His men had also helped eject the Soviets from the brickworks.

The senior noncommissioned officer didn't waste time: "The company's occupying the southern part of the firing pit. *Hauptmann* Kumm will be here shortly!"

A short while later, the company commander came running up, showing the men the positions that he wanted them to occupy.

Rudi Brasche and his section went into position in a corner of the outbuilding. The hole in the wall there was enlarged somewhat, so that there was a free field of fire to the brickworks administrative building that was about 100 meters away, as well as the chimney that was in front of it. There appeared to be a few Red Army men still there.

Grunge disappeared. When he returned, he brought along a large bale of hay. They took the tops off of the brick carts and positioned them so that they absorbed some of the bitterly cold wind from the northeast. Following that, they "upholstered" their new position with the straw.

✠

Rudolf Brasche was born in Halberstadt in the Harz Mountains on 17 August 1917. He entered the *Reich* Labor Service[1] in 1937, and he was released a year later in Genthin as a section leader.

On 18 November 1938, he received his draft notice and was conscripted into *Infanterie-Regiment 93 (mot.)* of the *13. Infanterie-Division (mot.)* in Stendal. He was assigned to the 2nd Battalion's 6th Company.

Brasche saw his baptism of fire in Poland with that company. During the advance from Radom to Pulawy, he became separated from his company in the woods. He was able to work his way through Polish positions and return to his unit. At the conclusion of the campaign, the regiment returned to its peacetime garrison in Stendal. At the end of April 1940, the division was moved to the border with Luxemburg.

At the start of the campaign in the West in May, Brasche rode into France on 10 May 1940 on a 3.5-ton squad truck, the Opel *Blitz*. The division encountered French colonial forces in Corbin. It was there that Brasche saw his first fighting in France; he also observed a *Stuka* attack for the first time and its horrific effect.

The German advance continued in the direction of Troyes. Together with his company, *Grenadier* Brasche then moved on to Homyly. The men entered the city, reached the bridge over the Seine at the southern end and took it by surprise.

Enemy assault detachments, supported by armor, attempted to regain the bridge. The first enemy armored car to attack was dispatched with an antitank rifle. Brasche took on the second one with two other

---

1. Translator's Note: The *Reicharbeitdienst* was a compulsory paramilitary organization for German males prior to their conscription into the armed forces. It was charged with building and improving infrastructure within Germany and its territories and, with the onset of war, in the occupied territories as well. Since the *RAD* was organized along military lines, it spared the actual armed forces which preliminary training when young men were conscripted.

comrades. He charged a hand grenade and tossed it into the vehicle. For this action, he was later awarded the Iron Cross, Second Class.

On the day the ceasefire was announced, the company was in Aix les Bains. It was there that Brasche was promoted to *Gefreiter* on 1 July 1940.

In August 1940, the division moved to Hollerbrunn, north of Vienna. In September, the division was sent to Rumania to act as trainers for that country's armed forces. Brasche's company took up quarters in Petersberg, an ethnic German enclave a few kilometers north of Kronstadt. On 10 November, the division took part in the birthday parade of King Michael.

When fighting started in the Balkans at the beginning of 1941, the division was moved south to perform frontier security duties. In May of that year, the division was moved to Oppeln, where it was reorganized and re-designated as the *13. Panzer-Division*. At the time, the division reported to the *III. Armee-Korps* of *General der Kavallerie* von Mackensen. Brasche could never have imagined that he would be standing in front of the commanding general just 18 months later.

At first light on 22 June 1941, Brasche assaulted across the Bug at Hrubieszow along with the rest of his comrades. The German strike was preceded by a preparatory artillery barrage conducted by 300 guns. On 6 July, the division penetrated the Stalin Line at Hulsk. Twenty-four hours later, it was outside of Shitomir.

On 20 November, Rostow and the large bridge over the Don were taken. In addition to the *13. Panzer-Division*, the rest of the *III. Armee-Korps (mot.)* of von Mackensen—the *14. Panzer-Division*, the *60. Infanterie-Division (mot.)* and Hitler's bodyguard brigade, the *Leibstandarte*—participated in the operations. The gate to the Caucasus had been flung open: the Soviet oil region was palpably close to the German forces.

But the Soviets did not stand idly by. Field Marshal Timoshenko advanced into the rear of the German armored corps with his 37th Army (General Lopatin) and his 9th Army (General Charitonow).

Initially, von Mackensen had to pull the *13. Panzer-Division* out of the front to combat the new threat. That was followed by the *14. Panzer-Division*. Both divisions were committed along the Tuslow River line sector.

Following that, the enemy attacked the southern outskirts of Rostow from the southern bank of the Don on 25 and 26 November. Three Soviet divisions—the 31st Rifle Division, the 343rd Rifle Division and the 70th Cavalry Division—participated in the initial operation. The Soviet offensive operations continued and, on 28 January 1942, they assaulted across the frozen Don. The sector of the *III. Armee-Korps (mot.)*, which extended along a frontage of some 115 kilometers, was simply too weak to hold out against the Soviet onslaught. The Germans withdrew to the Mius for the first time.

The next night, in their positions in the brickworks, the men of the headquarters company waited for the enemy. The stillness of the night was suddenly rent by the impacts of some mortars shells.

"That was in the other company," Grunge said.

Brasche looked over at the administration building. The Soviets would most certainly come out by the chimney, just as they had the previous night.

When a sound was heard in that direction, the men froze in what they were doing. They listened intently for about a minute, holding their collective breath. Then they heard it again—a strange sort of scraping. Brasche moved a bit in the direction of the sound. The wind hit his face like the blow of a whip. The strange noises were coming over from the right.

All at once, the darkness over by the chimney was eliminated by the muzzle flashes coming from the firing of several machine guns. Barely 50 meters in front of the German machine-gun position, figures jumped up from the snow and charged. Brasche engaged immediately. Gambietz prepared hand grenades for throwing, and Grunge prepared to insert another belt of ammunition.

Bricks suddenly came tumbling down from the chimney. A large wave of Soviets in white camouflage snow-suits appeared and then disappeared almost as suddenly in the snow trenches and pathways.

A short while later, the Soviet brought a rapid-fire cannon into position. It immediately started to fire. A few 2-centimeter rounds hunted down the German positions. Brasche let go a long burst above the steel gun shield on the cannon.

Gambietz saw Red Army men jumping up about 20 meters in front of him and tossed two hand grenades. Grunge fired with his submachine gun, and the attackers took cover. Then it turned quiet. But the deceptive calm was shattered a few minutes later when some "potato launchers"—the German soldier's slang for the Soviet 5-centimeter mortar—opened fire. The shells came sailing in from all sides and burst asunder in the main line of resistance. Bits of steel crashed with a loud clang into the frozen brick walls.

Suddenly, a horrible cry emanated from behind the men from the foxholes of the neighboring platoon. Hand grenades exploded, a Soviet submachine gun barked and then the deceptive calm descended again.

"Ivan's in the line!" a voice could be heard from the direction of the machinery plant.

Laupert called out: "My squad, follow me! Machine gun to remain here!"

The junior noncommissioned officer took off with his men. When they returned, Brasche and crew discovered that the Soviets had made a surprise appearance, took a machine gun and its gunner and then disappeared without a trace.

✠

In the nights that followed, there were four similar incidents. Small combat patrols penetrated into the industrial area at some point, grabbed a machine gun and then disappeared. Where they were coming from was a complete mystery.

Deep in thought, Grunge said: "We need to smoke out the pit over there, Rudi!"

"And how do you intend to do that?" Brasche replied.

"We'll take down the chimney so that it falls on the building—then it's all over for them!"

Gambietz immediately started to calculate how much they would need in the way of explosives. Even Brasche started to consider the thought. Then he came up with a plan: 'If the heavy machine guns and the mortar platoon can keep up the fire, then perhaps we can make our way through the snow to the chimney without being caught."

Working through the chain-of-command, the men were soon talking to the company commander, *Hauptmann* Kumm. He agreed to it and made the necessary arrangements for artillery support. At 2345 hours, the divisional artillery opened fire on the main enemy-occupied building of the brick works. Mortars—5-centimeter and 8-centimeter—also joined in.

The three men were able to make good progress as far as the small wall. They were pulling their demolitions—8 *Teller* mines—behind them on a sled and shoveled their way through the snow.

While the mortars kept the Russians' heads low, the three men took turns creating a pathway. Occasionally, a mortar shell hit the chimney, and the resulting shrapnel whizzed past the men's ears. After a seeming eternity, they got to their target. Gambietz created a small trench around the base of the chimney. The sounds of destruction filled the air—the sure sign that the artillery had finally found the range to the nearby enemy-occupied building.

"Ready!" Gambietz announced in a whisper.

They moved the *Teller* mines into place, inserted the fuses and started crawling back to their lines with the electrical detonation cord trailing behind them. *Feldwebel* Wegener was waiting for them with the rest of the platoon behind the low wall.

"You can do it, *Herr Feldwebel*!"

Wegener depressed the electrical igniter. There was a garish brightness at the base of the chimney. Then the giant cylinder tilted forward in the planned direction and dropped on to the enemy-occupied building with a thunderous roar.

Flames rose through the dust that had been raised. Wegener had the designated pyrotechnics fired—two red flares—into the nighttime air. That signaled the guns to stop firing. Once that was done, the entire company stormed forward towards the Russian positions.

Brasche and his two men stayed together. At the edge of the building, the muzzle flashes from two Maxim's could be seen. German mortars immediately took those two pockets of resistance under fire.

They then ran into the building, coughing and gasping through the haze. Submachine gun crackled. The men fired at the muzzle flashes.

Three minutes later, the last of the enemy resistance was broken. Brasche ran to the northern side of the building and spied out through the shot-out window into the downward slope of the depression. On the far side, there was a slight rise, from which the enemy then started firing with his light artillery.

In the basement of the building, they found an underground passageway, which connected the administrative building with the brickworks. It was most likely that the Soviet patrols had used that tunnel to practice their handiwork against the Germans.

Under the command of *Leutnant* Heinrich, a combat patrol was immediately formed, with Brasche's machine-gun being a part of it. They advanced along the underground tunnel and placed demolitions at the point where it opened into the depression. After the explosives had gone off, the enemy no longer had any opportunity to enter the underground system.

Brasche and his crew stayed busy over the next few days. On occasion, they also participated in patrols to the high ground on the far side of the depression.

✠

January 1942 had arrived. It was bitterly cold. On 12 January, *Jagdkommando Heinrich* of the headquarters company relieved the battalion's 2nd Company in the latter's positions. The bunker was to the right of the firing pits. The slope that led downward towards Kamjenka Valley from the bunker positions was protected by a minefield. On the far side of the valley—only 100 meters as the crow flies—were six enemy bunkers on a hilltop. From there, the Soviets had a completely open field of fire over to the German positions. The German force consisted of two infantry squads, an engineer squad and a heavy section with flamethrowers.

A few days later, the regimental commander, *Oberst Dr. Ing. Ritter von Weber*,[2] hatched a plan to eliminate the annoying enemy positions. Correspondingly, *Jagdkommando Heinrich* was pulled out of its positions and replaced by the 3rd Company.

The small *Kampfgruppe* advanced against the enemy positions after the divisional *Flak* opened fire a few hundred meters behind the

2. Author's Note: Of interest is also the fact that Weber had been involved in the development of the *MG 34.*

front lines. It reached the bottom of the depression, crossed it and then started ascending the steep slope. Brasche and his crew found a vegetated outcropping, which offered them some protection from above. About 30 meters ahead of them, a submachine gun was firing. Once it was silenced, the men continued and were soon on top of the hill. Gambietz started firing at Red Army men, who were defending. Brasche fired from the hip on the run against the muzzle flashes coming from the embrasures of an enemy bunker. *Leutnant* Heinrich entered the enemy dugout with three men. Once in their hands, the men turned the heavy Maxim machine gun on the Soviets. Flamethrowers broke the will of the enemy in the next pocket of resistance. The rushing sound of the 30-meter-long lance of oily flames could be heard as far back as Brasche's location. It was a terrible sound. He rushed through a communications trench, closely followed by Gambietz. Grunge, who had the ammunition cans, trailed by about a dozen meters. They fired on a small earthen bunker, hitting a heavy machine gun. They succeeded in breaking the enemy's resistance there.

The company occupied the hill, which then became known as the Heinrich position. The Soviets attempted to take back the bunkers four times. All of the attacks—two of them in battalion strength— were turned back. Brasche turned out to be a machine gunner of extraordinary merit. The tracer rounds of his machine-gun bursts danced among the barbed-wire entanglements, bewildering and shocking the Soviets.

Then the Soviets attempted a fifth time, this time supported by tanks. The *Flak* positioned on Hill 189 knocked out several of their number, and four of the armored vehicles ran over mines. Despite that setback, the Soviet infantry continued to advance, also winding up in the minefield. Trip-wire flares went off, as the Soviets hit the wire. The Soviet attack collapsed in the face of the combined automatic-weapons fires.

The remaining Soviet tanks then attempted to take out the *Flak*. They were reinforced by additional T-34's, which advanced firing, followed by new groups of infantry. Machine-gun and main-gun fires hit the bunkers. Brasche's machine gun was caught up in the whirlwind of a Maxim machine gun's fire with Grunge being able to pull Brasche back under cover in time.

The enemy tanks continued to advance. The Germans could smell the stink of diesel fuel and hear the ear-deafening roar of the steel tracks. Soon, the tank was on top of them. Biting exhaust fumes took their breath away. One of the frozen-hard trench walls collapsed, but the other side held firm.

"Let's get out of here," Gambietz yelled out above the thunder of the tank engine racing above them.

They crawled away from under the tank, made it out of the hole and found themselves staring into the faces of a few Soviets, who had taken cover behind the tank. The Red Army men were mown down by a burst from Grunge's submachine gun.

Suddenly, a *Flak* round slammed into the flank of the T-34, and it was engulfed in flames a few seconds later. But the threat had not been averted. Another attack wave was advancing on the German positions. They raced towards and around the defenders like a tidal wave.

"Back . . . back!" *Leutnant* Heinrich shouted, firing the designated pyrotechnics. Only half of the men could reach the original Radau Bunker on the far side of the valley.

✠

February passed. The Soviets took the positions six times; the Germans retook it six times. A bitter war was conducted on a small scale in Kamjenka Valley. Brasche and his men made a name for themselves in the fighting.

During the morning of 7 March, the Soviets attacked the German lines again, this time with tanks in support. Brasche's machine-gun section was in the thick of the fighting again. A Soviet sniper took Brasche in his sights; somehow, Brasche saw the muzzle flash, but the next thing he knew, he had been hit in the head and was knocked backwards unconscious.

When he recovered, he saw the face of his friend, Grunge. "What . . . happened?" he asked, hesitantly. Grunge was dressing his wound.

"Boy, were you ever lucky. The bullet went through the helmet. When it did, it was deflected up, so it only grazed your skull. When it came out, it somehow went down again and into your shoulder. There's a hole there, as well."

The button on Brasche's overcoat for retaining the shoulder strap had been smashed flat by the round. Brasche could not be sent to the rear by the medics until the Soviet attack had been turned back. He was sent to the field hospital. Gambietz took his place, and he also rose to the occasion during the next Soviet attack, which took place on the night of 7/8 March. He lost his left index finger in that engagement; it was shot off. Despite that, he continued to man the machine gun as the assistant gunner, when Grunge took over the gunning duties.

The enemy attack bogged down thanks to the likes of men like Grunge and Gambietz. On 27 May 1942, Gambietz was awarded the Knight's Cross for his quick thinking and heroic actions during those engagements conducted in the late winter. By the time Brasche returned to his company, Gambietz had been transferred.[3] Grunge, the powerful East Prussian, was still in the company, however.

It was at Hill 419 that Brasche returned to the company in September 1942. The division had gotten closer to the Caucasus by advancing from the Mius across the Don and the Kuban. It had gotten as far as Krasnodar and Maikop. It had then turned south and advanced through Mosdoc to the Terek. Twenty kilometers south of Mosdoc, it reached the foothills of the Kasbek Range, whose high point could be seen rising to 5,043 meters in the distance. From Hill 419, Brasche and his section and another six comrades moved to Hill 489, which the *Obergefreiter* had been directed to defend.

Leutnant Köhler, a forward observer from the divisional artillery, was the only officer on the hilltop. From the crest, he was able to effectively direct the fires of the guns. On 13 and 14 September, the enemy started to register artillery fires on the hilltop. Brasche's squad had 18 crates of hand grenades and a fairly large quantity of demolitions.

On the evening of 14 September, the Soviets started placing artillery fires on the hill. Shortly after midnight, the enemy infantry attacked. Two battalions' worth of Soviets were attacking the crests of Hills 419 and 489.

Brasche gave the men of his group clearance to fire.

The three machine guns began to rattle. Their salvoes tore great gaps in the ranks of the attackers. Despite that, a number of Red Army

---

3. Author's Note: Sadly, *Unteroffizier* Gambietz was later killed in action on 25 April 1944.

men reached the concealment of the belt of vegetation below the crest
and disappeared.

"I'll light up the area . . . then I want you to fire into it," Brasche
directed his men. He left his covered position and fired two white
cluster pyrotechnics across the slope. A dozen automatic weapons
bellowed. The rounds whizzed past Brasche and forced him to take
cover.

"Wilhelm, come over here!"

The East Prussian came gasping over, straining somewhat under
the weight of the two pouches of hand grenades he brought along.
They moved into the cover afforded by the rocky outcropping that
nosed out past the crest. When the Soviets started advancing across
the saddle, they started tossing the first of the 360 grenades they had
available. A large number of the attackers disappeared under the
raging explosions, but those who survived fired with everything they
had and continued to advance.

The Soviet battle cry echoed eerily through the nighttime din of
battle: *Urrä . . . urrä . . . urrä!*

Brasche and Grunge started tossing from the prone position.
The grenades rolled towards the feet of the attackers. The enemy
attack bogged down. None of the seven men of Brasche's squad were
scratched.

Hill 419, on the other hand, was completely overrun by the enemy.
The enemy then directed his fires solely onto Hill 489.

"Madel...give us cover...we're going to put out some mines."

A short while later, Grunge and Brasche crawled down slope
towards the saddle. Each had two *Teller* mines, which they emplaced at
optimal distances apart. They then armed them and strung detonation
cord back to their positions.

An hour later, the Soviets attacked the saddle again. When the
enemy had approached to within 400 meters, the 9 *MG 42's*—capable
of firing up to 1,500 rounds a minute—opened fire.

Runge called out: "To the left, Rudi!"

Brasche fired a flare and saw that a large group of Red Army men
had reached the area where the mines had been emplaced. He pulled
the igniter cord, and the Soviets met their death in a whirlwind of fire
that signaled the explosions.

Brasche then raised his flare gun again. The round shot skyward with a hiss. At the same instant, a round could be heard firing. Brasche felt a mighty blow. The pistol was forced out of his hand, and he felt a sharp stab of pain there. But he was only able to see a shallow tear.

Madel fired with his machine gun. A few seconds later, two other machine guns joined in. Then, the remaining two *Teller* mines detonated on the right flank. The enemy pulled back, when it started to turn light that morning of 15 September.

Three hours after the sun had risen, communications were reestablished with the battalion command post.

"There's only seven of us, *Herr Hauptmann*. We need help if we are to hold the hill!" the *Obergefreiter* reported to the commander.

"We'll send you whatever we can spare, Brasche. Give them cover and hold out!"

The promised reinforcements were unable to make it through, however, since they were caught in mortar fire. On top of the hill, the men could hear the racket. Finally, the battalion commander called the lonely outpost: "Brasche, the route to your position can be observed by the enemy. We can't send you anyone. The reinforcements were wiped out. We'll try to get through at night. You have to hold out until then. Your position is the key point of the entire main line of resistance. Everything depends on you and your squad."

With a curse, Brasche threw the receiver back onto the cradle and rang off.

"So . . . no reinforcements," Grunge said, as calm as ever. "I guess we'll have to take care of things ourselves."

The second night on the hill had descended. The barrage fires of the Soviets continued unabated, and the seven men—with drawn faces, dirty and unshaven—had to endure that ordeal. Brasche crawled from one man to the next. Hastening through the fires, which fell from the heavens and plowed up the hilltop, he reached the downward slope to the saddle.

"There they are again!" Grunge reported.

Brasche grabbed his binoculars. He immediately made out the enemy section that was sneaking its way up the hill.

"If we head out to the rock outcropping, we can get them with hand grenades, Wilhelm."

"Good, Rudi! I put a crate of 20 in the hole over there."

They informed Kneisel and his machine-gun crew of what they were doing, and then set off. They then unscrewed the arming caps on the hand grenades. Brasche then grabbed the trip wires that led down to the pyrotechnics he had placed on the vegetation another 60 meters down the hill.

The Soviets approached closer. The two sections of Soviets linked up. There were about 30 men in all, who apparently were attempting to catch the Germans by surprise.

When they reached the area around the vegetation, Brasche pulled the trip wires, and Grunge tossed the first few hand grenades. Brasche then joined in. The Soviets froze when they were illuminated in the chalk-white brilliant light. The hand grenades detonated, and Kneisel's machine gun let loose with long bursts of fire. Barely a minute after they had opened fire, the enemy force had been wiped out. At that point, the Soviet mortars started in.

"The Russian are coming from the north!" one of the machine=gun outposts reported.

Brasche and Runge ran along the plateau. They then heard the battle cry of the Soviets. Josef Topploczan, an ethnic German from Hungry, who was part of Brasche's section, pointed to the left. "Over there, Rudi!" he spat out, horrified; Soviets were spilling out of the nighttime shadows from that direction.

The attackers had already overcome the steep slope and were running across the plateau. Brasche and Grunge headed in their direction. Hand grenades detonated. After the short skirmish, the enemy had been eliminated, a group of 20 Red Army men.

The attack that followed placed the few German defenders in great jeopardy. But the enemy was again stopped with *Teller* mines and hand grenades. But the supply of hand grenades was dwindling.

"Bring up the demolitions!"

Brasche reached for the package that someone handed him. He looked down into the thick mass of enemy attacking in the moonlight and flung the 3-kilogram charge down towards them. It exploded with a thunderous detonation.

The Hungarian then jumped up and emptied a submachine gun into the Soviets that followed. A bright lance of fire soon headed towards him, flinging him backwards. He had stopped the attack, but at the ultimate price. When Brasche bent over his stricken comrade, he saw there was nothing more he could do for him.

The Soviets attacked three more times that night, but they were repulsed each time. When the sun rose in the morning, the hillside was strewn with corpses.

Throughout the day on that 17th of September, the six men on the hill strung wire and emplaced mines. Brasche reviewed his defensive plans.

When it turned dark, the men turned back another attack, the fourteenth. The brilliant flashes helped guide the way to the forlorn position for the reinforcements. The battalion had finally freed itself from a threatened encirclement and was able to try to send relief forces again, which reached the beleaguered forces and relieved them.

Brasche was given an immediate promotion to *Unteroffizier* for bravery in the face of the enemy. The battalion commander told him he could expect another surprise. On 26 September, it was confirmed that he would receive the Iron Cross, First Class.

Two days later, Brasche was wounded for the fourth time outside of Orschonikidse in the Caucasus when he helped defend against a Soviet attack. He did not wake up after being hit until he was in the military hospital at Kislowodsk. On 9 November, he was still in the hospital when he was listening to the news on the radio. At the end of the newscast, he heard the following:

> The *Führer* and Supreme Commander of the Armed Forces has awarded the Knight's Cross to the Iron Cross to *Obergefreiter* Rudolf Brasche, squad leader in a *Panzergrenadier* regiment. Together with his squad, Brasche turned back 14 Russian attacks in battalion strength and became the bulwark of the division, all on his own.

Two days later, he was ordered to the hospital commander. When he entered the commander's room, he saw a general officer was already there. He recognized the white-haired figure with the monocle in his right eye and came to attention.

"That is *Unteroffizier* Brasche, *Herr General!*"

General der Kavallerie von Mackensen, the commanding general of the *III. Panzer-Korps*, the man who had led the corps as far as the

Caucasus, stepped forward and waved to his adjutant, who was standing near the window.

"Dear Brasche, you most certainly already know that the *Führer* has awarded you the Knight's Cross. I have the pleasure of being able to present it to you personally."

After he had presented Brasche with the decoration, von Mackensen said a few words that remained indelibly etched in Brasche's mind: "Without men such as you, Brasche, our corps would have long since been overrun and destroyed by the enemy."

Rudi Brasche then went on convalescent leave. All of Halberstadt prepared a hero's welcome for him. During the subsequent convalescent leave, he also linked up with his friend, Richard Gambietz. That would be the last time they would see each other. Following his leave, Brasche went to the replacement detachment for the *Panzergrenadiere* of the division at Magdeburg.

In October 1943, he was transferred to the *1./Panzergrenadier-Lehr-Regiment 901*, where he deployed with the formation to Italy. The regiment remained in the Fiume area until January 1944, when it was moved to Nancy in France, where the *Panzer-Lehr-Division* was being formed.[4] The following month, the division was sent to Hungary to participate in the show of force there to stop the nation from leaving the Axis.

The regiment returned to France in May 1944. It was alerted on the morning of 6 June, when the Allied invasion at Normandy started. Although the division was ready to move almost immediately, it was not until 1700 hours when it was finally ordered to move out to counter the Allied landings. The reason for the delay was the Germans' hesitancy in declaring the Normandy landings as the actual invasion rather than just a deception measure.

Because the division had to move forward in broad daylight, it paid a terrible price even before it engaged in ground combat. More than 100 vehicles were destroyed during the march by Allied fighter-bombers.

---

4. Translator's Note: The *Panzer-Lehr-Division* was the largest armored formation in the German Army. It had the distinction of not only having two *Panzergrenadier* regiments, but all of the combat vehicles in the regiment were *SPW's*, an organization that was never seen in any other Army or *Waffen-SS* formation.

Brasche's company reached the area around Norrey during the morning of 8 June. It was intended to be the assembly area of the regiment, under the command of Knight's Cross recipient *Oberst* Georg Scholze. The formations were then sent to Tilly to reorganize. It was intended for the division to attack Bayeux during the morning of 9 June, but it received orders as its attack was already underway to return to Tilly.

During the night of 9/10 June, the entire division was ordered to deploy along two lines running Christot–Tilly (North)–Verrières and Bernières–La Belle Epine–Toteval–St. Germaine d'Ectot. That gave the division a sector of 17 kilometers to defend.

To screen the division's left flank to the west and the northwest, the *1./Panzergrenadier-Lehr-Regiment 901* of *Oberleutnant* Monz was sent in the direction of Ballery. In the fighting that followed against the tanks of the British 7th Hussars, *Unteroffizier* Brasche would again rise to the occasion. The British tanks were also on the move at the same time and their intent was to encircle Tilly by means of a pincers movement.

The 1st Company worked its way forward in a wedge. The 3rd Platoon, which was in the lead, moved along the road and reached the edge of some meadows and dense vegetation, behind which one of the characteristic hedgerows of the region was located. About 100 meters behind the 1st Platoon, the 4th Platoon brought up the rear with its heavy machine guns and mortars. *Oberleutnant* Monz was up front with his 3rd Platoon.

Brasche was with the 2nd Platoon, where he was part of a tank hunter/killer team outfitted with the *Ofenrohr*, the German equivalent of the bazooka. He had his section hold up when it approached a wooded defile that emptied out into the road. Brasche intended to move out again, when *Obergefreiter* Langemann called out: "Tanks to the left, Rudi!"

Brasche immediately moved back to a concealed position. As he dove to the ground, he heard the sound of several tank engines roaring. A few seconds later, the first Sherman appeared. Three more tanks appeared behind the lead one. They were rattling slowly up to the corner.

"Becker, report to the company commander: Tanks to the left . . . rolling right into the flank of the company."

Becker disappeared and Brasche ran over to the righthand side of the defile, diving into the ditch. He trained his "stovepipe" on the lead tank, whose tracks were already clattering much too loudly for him. The steel giant approached ever closer, with stinking exhaust fumes clouding the air behind.

The tank completely filled Brasche's sights by then. Brasche squeezed the trigger. A jet of flame exited the rear of the firing tube; the rocket-propelled grenade screamed towards the target and hit the vertical turret wall. As if lifted by an unseen hand, the turret came out of its race, whirled a few meters to the rear and landed with a crash on the tank that was following. At almost the same instant, the third Sherman fired and all hell broke loose in that sector around Tilly.

"Follow me!" Brasche cried out, grabbing the *Ofenrohr*. He ran west, parallel to the defile. Hannes Keck appeared next to him, with Hill and Langemann following behind with the additional rounds for the *Ofenrohr*. All of the combat vehicles were firing, as the squad made its way towards the bend in the road to the north. To the right of it, there was the sound of the firing of tank main guns, coupled with the rapid crack of automatic cannon. The tracers appeared trained towards the north, where the 3rd Platoon had to be.

"Keep going! If we knock out the last tank in the column, we've trapped the rest in the defile," Brasche gasped, as he ran.

They moved forward rapidly, crouching all the way. They were greeted by bursts of machine-gun fire, before they were finally out of the zone of death. They could make out the location of the last tank by the muzzle flash when its main gun fired.

Brasche broke his way through the vegetation to the defile. All at once, he saw the turret of the Sherman approaching. He quickly took up position. A round was inserted into the tube. Once again, the telltale jet of flame shot out the back. The projectile bored into the enemy tank. With hammering blows, the ready ammunition in the tank went up a few seconds later.

At the location of the 4th Platoon, the 8-centimeter mortars went into action. It was not a second too soon, since enemy infantry was coming forward behind the tanks. The mortar shells landed among the widely dispersed enemy squads. The enemy took cover.

"Hill and Langemann, follow me! Everyone else, cover us!"

Brasche ran through the vegetation to the edge of the defile. Right next to him, he felt the concussion of the report of a main gun firing. Then there was a second muzzle flash.

Suddenly, Brasche saw a squad of English soldiers. He quickly grabbed his submachine gun and let loose three bursts of fire, while Hill approached the Sherman. He held a bundled charge, climbed up onto the tank and pulled open the hatch that had not been secured. He dropped the charge into the fighting compartment, and Hill jumped as far clear of the tank as he could. The explosion eliminated all life within the confines of the steel colossus.

At the same time, Brasche crept through the underbrush of some hazelnut trees. He worked his way through the hedgerow "wall" and saw another Sherman about five meters away.

That combat vehicle was firing to the south in the direction of the 4th Platoon, which continued to fire its mortars. Brasche pulled four hand grenades from his belt, lashed them together, took off the igniter cap from the center one and continued sneaking up. Langemann, Hill and the others gave him covering fire, so he was able to reach the rear deck of the tank. He heard voices and heard the snapping shut of the cannon breech, before he forced his improvised shaped charge under the turret overhang that was over the rear deck. He pulled the igniter and ran as fast as he could. He took cover when the hand grenades exploded.

A lance of flame shot out of the engine compartment and hatches popped open. The crew abandoned its burning tank. Soaked with sweat, Brasche rejoined his comrades.

Oberleutnant Monz, who had returned with the 3rd Platoon, ordered Brasche's squad to cover the far edge of the defile. He had the remaining two squads of the 1st Platoon adjoin Brasche's men to the right.

Concealed by the vegetation, Brasche and his men reached the other end of the defile. Once there, they identified enemy forces in a patch of woods across the open terrain.

"At least a battalion," Langemann said, lost in thought.

"We'll hold them back with the *Ofenrohr*!" Brasche announced, already taking aim at something.

The round achieved a monstrous effect and kept the enemy quiet for the time being. *Oberleutnant* Monz had his company take up defensive positions.

✠

In its first fighting in Normandy, the 1st Company had achieved a major local success. The fact that the armored forces had been held at bay was thanks to *Unteroffizier* Brasche. His achievement was singled out for praise in a division order-of-the-day on 11 June.

Two days later, on 12 June, the defensive situation in the Tilly sector had stabilized. The 1st Company was positioned in a patch of woods in the vicinity of Lingèvres. *Hauptmann* Phillips, the commander of the *5./Panzergrenadier-Lehr-Regiment 901*, had turned back the numerically superior enemy forces in Tilly proper.

During the afternoon of 12 June, Monz's company was ordered forward in order to establish a blocking position. It was believed the enemy would continue his efforts to outflank the division in that sector.

The company pushed its way forward slowly. On this occasion, the 1st Platoon led the way, moving parallel to a road on the right. The 4th Platoon, as was always the case, brought up the rear with its heavy weapons. As it turned dark, the company reached a large open meadow, which was crisscrossed with haystacks and mound-shaped vegetation. Brasche's squad stopped at a hedge that bordered the meadow land.

"There's a ditch here, Rudi. That would be a good position!" one of the men stated.

The junior noncommissioned officer jumped into the ditch and placed the *Ofenrohr* on its edge. He tried to look out into the meadow from a hole in the vegetation. It proved impossible.

"Dig in a bit deeper," he ordered, after thinking it over.

While the squad went to work in a sullen mood, Brasche cut a hole in the hedge with his entrenching tool and positioned the *Ofenrohr* in it. He told Hannes, one of his men, to cut another firing port in the hedge for the other *Ofenrohr*. Following that, Brasche went around the hedge to its eastern face. There he met one of his friends, *Unteroffizier* Görentz.

"What do you think, Karl-Heinz?" he asked.

"Can't see anything. Maybe we can play some cards in Wetterau's radio track later on. Let's meet there!"

When Brasche saw his company commander coming, he snuck back to his squad. A short while later, *Oberleutnant* Monz was at Brasche's position.

"Stay alert, Brasche! The enemy has to be somewhere right in front of us."

The company commander continued making his rounds. Five minutes later, he came back from the location of the 3rd Platoon. The commander was accompanied by the headquarters section leader, Peter Kollmannsberger.

Half an hour went by before things started to come to life out in the pastureland in front of them. Barely 40 meters in front of the hedge, a tank engine roared to life. Flames shot out of its exhaust stacks. The first powerful silhouette moved along the hedge towards the eastern corner of the pasture. The droning increased, and Brasche saw that four tanks were approaching the wall of vegetation. If they succeeded in overrunning the hedge, they could also bury and crush the 1st Platoon underneath their tracks.

Without thinking much about it, Brasche grabbed an *Ofenrohr*. Langemann jumped up and helped him. They ran through the ditch to the bend in the hedge, and they succeeded in passing the slowly moving tank. At the corner, Brasche saw a gap. "In there!" he whispered to Langemann.

They threw themselves down next to the long tube of the rocket launcher. The first tank was already approaching them. Brasche took up a sight picture and fired. The bellowing whoosh of the firing was almost indistinguishable from the dry crack of the impact and subsequent explosion. A bright red flame shot out of the tank.

At almost the same time, the night was lit up by the red glow of the firing of many tank main guns. The Shermans that had approached close to the hedge stopped where they were. Brasche took aim at the next one. That tank was also engulfed in flames a few seconds after it had been hit. The remaining two tanks rolled back across the pasture, with the two burning combat vehicles illuminating the eerie landscape.

At least 40 mains guns were firing at that point. The men ran back to their squad and fired a few more times with the *Ofenrohr* against the enemy. The mortars from the heavy platoon were firing and, in the brilliant light flashes, Brasche could see that enemy infantry was following the tanks.

They fired with everything they had from their submachine guns and *MG 42's*. An enemy squad charged them. Brasche aimed for the muzzle flashes of submachine gun. He saw tracer rounds headed towards him. Something smacked into his upper left arm and threw him back into the ditch.

"The war's over for you!" Langemann stated, laconically, as he dressed the wound for several minutes. "Nothing too bad, but it's bad enough, Rudi!"

In the course of engaging a heavy British tank, *Oberleutnant* Monz was also badly wounded. Despite the loss of the two senior leaders, the men were able to hold their positions once again. For the second time, it was largely thanks to Brasche's efforts that an enemy tank attack was halted.

The division was able to hold out in the Tilly area of operations until 18 June 1944. Brasche's efforts were singled out for praise in a division order-of-the-day dated 15 June.

The junior noncommissioned officer wound up in a military hospital in Tuttlingen. At the end of August, he was returned to the replacement detachment of his regiment at Küstrin. Once there, he discovered two things. One was that his friend Richard Gambietz had been killed in the course of defensive operations at Tiphina along the Dnjestr. The second thing he discovered was that his friend, Wilhelm Grunge, who was still with *Panzergrenadier-Regiment 93* as a squad leader and *Obergefreiter,* had received the Knight's Cross on 3 July 1944.

That meant that all three *Obergefreite* of Brasche's original machine-gun team had eventually been awarded the Knight's Cross.

✠

Brasche became an instructor for *Panzergrenadier* replacements, but he wanted to return to the field. His wish was granted, and he returned to the headquarters company of the regiment as part of the flamethrower platoon and participated in the Ardennes offensive. Brasche manned the heavy machine gun of a flamethrower *SPW*. He survived the initial offensive and the subsequent retreat, which was initiated on 5 January 1945.

On 1 February 1945, he was promoted to *Feldwebel.* His last combat operation was along the Üdem Lowlands. The regiment attempted to hold up the advance of British General Horrocks's XXX Corps. Caught in an artillery barrage, Brasche was wounded in the shoulder. That meant the war really was over for Rudi Brasche.

Surviving the war, Brasche established himself in his hometown, rebuilt his life and passed away in Bavaria on 22 November 1975.

A badly wounded German soldier is carried to the main clearing station by two Soviet prisoners of war.

Oberleutnant Steglich sees the bottom of a 56-ton *Tiger* during an exercise designed to get soldiers familiar with the experience of being overrun by enemy tanks.

A Russian Maxim machine gun and crew. It was the standard Soviet machine gun in operation until 1943. It had a maximum rate of fire of 500 rounds a minute, compared to the *MG 42*, which could fire up to 1,500 rounds a minute.

Two out of two million dead in the Soviet theater of war. This crew was killed next to its Maxim machine gun. This photograph and the previous one appear posed. Possibly they are stills from a propaganda film.

Albert Brux

CHAPTER 3

Oberst Albert Brux

RACE TO MAIKOP

The sun rose blood red over the horizon on 19 July 1941. *Hauptmann* Albert Brux was in the forward positions of his battalion when a Soviet division attacked the Perewos bridgehead along the Irpen southwest of Kiev. From prisoner statements, Brux knew that it was a newly introduced division from the Caucasus.

"Let them approach to within 100 meters," he ordered.

The Soviets began to bellow their battle cry: "Urrä . . . urrä . . . urrä!"

"Now, Löffler!" the *Hauptmann* ordered the machine gunner in the forward dugout. A long burst of fire headed towards the enemy, who had already attacked twice before on the previous day. At the same time, another dozen machine guns joined the fray. *Hauptmann* Brux observed the first attack wave of the Caucasians dissipate, practically dissolve, and disappear into the crater-filled landscape.

Soviet artillery then commenced firing. A salvo of artillery shells impacted into the area in front of the positions. The curtain of dust and haze grew thicker. The flames of detonations could be seen through the gray curtain, as well as muzzle flashes from the artillery. In between, silhouettes of Soviet soldiers could be made out.

"Off to the right . . ." *Oberleutnant* Klaus called out.

Two machine guns swung over in the direction of the attackers, who were appearing there. The antitank guns on the right flank also joined in, sending rounds into the ranks of the Red Army men. The attack was turned back.

Brux then placed men from the reserve company into the front lines and took the 1st Company, which had borne the brunt of the attacks the previous day, out.

"Keep the mortars ready! Antitank and heavy machine guns orient on the depression in front of us."

Standing next to his riflemen up front, *Hauptmann* Brux issued his orders. Thinking through the scenarios, Brux attempted to determine what the Soviets' next steps might be. He used all available assets in his defensive planning to employ against the next Soviet attack, which was only a matter of time.

Hauptmann Brux had been the acting commander of the battalion since July. He received command the same day he had been shot in the shoulder as is 1st Company broke through the bunkers of the Stalin Line. The battalion commander at the time had been badly wounded in the same series of attacks. As the senior officer of the battalion, Brux assumed command and stayed with the troops.

They didn't have to wait long for the fourth enemy attack. The Soviets departed their attack positions, and all of the weapons in the bridgehead opened fire. Once again, Brux was up front with his men, directing the battle. The Soviet attack collapsed even before it had reached the barbed-wire entanglements.

When it turned dark, relief forces moved forward. Weaker elements of the *25. Infanterie-Division (mot.)* had reached the bridgehead. In all, the Soviets would charge the bridgehead eight times, employing at least three regiments of men.

Hauptmann Brux did not have his battalion move all the way back to the designated resting area. On his own initiative and accurately gauging the situation, he expected he would be needed to help fend off more attacks. He positioned his forces right behind the bridgehead area.

Early in the morning of 20 July, the Soviets moved out to attack again. They overran a large portion of the new forces manning the bridgehead, whereupon *Hauptmann* Brux and his battalion moved out to launch an immediate counterattack.

"Move forward, men! Into the trenches! Let's get back the men taken prisoner!"

He led the charge at the front of his men. They reached the main line of resistance, cleaned out the trench lines and threw back the enemy.

As the men continued to advance, they reached the former battalion command post, where nine Soviets surrendered. Brux was long overdue for the award of the Infantry Assault Badge.[1]

✠

Albert Brux was born on 11 November 1907 in Lauban (Silesia). He entered the army in career status in 1926, as part of *Infanterie-Regiment 8*. He received his officer commission to *Leutnant* in 1934 and was promoted to *Oberleutnant* a year later, with an effective date of 1 February 1934.

On 1 October 1936, he was transferred to the newly formed *Infanterie-Regiment 66* in Magdeburg. The regiment was a part of the *13. Infanterie-Division*, which was reorganized as a motorized division in 1935. Brux's regiment was reorganized and redesignated as *Schützen-Regiment 66*, a designation it retained until June 1942, when it became *Panzergrenadier-Regiment 66*.

During the war, Brux served in a variety of positions within the regiment: signals officer; company commander; battalion commander; regimental commander.

In the Polish campaign, Brux commanded the *1./Schützen-Regiment 66*. He had his baptism of fire at Kock. Art the end of the campaign, he was awarded the Iron Cross, Second Class.

In the war against France in May 1940, he was still a company commander. For the taking of La Fère and the rapid capture of a bridge over the canal of the same city, he was later awarded the Iron Cross, First Class. Then, after the successful fighting at Rhône, he was promoted to *Hauptmann* ahead of his peers for bravery in the face of the enemy.

The division commander, *Generalmajor* Friedrich-Wilhelm von Rothkirch und Panthen, was awarded the Knight's Cross to the Iron Cross on 15 August 1940 for the success of the *13. Infanterie-Division (mot.)* during the campaign in the West.

---

1. Translator's Note: The Infantry Assault Badge—*Infanteriestrumabzeichen*—was awarded after three separate ground engagements. In this case, Brux had earned six qualifying engagements just in the bridgehead fighting alone.

Following the campaign, the division was reorganized and redesignated once more, becoming the *13. Panzer-Division.*

At the beginning of September 1940, it was sent to Romania to act as an instructional and training force for the Romanian Army. It took up billets in Petersberg, five kilometers north of Kronstadt, in the heart of the ethnic German portion of the country. On 10 November 1940, the division participated in the birthday parade for the monarch King Michael. In the area around Rocsani, the division conducted reconnaissance of approach routes to the Soviet frontier.

When the campaign in the Balkans started on 6 April, the division moved to the frontier and performed security missions.

In May 1941, it was moved to the area east of Oppeln, where it was allocated to the *III. Armee-Korps (mot.)* of *General der Kavallerie* von Mackensen. Around noon on 22 June 1941, it started its part in the campaign against the Soviet Union by crossing the Bug at Hrubieszow. Brux's battalion, outfitted partially with *SPW's*, was frequently attached to the division's tank regiment—*Panzer-Regiment 4*—almost to the point that it became a standing *Kampfgruppe.*

Hauptmann Brux followed the tanks with his 1st Company, when the division finally broke through southeast of Wlodzimiersk and gained operational freedom of movement. Also part of the corps at the time was the *14. Panzer-Division,* the *"Leibstandarte SS Adolf Hitler"*—a reinforced brigade composed of Hitler's *SS* bodyguard formation— and *SS-Division "Wiking,"* another *SS* formation, that was composed of small contingents of foreigners of Germanic extraction and augmented by large numbers of German *SS* forces.

The division fought its way forward through the broad brush country. On 6 July, it reached Hulsk, east-southeast of Zwiahel, which was part of the Stalin Line, a series of prepared fortifications designed to protect the actual frontier with the Soviet Union. It was bristling with bunkers and field fortifications. Zwiahel was one of the lynchpins of the entire defensive network. The effort by the *14. Panzer-Division* to take the city in a *coup de main* failed. The *13. Panzer-Division* succeeded, however, where its sister division had failed. Despite a shoulder wound, Brux stayed with the troop and performed duties as the acting commander of the battalion until November 1942.

From 20 to 23 July 1941, the corps wrested control of the area around Fastow, which served as a prerequisite to the further advance to the southeast.

On 24 July, Brux's battalion joined forces with *Panzer-Regiment 4* and prepared for further offensive operations. The next objective was Smela. By the evening of 30 July, the area around Korssum had been reached. On the east flank of the division, *Hauptmann* Brux and his men attacked enemy forces west of Korssum on the morning of 31 July. Brux, in trademark fashion, led his forces from the front.

"Let's go!" his voice echoed through the radio sets, as the men headed at high speed towards the enemy's blocking position. By moving quickly, they outran the ability of the enemy's guns to adjust fires.

"Dismount . . . Attack!"

A short while later, they were in the enemy's positions. A short, sharp fight started, which ended in close combat. Rounds were fired . . . hand grenades exploded . . . entrenching tools were swung.

The Russians, surprised by the speed and the ferocity of the attack, surrendered in droves and threw his weapons away. Thanks to the efforts of *Hauptmann* Brux and their men, the division then had a clear path at Korssum and enabled the capture of the city.

The small band of men captured 10 15-centimeter guns, 3 antitank guns and 3 heavy mortars. The number of prisoners taken reached 500.

During the period that followed, the pace seemed to increase. The next major objective of the division was Maikop, with the *14. Panzer-Division* ordered to take the bridges over the Dnjepr at Krementschug. The Soviets blew up those bridges in the nick of time, however.

Early on the morning of 9 August, the men of Brux's battalion mounted up, linked up with the tanks and headed east towards Krjukow. On the way, they caught up with trains elements. Brux had to order his men not to engage them. They had bigger fish to fry. It was only in the case that they were engaged that they were to respond. The battalion continued eastward. On 9 August, Krjukow was taken. It was there that Brux discovered that the division had submitted him for the Knight's Cross for his actions in July.

On 25 August, Dnjepropetrowsk was reached. Brux was among the first to enter the city. The light vehicles of the division crossed

the Dnjepr on the bridges that were still standing or had been hastily
put back into operation by engineers. The soldiers dug in, once a
bridgehead on the far side was established. The men were subjected to
almost constant artillery and aerial attacks.

With the taking of Dnjepropetrowsk, the entire bend of the Dnjepr
from there to Chersson was in the hands of *Generaloberst* von Kleist's
Panzergruppe 1.

Hitler's new directives for the campaign in the East, dated 21
August 1941, were of special import for the men of the *13. Panzer-
Division* and the corps:

> The most important objective to be taken before the onset of
> winter is not the capture of Moscow; instead, it is the capture of
> the Crimea, the industrial and coal regions of the Donez and
> the interdiction of the importation of oil for the Russians from
> the area of the Caucasus.

That meant that the German Armed Forces in the Soviet Union
were to orient more to the south and southeast instead of directly east.

On 12 September 1941, *Hauptmann* Brux finally was presented
with his Knight's Cross.

✠

Offensive operations recommenced in the latter half of September,
and *Hauptmann* Brux again demonstrated his tactical prowess. It
was a time of maneuver warfare once again. The *13. Panzer-Division*
participated in the pocket battle of Kiev, in which the Germans fielded
three field armies, two armored groups and a tactical air force. Facing
them was a Soviet force of seven field armies. The attack started for the
division on 27 September and, by the next day, the enemy bridgehead,
which was still holding out, was scattered.

The field army then ordered the *13. Panzer-Division* to advance
north on 30 September, so as to link up with the forces approaching
from that division. In the armored engagements that followed, the
Soviets lost 47 tanks. The motorized infantry of *Hauptmann* Brux were

in the lead and crossed the Oriol at Pereschtschepinio. On 1 October, the division reassembled at Golubowka.

The division then overran the enemy at Rasdory and Troizkoje in a rapid thrust. It then proceeded in the direction of Nowonikolajewka. On 5 October, Brux's men entered the city. The enemy attempted to break through his encirclement in the sector of the *13. Panzer-Division* at Fedorowka. The enemy's efforts failed.

Later in the month, the division advanced along the coast line of the Sea of Asov in the direction of Rostow. It captured a bridgehead over the Donskoj-Tscheluk and took another one later that evening north of the Krym. On 23 October, Brux's men had to fend off strong Soviet counterattacks. Once the Soviets had been contained, the advance on Rostow continued.

The bridges over the Don at Rostow were captured intact by forces of the *Leibstandarte SS Adolf Hitler*. For all practical purposes, that meant that the gates to the Caucasus had been swung wide open.

Of course, that fact was not lost on the Soviets, either. It was no surprise, then, that the 9th and 37th Armies of Marshall Timoshenko advanced into the ever-widening gap between the *17. Armee* and *Panzergruppe 1*. The Soviet operations took place far to the rear of the *III. Armee-Korps (mot.)*.

In the face of the critical situation, von Mackensen turned first the *13. Panzer-Division* and then the *14. Panzer-Division* to confront the enemy along the Tuslow River line, where heavy fighting ensued. The corps front ran an astounding 115 kilometers and, for that reason, was not able to withstand the tremendous Soviet pressure for long. *Generalfeldmarschall* von Rundstedt requested permission from the supreme commander to abandon Rostow. Hitler forbade such a move. The field marshal refused to obey that order and was relieved.

On 1 December, von Rundstedt's successor, *Generalfeldmarschall* von Reichenau, did the exact same thing that had previously been requested and moved the front back to the Mius. Hitler approved that move, primarily because he had no other choice. The winter fighting along the lower Mius started. The division set up defensive positions at Prokowskoje, north of Taganrog. The riflemen took up positions under the icy breath of the raging *buran*, which was the Soviet version of near gale-force winds. Meter-high snow made almost all movement all but impossible.

It was in those positions that Brux was promoted to *Major* on 1 February 1942.

After the snow had melted and the spring thaw and mud period had set in, the *13. Panzer-Division* moved out again towards the Don. This time, it was a part of the *LVII. Armee-Korps*, which reported to the *17. Armee*. Once again, the attack objectives were Rostow and Bataisk. *General* Kirchner's corps was charged with attacking Rostow. Kirchner was ably supported by his chief of staff, *Oberst i.G.* Wenck, who would later go on to command a field army by the end of the war. The city at the mouth of the Don was to be taken under all circumstances. The bridges there were necessary for the continued advance.

At the same time, the *III. Armee-Korps (mot.)* of von Mackensen advanced on Rostow from the north. The Soviets had not been idle in the intervening time. They had transformed the city into a fortress bristling with weapons and fortifications, protected by a broad minefield. On 22 July, *Schützen-Regiment 93* started its attack from the west. Brux's battalion was attached to *Panzer-Regiment 4*.

Brux and his men assaulted along the Stalino–Rostow road. Once they were north of the city, they were greeted by heavy fire. The tanks took out the enemy's antitank guns. A short while later, the motorized riflemen reached the city's edge. Brux ordered his men to dismount and clear the buildings. They entered the city, where they found that each building had to be taken individually. The attack was continued the next day.

"Look out, Gaza . . . off to your right!" Brux warned the commander of his 2nd Company, when he identified two antitank guns. "I'll give you covering fires. Break through the enemy positions, cross the river and take the road bridge." While the 2nd Company took that objective in bitter fighting, Brux had the flank of the company screened.

Brux's men were given excellent support from the tanks. Obstacles and barricades were put out of commission under their direct fires. The division's motorcycle battalion—*Kradschützen-Bataillon 43*—took the north bank of the Don and rolled past the harbor and industrial facilities towards its objective, the east bridge over the Don. Before the motorcycle infantry could reach it, however, a portion was blown up, collapsing into the river. While the accompanying tanks continued to engage pockets of resistance, the divisional engineers went to work.

At the same time, Brux and his 1st Battalion entered the most fiercely defended quarter of the city, the area around the main post office and the NKVD headquarters. The Soviets defended with great ferocity, and Brux's riflemen could only advance step-by-step.

During the night, Brux had his men provide security for the tanks that were attached to his battalion. Several Soviet hunter/killer teams were eliminated.

On 24 July, the post office was finally captured. In the NKVD headquarters, however, a few formations continued to hold out. Brux requested additional tanks, which came from the *22. Panzer-Division.* The tanks were able to pepper the building with so many rounds that Brux's men could finally enter.

In a dramatic struggle, Stalin's security forces fought from machine-gun nests and other pockets of resistance. Brux's men had to face snipers and hundreds of Molotov cocktails. The Soviet forces were well versed in all of the tricks of the trade and were iron-hard fighters. Door handles were booby-trapped. Death came from below and above, from the basement and from the attic ways. The nightmarish scene was accompanied by dust, smoke and haze, tracers rounds and pyrotechnics and the deafening roar of firing antitank and antiaircraft guns.

After the vicious fighting, Rostow finally fell on 27 July and the armored vehicles of the *13. Panzer-Division* started rolling across the bridges of Rostow to the south. For his significant contribution to the victory, Brux submitted the commander of his 2nd Company, *Oberleutnant* von Gazen, for the Knight's Cross, which he received on 18 September 1942.[2]

✠

The advance into the Caucasus started. Brux and his men were there, every step of the way, usually with the tanks and well ahead of the rest of the truck-borne rifle battalions. In the open expanses of the

---

2. Author's Note: Von Gazen continued to have an illustrious career. He was the 504th recipient of the Oak Leaves to the Knight's Cross to the Iron Cross on 18 January 1943, while serving as *Hauptmann* and acting commander of the *I./Panzergrenadier-Regiment 66*. As a *Major* and the acting commander of *Panzergrenadier-Regiment 66*, he was the 38th recipient of the Swords to the Oak Leaves on 3 October 1943. At last report, he was still alive.

steppes, the tankers and the mechanized infantry demonstrated what a powerful weapon armored forces could be.

On 1 August 1942, the division was attached back to the *III. Panzer-Korps* of von Mackensen. He later wrote:

> After seven months of unwanted separation, my old, tried-and-true *13. Panzer-Division* was attached back to me again. Coming from Rostow, it had reached the city of Ssalsk, crossing the Gigant, constantly fighting, the farthest forward division of the field army. It quickly formed a bridgehead over the Ssandata at Nikolajewka.[3]

Brux and his men continued the assault south. On 2 August, Nowo Alexandrowskaja was reached. The trucks and *SPW's* followed the fleeing enemy, passed trains columns, blew a path through enemy forces and rolled along dusty roads to distant objectives.

At Armawir, Brux and his men reached the Kuban. After the lead tanks had crossed the bridge, it was blown up in the face of the following infantry.

The engineers were sent forward. By the early morning of 5 August, a bridge capable of supporting armored vehicles had been erected. The remaining tanks and other armored vehicles crossed the bridge, advancing in the direction of the enemy positions. Firing from the vehicles, the grenadiers cleared a path. A tank ditch was smoothed out and crossed.

"The faster we advance," *Generalmajor* Herr, the new division commander, said, "the easier it becomes. The enemy must be kept on the run!"

They crossed the raging Laba at Kurgannaja. In the terrain between the tributaries, the Soviets fired at them from foxholes and trenches. Tanks were able to break the resistance. On the evening of 8 August, Brux and his men were west of Dondukowskaja. There he received orders from *Generalmajor* Herr to continue the advance on Maikop without consideration of losses. Maikop was the administrative center for the important oil region; it was the operational objective of the *III. Panzer-Korps*.

---

3. Author's Note: See von Mackensen, *Vom Bug zum Kaukasus.*

On the morning of 9 August, Brux's vehicles rolled out as the spearhead of the attack. Fleeing enemy columns could be seen.

Brux radioed his units to go around them. They passed the enemy formations and left them behind. It appeared as though the battalion had not even been identified by the Soviets as an enemy force.

It was not until just outside of Maikop that Soviet security forces opened fire. Firing to both sides of their vehicles, Brux's men cleared a path into the city. The *Kampfgruppe* reached the city center and then continued on.

One of the patrols that had been sent forward reported an intact bridge.

As *Kampfgruppe Brux* headed in that direction, it received fires on both sides from enemy dugouts. Brux directed the 1st Company to move across the bridge and remove any demolition charges. The 2nd and 3rd Companies were to dismount and eliminate any enemy forces guarding the bridge.

The men dismounted and assaulted. Hand grenades detonated. Brux could clearly hear the sound of ricochets and the hissing of rounds from light antitank guns.

He fired his submachine gun as he ran forward, taking cover behind a wall. He loaded another magazine and then ran on. Red Army men started to come his way. He eliminated the enemy in close combat.

A short while later, they were on the bridge, running across it. The bridge, which had been prepared for demolition, was taken intact, due to the elements of surprise and the quick moves of the German force.

Brux had a radio message sent to the division: "Maikop bridge in our hands. We are establishing a bridgehead."

The men at the bridgehead could hear the sounds of heavy fighting behind them in the city all night long. Von Mackensen later wrote the following about this operation: "An especially risky operation saved the iron road bridge from being demolished by the Russians."

The next morning, Brux's men moved out to expand the bridgehead. They were greeted by heavy mortar fires. A shell exploded right in front of the officer. Shrapnel from the shell wounded the field-grade officer for the fourth time. Despite his wounds, he remained with his battalion.

Brux then participated in the operations designed to take Ordshonikidse and the Grusinian Military Road. The attack started on 25 October 1942 and reached Stary Tscherek the next day. The latter city was protected by a large minefield, which caused a number of Brux's vehicles to be damaged or destroyed. The advance continued along the Tscherek River in the direction of Pssyganssu. On 28 October, the grenadiers entered Shemgala. The Germans had entered the Caucasus.

✠

On 1 November, the *13. Panzer-Division* was 15 kilometers from the Caucasian capital. It was also in a position to threaten the lines of communication available to the Soviets through the Central Caucasus, the Grusinian Military Road. On 6 November, the division was cut off from its lines of communications by two Soviet rifle corps. In desperate fighting, the *Panzergrenadiere* got some breathing room for the division. The men found themselves fighting on all sides, and it was *Major* Brux who demonstrated a knack for mastering crisis situations through rapid decisions.

On 9 November, von Mackensen ordered a withdrawal. By 10 November, the division had made it as far as the Nish Ssaniba. On 12 November, the division rejoined the corps. By then, some of its elements had also approached to within 5 kilometers of Ordshonikidse, after having withstood 14 attacks by enemy formations in the past few days.

✠

On 1 January 1943, Brux was promoted ahead of his peers to *Oberstleutnant* as a result of the performance over the recent past. Just a few weeks before the promotion, he had assumed acting command of the regiment.

That year marked the end of any advances in the Caucasus. In a span of 30 days, the corps retraced its route from the Terek to the Don, as far as the Kuban bridgehead. The military bridges at Ust-Labinskaja were held open for all of the other divisions against a vastly superior enemy. It was not until 30 January that the bridges were blown sky high. By then, all of the German forces had safely pulled back. On 23 January 1943, *Oberstleutnant* Brux received the German Cross in Gold.

In the spring and summer of 1943, the *13. Panzer-Division* had a relatively peaceful time on the Crimea Peninsula, where it underwent reconstitution. On 1 August 1943, Brux was again promoted early to *Oberst.*

When the Soviet 2nd Guards Army, together with the 5th Shock Army, overran the *294. Infanterie-Division* between Kalinowka and Hill 175.5 and began pouring west through the gap, the *13. Panzer-Division* was thrown into the breech in expedited marches from the Crimea. *Panzers* and *SPW's* of the division, augmented by the guns of *Sturmgeschütz-Abteilung 259,* hit the enemy in the flanks. The attack force was able to force its way 7 kilometers north into the Soviet assault wedge, but then the attack bogged down. On 30 August, the division— supported by the *Stukas* of *Major* Rudel—were able to relieve the encircled *336. Infanterie-Division.* The fighting along the Mius slowly reached its culminating point for the Soviets when *Oberst* Brux was badly wounded once again. *Major* von Gazen assumed acting command of the regiment and led it successfully in those weeks of hard defensive fighting.

✠

By January 1944, *Oberst* Brux had recovered. He returned to the front, where he was assigned as the commander of *Panzergrenadier-Regiment 40* of the *17. Panzer-Division.* Given command of a *Kampfgruppe,* he received the mission to break through the Soviet positions south of Tschaschkow. Together with another armored division, it was to press forward, cut off and destroy the attack spearheads of several Soviet divisions that were pressing on Uman.

Moving at night, Brux and his men passed through two villages occupied by the enemy. A Soviet attack on the flanks was turned back and a bridgehead of decisive importance established. The Soviets attacked Brux's forces without a break for two solid days. Tanks and infantry tried to roll up *Kampfgruppe Brux*—an effort doomed to failure.

The *Kampfgruppe* succeeded in stopping the enemy armor attacks again and again, even though it had few heavy weapons. Supporting Brux were just a *Wespe*[4] and an assault gun. Two men of a motorcycle messenger section turned back an entire Soviet company. A *Hauptmann*, whose right arm had been blown off, had to be taken to the rear on Brux's orders. He refused to go. He wanted to stay and continue to fight.

Enemy penetrations were sealed of and eliminated by Brux's reserves. As always, he was an example to his men, always out front and never asking his men to do anything he wouldn't personally do. The men under his command achieved remarkable things under his gifted leadership.

On the third day, the force was reinforced by a handful of tanks. It was then able to close the ring trap behind the enemy's lead forces. The Soviet forces were eliminated. The fighting there helped establish the Germans for their large-scale relief operations aimed at the Tscherkassy Pocket.

But *Oberst* Brux would not see that fighting. He was badly wounded once again and was sent to a military hospital in the homeland. His sixth wounding also meant he would not see any combat for some months. He was awarded the Oak Leaves to the Knight's Cross of the Iron Cross on 24 June 1944 for the operations he conducted in January of the same year. He was the 504th recipient of the award in the German Armed Forces.

Brux attended a division commanders school at Hirsschberg from 1 October 1944 to 20 November 1944. He was acting commander of the *17. Panzer-Division* on the 2 December 1944 until he was captured by the Russians on 13 January 1945. Brux was released from captivity 16 January 1956.

Brux passed away in Mainz on 16 December 2001.

---

4. Translator's Note: The *Wespe* (wasp) was a 10.5-centimeter self-propelled gun mounted on a *Panzer II* chassis.

Panzergrenadiere on the advance. Many of the elements of a *Panzergrenadier-Division* are evident: *Sd.Kfz. 251* half-tracks (a command version with a star antenna is in the foreground); an *Sd.Kfz. 222* armored car and motorcycle infantry.

Georg Feig

CHAPTER 4

Oberstleutnant Georg Feig

ALWAYS IN THE LEAD

The woods were behind us. We stood there as if on balconies, looking down into the Meuse Valley, emotion welling up. There it was, the respected city of Sedan. On the other side of the Meuse, we observed the high ground of Frénois. Through the haze of the day, we could identify the bunkers of the Maginot Line. That's where we wanted to go!

That's how *Oberleutnant* Georg Feig, the commander of the *7./ Schützen-Regiment 1 (1. Panzer-Division)*, set the scene on that morning of 12 May 1940. The division's mission was to take the crossings over the Meuse.

The riflemen dismounted form their trucks. *Major* von Jagow's 2nd Battalion approached Sedan in a widely dispersed skirmish line.

A halt was called in a quarry, and a French battery started to register its fires there. The approach lasted all day; it was continued on 13 May. The riflemen spent the day in a large park near a factory. By then they had gotten quite close to the Meuse. Their hour arrived at 1600 hours. "Get ready to move out!" the voice of the *Oberleutnant* echoed over to his 120 men. In the skies, the sounds of aircraft could be heard. One of the men commented that it must be bombers and *Stukas*.

Prior to the attack, Georg Feig was accompanied by a messenger. There was the sound of a single round being fired from the far side of the river. The messenger lay dead at Feig's feet. As if in terrible response, the *Luftwaffe* started its preparatory bombardment almost immediately thereafter. It seemed as though the world on the far side of the river had disintegrated.

"Assemble behind the wall!"

The men moved by leaps and bounds to the protective wall running along the banks of the river. When the last *Stukas* roared against their targets, Feig gave his final order on the near side of the river: "Let's go!"

With the roar of exploding bombs in the background, the riflemen jumped up and over the wall. The *Oberleutnant* jumped into one of the assault craft that were waiting for the men, which had been secreted forward the previous day by engineers. The men of the company followed and shoved off.

The men were stopped on the far side of the river by an artfully constructed wire obstacle. Feig ordered his men to emplace bundled charges, since it would take too long to try to cut their way through.

Two charges exploded thunderously a short time later. Fortunately, the French were not covering the obstacles. The men then crawled their way through the two lanes that had been blasted open.

The men then crossed a river path in a single bound. The company advanced through a village towards the enemy's defensive lines. The men could see the first concrete pillboxes. *Major* von Jagow appeared in the company's sector.

"Good work, Feig!"

But the day's work was not done. The men encountered additional obstacles. They also started to receive light fires from the flanks. But the men were able to break through, bypassing the bunkers and attacking them from the rear. The men manning the bunkers came out, surrendering. The French artillery, farther to the rear, continued to fire, however.

Feig ordered his men into the woods in the direction of the French artillery. They entered the thick vegetation and found themselves facing the guns a short while later. The cannoneers fled. *Oberstleutnant* Balck, the regimental commander appeared. The company commanders assembled around him to get new orders. The commander was a man of few words: "We've got a small lane through the enemy. Let's break through!"

Oberstleutnant Balck placed himself at the head of his men and moved out; the assault began. At midnight, the high ground around Cheveuges was reached, followed by the *Bois de la Marfée*. The riflemen occupied the woods; they were already behind the French artillery. It was not until the next day that the regimental vehicles caught up, having crossed the river on an expedient military bridge.

On 22 May 1940, *Major* von Jagow was killed. *Hauptmann Dr.* Eckinger took his place in commanding the 2nd Battalion. Feig moved from command of the 7th Company to the 8th.

On 13 June—a few days after the second phase of the campaign in France had started—the Rhine-Marne Canal was in front of the motorized infantry of the division's rifle brigade. If that could be crossed, then it would no longer be possible to prevent the Germans from breaking through behind the Maginot Line. Consequently, the capture of the bridge over the canal at Etrépy was the essential mission of the division.

Oberleutnant Feig was positioned with his 8th Company as flank guard of the regiment. The officer was in the process of cleaning up a bit when his company was alerted. With a curse, he put his still-dirty uniform on. A few minutes later, his company moved out behind the advancing regiment. He received a radio message: "*Kompanie Feig* up front!"

Picking up the pace, the company soon closed up to the rear of the 3rd Battalion. In accordance with regulations, a messenger was sent forward to the battalion commander: "May we pass?"

Major Richter answered immediately: "Of course, Feig!"

"What's going on, *Herr Major*?" Feig asked as he passed the battalion commander.

"The enemy situation isn't clear" was the answer he received.

Major von Studnitz, the commander of the 1st Battalion, also let Feig's men pass. He called out as Feig passed by: "Don't go so fast. Be careful!"

Despite the warning, the drivers of the 8th Company continued to press the pedal to the metal. They soon closed on their 2nd Battalion, which was in the lead. *Hauptmann Dr.* Eckinger called out to Feig: "Take over the point!"

Von Richthofen's company was passed and then the men of the 8th were out front and in no-man's-land. Occasionally, squads of retreating French soldiers could be seen. The summer sun burned down unmercifully on the riflemen. Dust wafted skyward. A French vehicle approached them with four men in it. The vehicles of the 8th Company paid it no heed and continued racing forward.

Oberleutnant Feig was in the sidecar of a motorcycle out in front of his company. He kept on exhorting his men to move faster and take more terrain.

Despite the rush forward, Feig still had not received his actual new mission. Nonetheless, his company crossed bridges and rolled through woods. From a slight rise in the land, he spied a village and then rolled towards it. A hard blow then shook the motorcycle. It flipped over. The driver and the company commander flew into the roadside ditch. A rifle round had blown out a tire.

"Take cover!" Feig called out as his driver started to raise his head. The French continued firing. The first trucks of the company came rolling forward and stopped. Feig and his driver climbed aboard one of the vehicles.

"Head to the right . . . fire when ready!"

One truck after the other moved out, the men firing from the vehicles. The enemy started to pull back into the village. The lead group of Germans was taken under fire from a tavern. The men quickly dismounted and stormed the building. The enemy continued withdrawing and the village was soon in the hands of the 8th. The pursuit then continued towards Sogny. Once there, the men ran into horse-drawn French guns. The crews were in the process of eating breakfast. A few rounds quickly brought the idyll to an end.

Hauptmann Eckinger and *Oberstleutnant* Balck arrived at Feig's location. Balck issued orders: "The attack objective is the bridge at Etrépy. I am committing two reinforced companies to take it, yours and Richthofen's. You are to take the bridge by surprise. I'm giving you Weber's engineer platoon for support."

Von Richthofen's company started to move past the 8th. It rolled forward, fought its way through Jussecourt and reached the canal, but it was unable to gain a bridgehead there, since it was being engaged.

Feig followed and, as a result of the skirmish that von Richthofen's men were involved in, he was able to approach unobserved. The men dismounted. Feig saw the men of von Richthofen's company being engaged. Feig had his company mount up again and ordered it to bypass the village to the west.

It rolled out and approached a patch of woods. From there, they could observe the bridge over the canal. Feig had the men halt there. Together with his headquarters section leader, *Feldwebel* Sigrist, and a messenger, *Gefreiter* Jöckel, they moved along the edge of the wooded area towards the objective. They soon approached relatively closely and were able to observe that the bridge had been prepared for demolition. They saw the thick cables that disappeared into the bridge's construction.

By then, the company had completely dismounted and was approaching. "Across the bridge, *Herr Oberleutnant?*" *Leutnant* Weber asked. Feig shook his head: "Too dangerous. The enemy will blow it up when we're on top of it. We'll try this a different way."

Feig had one of his platoons remain behind to provide cover. The rest of the men moved somewhat downstream from the bridge to a place where they could not be observed, and the engineers started ferrying the company across on the handful of rafts they had brought with them. On the far bank, the men then approached the bridge from behind. The company encountered French colonial forces, some 200 in all, who quickly surrendered without a fight. A short while later, *Leutnant* Weber cut the detonation cables. After he had done that, Weber and Feig crept across the bridge, hoping there were not any undiscovered charges.

They made it across without incident. The company's trucks were brought forward, and the company soon had the only intact bridge in the entire corps sector completely secured. Feig had achieved that notable success without losing a single man.

✠

Georg "Schorsch" Feig was born on 27 February 1899 in Annaberg in Saxony. He attended grade and trade schools there, starting work at age 17. On 21 June 1917, he entered the Army, being assigned to *Grenadier-Regiment 101.* He joined the regiment in France. On 12 September 1918, he received the Iron Cross, Second Class, a high award for an enlisted man at the time.

Following the war, he entered the reserves. In 1934, he participated in exercises conducted by *Infanterie-Regiment 10* and *Infanterie-Regiment 11.* A year later, he trained with *Schützen-Regiment 1* of the newly formed *1. Panzer-Division.* He was a *Gefreiter* at the time. He became an *Unteroffizier* in 1937 and, a few months later, a *Feldwebel.* Following the next training exercise at Weimar in 1938, Feig received a commission as a *Leutnant,* and he remained on active duty as a professional soldier.

In Poland, *Leutnant* Feig served as a platoon leader in the regiment. As already outlined, he served as a company commander in the regiment during the campaign in the West in 1940. As a result of his actions at the canal bridge, he was later awarded the Armored Assault Badge in Bronze.

As a result of the expansion of the armored force, elements of *Schützen-Regiment 1* were used as cadre for the formation of *Schützen-Regiment 113.* Feig became the commander of the regiment's 3rd Company.

The next way station in Feig's military carrier was to be the campaign in the East.

✠

During the night of 21/22 June 1941, Feig's company moved to within 200 meters of the frontier, where it set up all-round security. No one slept that night. All of the men were near their vehicles. Just before the start of the attack, the patrols were sent out. The building housing the Soviet customs officials was empty.

"Get ready!" *Oberleutnant* Feig commanded, in a half whisper, when his watch showed a minute before 0300 hours.[1]

Five minutes after 0300 hours, the 3rd Company started to move out. The war against the Soviet Union had started. Behind the men, the rocket launchers were hissing and the thunder of the onset of artillery ended the silence.

The riflemen rolled forward rapidly from Shäcken towards Stirbaitiai and Kelmyne in the direction of the border. The company was greeted by weak rifle fire. One round knocked *Unteroffizier* Sturm, the leader of the messenger section, from his seat. He was the first man of many in the company to be killed in the campaign in the East.

After it turned light, the enemy resistance increasingly stiffened. Russian artillery fire began to respond. The small river at Ezeruna was

---

1. Translator's Note: The Germans used middle European time when compiling official reports, which was two hours behind the local time. Thus, the attack started at 0500 hours on the morning of 22 June 1941. The official time will be used throughout this section and all of the other sections of the book.

forded; a tank ditch in the process of being constructed was crossed. Moving through Budvieciai, the company reached Dapkinskia.

All of a sudden, all hell broke loose. A Soviet battery, firing with everything it had, held up Feig's trucks. A few German tanks that headed towards the enemy got stuck in marshland. Feig ordered his men to dismount.

The men deployed in a broad skirmish line and approached the Jura. Feig saw enemy positions along the river and in the high ground beyond. He was also able to identify an enemy artillery observation post. He ordered his men to fire at the observation post first. Machine guns hammered away. Other vehicles started to get stuck in the marshland. Feig directed measures to have the terrain marked for the vehicles that followed. The bunkers and field fortifications of the Soviets were systematically engaged and destroyed. The first tanks finally made it through to the riverbank, forded the river and then climbed up the steep embankment on the far side.

Eckinger's battalion, which had been transferred to *Panzergrenadier-Regiment 113* as well, closed in on Feig's company, entering some wooded terrain. It did not come out again, with the exception of its advance guard, Kirchner's platoon, which linked up with Feig's men at Alanga.

The *Oberleutnant* received orders to continue the advance without the rest of the battalion. It was to take the train station of a village in front of it. All of sudden, great clouds of smoke arose in front of the men. The radio came alive: "Feig, this is Eckinger, over . . . "

Feig answered and listened.

"Where are your lead elements? Have the lead elements halt!"

A short while later, the battalion commander came racing up in a vehicle. He spat out: "Feig, what are you doing here? Where are you trying to go?"

Feig answered, with a laugh: "Is the battalion also coming?"

Angry, Eckinger responded: "It's disappeared!"

"I hope it didn't return to the border!" Feig said, mischievously.

Together, the men continued the advance on the train station, which they reached without enemy contact. The train station served as a detraining point for a Soviet base at the city of Tauroggen. The Soviets had set everything on fire, which was the cause of the clouds of smoke the men had seen earlier.

As the fighting around Tauroggen continued, Feig was ordered
to advance to the major road leading out of the city to the northeast.
Once again, he was engaged by Soviet artillery. With assistance from
the tanks of the *I./Panzer-Regiment 1* of *Major* Grampe, the battery
was put out of commission. That marked the end of the fighting on
the first day of the campaign. By then, Eckinger had "found" his lost
battalion again.

✠

In the weeks that followed, the division advanced rapidly eastward.
It was relieved from attachment to *Heeresgruppe Nord* outside of
Leningrad and moved to *Heeresgruppe Mitte.*[2] It was to be part of the
final push on Moscow.

The division's attack started at 0615 hours on 2 October 1941. Ten
days later, the attack towards the Volga was initiated from Staritza.
Leading *Kampfgruppe von Heydebrand* in the direction of Pogoreloje–
Goroditschtsche was Feig's company and that of the *3./Panzer-Regiment
1* of *Hauptmann Graf* von der Schulenburg.[3] Feig later recounted his
experience in an article entitled "Kalinin":

> From a slight rise, we were able to observe a Russian tank crew
> work on its vehicle along the Volga. We helped them along a
> bit by seeing to it that they finished more quickly. Although
> the round from the antitank gun did not hit it, the tank soon
> disappeared from view.
>
> We went to sleep in our *SPW's*. All of a sudden, we were
> roughly awakened. Eckinger was calling his men and told me:
>
> "Get moving . . . it doesn't matter, just get moving!"
>
> "Where . . . what's the mission?"
>
> "No idea . . . just go!"
>
> He gave me a wave of the hand, indicating the basic
> direction. My company rolled out in short order. We moved
> down to the road and reached a small airstrip when we moved
> past Staritza. Two or three machines were able to take off.
> The rest were unable to get airborne; they were captured.

2. Translator's Note: Army Groups North and Center, respectively.

3. Translator's Note: The term *Graf* is a term of nobility and corresponds to count.

Around 1600 hours, our sister regiment had taken the city. We thought we might spend the night there, but things turned out differently. We continued to move. It was directed that a large railway hub northeast of Moscow be taken . . . the railway bridge at Kalinin on the Volga. That could be interesting. We were faced with a movement of 80 kilometers.

The engines roared; the division moved out again. My company was in the lead. Four *Panzer III's* under *Leutnant* Otto were attached in support. One of the tank commanders was the well-known Strippel.[4] It was a good combination that had always done well.

Since it was already starting to turn dark at 1700 hours, we didn't think we could go much farther that day. But, once again, things turned out differently. The pace of the march increased. We weren't worried about Russians left behind in a patch of woods; Eckinger's armada was following us, after all. We still had some visibility. But what was that moving ahead of us?

Russians! A column of cars with Red Crosses painted on them. We quickly caught up and then passed them. A short while later, there were more vehicles in front of us. This time, it was heavy guns. Catch up to them!

Just like we had with the medical vehicles, we linked up with the vehicles and then passed them. We stopped the lead vehicles. Our orders, after all, had been: "Take the bridge quickly and under all circumstances!"

In the meantime, it had turned dark. We continued to move. The tanks, which had been moving cross-country to the right and left of us previously, joined us on the road. With mixed feelings, we moved on. We stopped frequently to listen out into the night.

Sounds in front of us! The trampling of horses—off that way!

---

4. Author's Note: Hans Strippel was a long-time tank commander, who was later awarded the Knight's Cross to the Iron Cross as a *Oberfeldwebel* and platoon leader in the *2./Panzer-Regiment 1* on 22 January 1943. On 4 June 1944, he received the Oak Leaves to the Knight's Cross as the 485th member of the German Armed Forces to be so honored. At that time, he was still an *Oberfeldwebel* but had been reassigned to the *4./Panzer-Regiment 1*.

We passed columns of infantry, motorized elements, horse-drawn elements, ammunition-vehicles, field messes that were still cooking. The vehicles seemed to have no end. We passed more and more Russians. It started to become chaotic; the confusion of the Soviets knew no limits. Whenever a vehicle blocked our path on the road, it was pushed aside by a tank. Four Russians had fled to my vehicle; they went on the nocturnal raid as prisoners.

Then we moved in the midst of the Soviets. A Russian unit of some sort was in front of my lead vehicle; there was a Russian truck right behind me. My heart started to beat somewhat irregularly. I sent out a radio message: "Turn off your lights! Don't fire! Don't talk!"

Far to our rear, the elements following us were slugging it out with the Russians. Around us, it was quiet. Whenever we halted, Russians would walk past out vehicles. In the pitch-black night, they did not hear us. When Eckinger asked what element was up front, we answered that it was the Russians!

We moved through the villages of Saschejkowo and Spasskoje. Whenever our route was blocked, the tanks swung into action and swept the road clear. And that didn't seem to make any difference to the Russians. They had still not identified us, and the movement into the dark night continued. We could no longer halt, since the Russians were pushing hard on us from behind. Eckinger kept on asking: "Where's the lead element?"

We didn't know. All we knew was that we were on the road to Kalinin. Suddenly, we were confronted with a sensational sight: a dome of light above the city of Kalinin that was created by searchlight batteries on the outskirts. We had closed to within 10 kilometers of the city and the railway bridge!

We moved through an extended village along the road: Danilowskoje. Russian infantry marched past us to the left and the right along the road. We were right in the middle. It was imperative to keep our nerves and consider what our options were.

It would have been suicide to move right into Kalinin. I decided to leave the road, which had become wider in the village, and turned off to the right and into the houses. I sent a message to Eckinger: "Lead elements at the northeast outskirts of Danilowskoje. Halting. Close quickly!"

While the Russians continued to march on, we turned off. Everything went well. No one showed any concern about us. *Hauptmann* Eckinger showed up in the night.

"Were we ever lucky!" His usual smile was nowhere to be seen. So far, the following had been captured: 1 tank, 47 prime movers, 13 gun, 525 trucks, 15 trailers, 5 field messes, 54 horse-drawn wagons, and 11 staff cars. One hundred fifty prisoners had been taken.

The battalion spent the night there. The next morning, Eckinger assembled his commander to issue orders. Eckinger directed everyone to dismount and continue the assault on foot. The vehicles were to be brought forward later under the direction of Feig. Eckinger wanted him to rest, and he directed *Oberleutnant* Körber to assume acting command of the company. Feig would hear nothing of it. Eventually, Eckinger relented, and Feig was back at the helm. The only concession he allowed was to form the trail element of the battalion. The axis of advance continued through the woods that paralleled the road to Kalinin. After a while, the men could see the waters of the Volga shimmering in the sunlight.

The pace of the advance was not fast enough for Feig, however. He took his leave of his commander and raced forward, where he linked up with riflemen from the division's sister regiment. After conferring with the company commander, *Oberleutnant* von Bubenheim, he took off again to the very front.

He asked the men in the point element why they were being so careful. He told them he was going forward to check things out. He told the men to be on the lookout for him to return in the same area. He went on alone through the woods. From the edge of the wood line, he could see the cityscape of Kalinin. Closer by, he could see a sawmill. After observing for a while, he snuck up closer to it.

Suddenly, about 200 meters distant, he saw two Soviet guns. Their barrels were trained on the road leading out of Danilowskoje. Out in the open, an antiaircraft machine gun was posted. Two Red Army men were manning it, smoking cigarettes. Feig had seen enough; he ran back to von Bubenheim's company. He asked for forward observers to be brought forward. The observers arrived a short while later. Feig led them to a vantage point, where they climbed trees and directed fires against the sawmill. Both of the guns and the machine gun were eliminated after being engaged by the artillery.

Generalleutnant Kirchner, the division commander and recipient of the Knight's Cross to the Iron Cross (20 May 1940), came up front and ordered the stalled forces to attack. Von Bubenheim's company moved out, but it soon bogged down in the face of heavy fires. Feig then moved out with his 3rd Company. The company was also forced to take cover in a field with tall standing grass. Eventually, however, the voice of *Leutnant* Gayen could be heard echoing out in the late afternoon: "Get up . . . move out!"

Feig could see men jump up, only to disappear again a short while later. Feig followed soon thereafter, followed by more of his grenadiers. The men ran forward, reaching a trench line in front of the Volga. Feig peeked his head over the edge; no Soviets could be seen. He didn't seem to hesitate: "On to Kalinin!"

A heavy machine-gun platoon was attached to Feig in support. It arrived as it turned dark and was given the mission of protecting the company from the rear. In the meantime, von Bubenheim's company had been able to get moving again. The sound of rifle fire could be heard coming from its sector.

A few Soviets could be made out in the darkness. The riflemen snuck up on them and took them prisoner, until it was determined they were curious civilians, including some women.

The advance was continued in the darkness. Out in front was the previously mentioned *Leutnant* Gayen, an aggressive officer, and several men from his platoon. They were far ahead of the company. Even Feig could no longer see them, since it had since turned completely dark. The trench eventually stopped, and the men found themselves next to the banks of the Volga. To the rear, white pyrotechnics were cascading through the nighttime sky. In the weak light they provided, Feig could make out the silhouette of a bridge up ahead. He could hear half-whispered calls. Was that Gayen? There was only one way to find out.

Wire obstacles and Spanish riders[5] formed the inner ring of defenses for the bridge. Feig finally reached the end of the obstacles and found himself in front of a high embankment. The railway tracks on top left no doubt that they were at the right spot. Feig had reached the attack objective, even if it was only with a handful of men.

A wooden ladder led up the side of the steep embankment. There were four men on top of the embankment. Feig recognized Gayen and the others. Two Red Army men were sitting on the ground; the bridge guards had been surprised by Gayen and his men and taken prisoner.

Up to that point, everything had gone well. But extreme care was still needed. The company had still not closed up when a train approached. It thundered past. The fireman and the engineer had their heads way out of the cabin. Sounds were then heard from the other side. Three Soviets, cigarettes in their mouths, approached and climbed up the ladder.

Feig was quick: "Gayen the first one . . . Heise the second . . . I'll take the third!"

The relief force was taken completely by surprise and overcome.

"Where's the rest of the company, *Herr Oberleutnant?*" *Gefreiter* Götz asked.

Right after he said that, the sounds of rattling mess kits could be heard on the bridge. Another six Red Army men approached. Suddenly, there was a crashing sound on the far side of the embankment. Hand grenades were thrown. On the far bank of the Volga, muzzle flashes could be seen coming from a bunker.

A few seconds later, the German heavy machine-gun platoon replied. Tracers slammed into the embrasures of the bunker; a short while later, it was on fire.

The men on the embankment were being taken under fire, however. Machine-gun rounds whizzed past them. The *Gefreiter* was hit and killed. *Leutnant* Gayen was wounded. That left three of them, along with the five prisoners. In that moment of grave danger, Feig heard a voice shouting: "*Kompanie Feig . . . Kompanie Feig!*"

Feig ran in the direction of the voice and called his men up on to the embankment. The south side of the bridge was in their hands. The battalion commander arrived: "Good job, Feig!"

---

5. Editor's Note: A form of barrier consisting of 3 or 4 pronged concrete or metal obstacles intended to impede vehicles, particularly tanks.

A short while later, Feig received the report that all of the spans
had been searched and no demolitions had been found. Feig then
devoted his attention to the enemy bunkers on the far side. A short
while later, the bunkers had been put out of action. The company
then moved into the rail yards and was able to spend the night in the
warm boiler room of the station on the outskirts of the city

✠

On the morning of 14 October, the company was pulled out of the
line. The tanks had made it forward, and the division received new
orders from the corps: "Take the city of Kalinin and the road bridge 2
kilometers farther east."

Once again, Eckinger's battalion was in the lead. When the 3rd
Company reached the railway underpass leading into the city and
approached the apartment buildings near the embankment, it
received fire. The squads worked their way around the underpass.
Using fire and maneuver, the enemy resistance there was soon broken.
The advance continued rapidly. The German forces fighting in the
city center were held up. *Major* Eckinger appeared in his *SPW*; Feig
reported to him. The battalion commander ordered the assault to be
continued on foot in the densely built-up area. The men worked their
way forward, building-by-building, block-by-block. Shortly before the
road bridge, they started to receive fire from a heavy machine gun. A
flamethrower tank attached in support of the battalion moved forward
and quickly eliminated that threat.

A short while later, the men were standing along a canal, but the
dream of quickly taking the bridge seemed to have disappeared, since
Red Army men were arrayed along the far bank. One of the men
was hit in the head and killed. The remainder took cover behind a
small church and a low wall. The Volga was flowing to the left; in the
background, about 250 meters away, was the bridge. The canal was
right in front of the 3rd Company; the Kalinin sports stadium was on
the far bank. Off to the right, Feig could make out tall governmental
buildings. Large roads were leading off in all directions.

Soviets started to appear everywhere. Soviet artillery was brought
into position in the park-like landscaping near the governmental
buildings. Trucks were bringing in infantry. Farther off to the right, an

antitank gun was brought into position. The 3rd Company was taken under fire over open sights by the enemy gunners.

"I'll run across the canal bridge!" *Gefreiter* Götz volunteered.

"Stay here!" Feig immediately replied.

Eckinger appeared with the men.

"What's going on, Feig?"

"A quick capture is out of the question . . . it's turning to shit!"

"Well, let's look at things from above!" The *Major* turned and headed for the church steeple. Once in the tower, the men looked for options. How to get across the canal? Feig had the mortar section leader summoned. Two minutes later, he was standing in front of his company commander.

"Do you have smoke rounds?"

"*Jawohl, Herr Oberleutnant!*"

"Fire some rounds off to the left towards the government buildings. Fire a second group into the intersection over there. Make it snappy!"

The mortars went into position. Feig assembled his 66 men.

"Once the smoke starts, we're going to run across the bridge, turn left on the other side and test our luck!"

The dull thuds of the mortars firing began to be heard. It was exacting work. Within a few minutes, however, everything was covered in a thick blanket of smoke.

"Let's go!"

The men raced off, thundered across the wooden trestles of the bridge and reached the wooden fence surrounding the stadium—all without being fired at.

"Now . . . on to the bridge!"

The Soviets had pulled back for some reason. Only a single guard was left at the bridge. He had a large cape draped over him to protect him from the elements. His back was turned to the attackers. Feig found it impossible to kill him when he was completely unaware of what was happening: "Scram . . . disappear!"

The Soviet whirled around, discovering the Germans there to his horror. He ran away as fast as he could. The men closed up to the bridge, their lungs practically bursting. A cable was discovered and cut.

"Let's go to the other side!"

The span was 250 meters long. As he was running, Feig saw an artillery piece, a machine-gun bunker and positions on the other side.

The men started to receive intense fire. Would the bridge go up in the air, after all? The Volga flowed on, deep below the span.

But the men were lucky—they made it across without the bridge going up.

"Take cover . . . disperse widely!"

They hit the ground. The enemy fire suddenly stopped. When Feig turned around, he could see a *SPW* on the bridge, followed by a *Panzer III.* Eckinger was coming to the rescue.

Major Eckinger worked his way out of the *SPW.* He struggled to say something when he reached Feig's location. With a raspy voice, he greeted his company commander: "Feig, you earned the Knight's Cross for this!"

Eckinger, the only Austrian officer in the regiment, seemed visibly moved by the terrific accomplishment of his company commander.

A company from *Panzergrenadier-Regiment 1* came forward to relieve Feig and his men. Feig and his company walked back across the bridge. Later on, Eckinger talked about his thoughts as he saw Feig's audacious movements: "Feig was running to his own death! That's what I was thinking. I climbed down the church tower and climbed aboard the *SPW* . . . all of it one continuous motion. I grabbed a *Panzer III* that was approaching, and off we went!"

Feig was equally lavish in his praise for Eckinger: "A one-of-a-kind commander!" The men of his company would have wholeheartedly agreed with that statement.

As a result of his quick actions, Feig had taken an important bridge intact. He was submitted by his regimental commander for the Knight's Cross. *Generalmajor* Krüger endorsed the recommendation, as did the commander in chief of *Panzergruppe 3.*

The advance continued. After the war, Feig recounted the events that followed several days later:

> All at once, there was main-gun fire up front. [Feig's company was bringing up the rear.] The adjutant of the *I./Schützen-Regiment 113, Leutnant* Wendt, a tall man, came towards the rear, where we were. His face was pale and anguished. Sitting in a motorcycle sidecar, he shouted out with tears in his eyes: "Eckinger's been killed!"

It took a long time before we could recover from that horrific news. But we had to continue somehow. Wendt came to me: "*Herr Oberleutnant,* move up front as fast as possible with your company and screen. The battalion's in pieces."

"Let's go! . . . Move out!"

Gaining my composure and smoking a cigar, I sat on the front of my *SPW,* not thinking much about it. We went past the companies of the battalion. Slowly, gradually, the faces turned to look up at me. "If Feig is coming up front smoking a cigar, then things can't be so bad!" That's what they seemed to be thinking.

Major Eckinger had been killed while standing in his *SPW.* The round from a T-34 had penetrated the crew compartment of the vehicle. Several others in the vehicle were killed; the rest wounded. During the night, the dead and wounded were evacuated. *Oberstleutnant* Wend von Wietersheim assumed command of the battalion. The battalion's lead elements had been encircled by freshly introduced Siberian forces.

The next morning, efforts were made to relieve the encircled elements. The relief attack was able to advance somewhat, but could not make it all the way through. *Feldwebel* Emil Emmert, one of Feig's best platoon leaders, was killed in the latest round of fighting. Orders were received on 20 October for the encircled elements of the battalion to break out. Feig was bent over a map, studying his options, when a Soviet machine gun began to hammer away. The rounds shattered whatever remained of the glass in the windows of the house that was being used for his command post. Feig was hit in the upper thigh. With the petroleum lamps extinguished, the men attempted to get their uniforms back on in the darkness. Minus socks, Feig quickly put on his boots and headed out the door. He needed to organize his men to fend off the enemy attack.

"Where's the *SPW* with the AT gun?"

Sauer, the *SPW* driver, came running up. He was minus his uniform jacket: "We're up the road a bit, *Herr Oberleutnant!*"

"Go get it, Sauer!"

Gefreiter Sauer took off and crept towards his *SPW,* which was already flanked on two sides by Red Army men. He stealthily entered from the rear, slid as noiselessly as possible into the driver's seat and pressed the starter button. As luck would have it, the engine sprang to life immediately, and Sauer started backing up, eventually reaching the courtyard where Feig and the company headquarters were located.

He had Könnitzer, the gunner, climb aboard: "Get in there . . . fire away . . . it doesn't matter where . . . just make a lot of racket!"

Suddenly, a house on the other side of the village road burst into flames. Feig found a piece of wood to use to support himself, since he started feeling weak form his wound. In the light of the flames, he was able to make out the enemy machine gun that had caused so much havoc.

"Hand grenades!" he ordered.

The company eliminated the immediate threat, but the Soviets managed to consolidate their positions to within 200 meters of Feig's company by first light. Feig finally had some time to have a medic check his wound. The round had passed completely through his upper thigh. He was taken to a dressing station. Eventually, the battalion elements were relieved, and Feig and the other wounded were taken back to the Volga, where waiting boats took them across the mighty river. At the Kalinin airfield, Feig was flown back to Germany for treatment. He convalesced in a hospital through the rest of that terrible winter of 1941. When it turned summer, he was released for convalescent leave. By then, he had already received his Knight's Cross (4 December 1941) and, a few weeks later, promoted to *Hauptmann*. He was attached to the Army High Command for a short period, before he returned to the *1. Panzer-Division* in September 1942.

Generalmajor Krüger appointed Feig as the commander of the *II./Panzergrenadier-Regiment 113*, which was undergoing a battlefield reconstitution at Popzowo. Within a short period, the battalion was ready for combat operations again. On 13 September, the battalion was employed on Hill 210.3 in the vicinity of Grebenkino.

The expected Soviet winter offensive started in the latter part of November. By 25 November, it forced a penetration to the south along the road from Belayj between Wypolsowa and Demechi. Feig's men, supported by armor, were ordered into the breech southeast of Beloyj.

Hauptmann Feig, his adjutant and the battalion physician were on the lead *SPW*. The remaining vehicles of the battalion followed closely behind. There were heavy snow squalls, and the air was icy cold. They started to receive fire from the crest of a hill, where the village of Motschalniki was located. *Dr.* Loida, the physician, was mortally wounded and collapsed to the floor of the vehicle. *Oberleutnant* Stengel, the adjutant, was wounded. The 5th Company, supported by several tanks attacked Motschalniki, but it was turned back. The company commander, Heinz Kirchner, was wounded so badly that he expired the next day.

The Soviets then attempted to eject *Hauptmann* Feig and his men from their positions outside of the village. They attacked with infantry, supported by tanks. The Soviet attack was turned back. Taking advantage of the fog and the thick snowfall, they approached again; this time, even more closely. The second attack ended in failure as well, however. Finally, in another effort, the Soviets succeeded in disrupting the rearward lines of communications at Nikitinka. The final operation resulted in Feig and other elements being cut off from the division's main body.

The *Panzergrenadiere* built positions in the snow. Feig established his headquarters in an outbuilding in Chirewo. The fighting raged back and forth for days on end. Feig made his rounds of the perimeter daily. One morning, when it was especially bright out, he headed for the left wing of the battalion. Separated from the rest of the battalion in a shallow depression was Nebel's company. On has way there, Feig observed a company of Soviets on the move. They had an antitank gun on a sled with them.

"Keep alert!" Feig told the company, when he arrived. "The Russians have something up their sleeves!"

Feig was offered a cup of warm milk, which he eagerly drank. As he was drinking, the Soviets attacked on two sides, forcing the company out of its positions. The onset of a snowfall and thick fog, which had rolled in, made it easier for the men to withdraw. In the main body of the battalion, however, the word was getting around: "The old man's gone!"

The Soviets then attacked along a broad front with tanks. The success in Nebel's sector had apparently encouraged them to attempt greater things. *Oberleutnant* Stengl led the battalion in the commander's absence and did a splendid job turning back the Soviets. Four T-34's were knocked out. It was not until the afternoon that Feig was able to make it back to the command post, after he had spent the day with Nebel's company.

It grew increasingly colder. The thermometer dipped to -30 (-22 Fahrenheit). On 4 December, a *Kampfgruppe* from the division was able to break through the Soviet forces arrayed along the road and relieve Feig's battalion. The men could finally enjoy a hot meal again.

In an attack that followed, the battalion was able to take Hill 214.8, an important terrain feature, and then reach Dubrowka on 8 December. On 9 December, the 5th Company was able to establish contact with the *12. Panzer-Division* on the left flank. It was time for the enemy forces that had pressed ahead to be encircled. Day and night, the Soviets attempted to get out of the pocket that had been formed. The fighting was brutal, but the men were motivated by the fact that the high command had promised to relieve the hard-fighting division. The promise was kept, and the division was pulled out of the line two days before Christmas 1942. Just a few days previously, the Armed Forces Daily Bulletin had singled out the *1. Panzer-Division* for praise:

> An armored division from Thuringia and Hessia, which has been in continuous combat in the east, knocked out its 1,000th enemy tank in the defensive fighting south of Totopez.

The division was being sent to France for reconstitution. The battered *II./Panzergrenadier-Regiment 113* assembled on Christmas Eve and road-marched back to the trains. It had only 12 operational *SPW's*. In the afternoon, the regimental commander appeared and presented some well-earned decorations. *Oberst* Wend von Wietersheim had also been singled out for recognition as a result of his leadership skills in the fighting around Totopez. On 12 January 1943, he was presented the Oak Leaves to the Knight's Cross to the Iron Cross, the 175th member of the German Armed Forces to be so recognized up to that point.

During the evening on Christmas Day, the battalion was loaded on trains at Semlewo. The journey took the men back to Germany for a well-deserved home-front leave, before reporting to France for the reconstitution. On 31 March 1943, Feig was promoted to *Major*.

✠

As part of the reconstitution, both of the *Panzergrenadier* regiments of the division received the latest versions of the *SPW's*, including some variants with short 7.5-centimeter infantry guns, 8-centimeter mortars, 2-centimeter *Flak* and 7.5-centimeter antitank guns.[6]

After the refitting in France, the division was sent to Greece for security duties. The Germans feared an Allied invasion of Greece and the armored division was considered to be "insurance" against just such an effort. The effort apparently worked, since Radio Cairo eventually reported that three armored divisions had moved to the Greek mainland.

At the beginning of July, *Oberst* von Wietersheim was transferred out of the division. Taking his place at the helm of *Panzergrenadier-Regiment 113* was *Major* Bradel. On 9 September 1943, all of the Italian forces in Greece were disarmed by the Germans, when the Italian government left the Axis. The effort involved taking away the weaponry of the Italian 11th Army. The Italian military was treated chivalrously, with the officers allowed to retain their side arms.

It had been 10 months since the division had seen action in the East, when the first transports headed there from Kumanovo on 25 October. *Panzergrenadier-Regiment 113* detrained in Talnoje, after having moved through Hungary. The headquarters of the 2nd Battalion was unable to detrain at its originally designated location at Christinowka and had to detrain at Uman instead. The Soviets had launched an offensive against Kiev and had already reached Shitomir. A company of Feig's men was committed at Kornin, with Feig's men taking the village.

Following that, Feig was ordered to billet at Gnilez. Attached in support to him was the *III./Panzer-Artillerie-Regiment 73* and a platoon of antitank forces. Feig and the antitank officer, *Leutnant* Kunz, moved ahead of the *Kampfgruppe* towards Gnilez. Since other elements of the division had already moved through the town, Feig did not give his decision a second thought. They entered the town and drove all the way through to the outskirts. A Soviet truck was on fire there. A Soviet soldier lay next to it on his stomach. When Feig and Kunz approached the supposedly dead man, he threw a hand grenade. Kunz received shrapnel and bled from his forehead. The Russian was killed in the

---

6. Editor's note: Basically a 7.5-cm *Pak 40* towed gun, without its wheels and trails, was mounted in a *Sd.Kfz. 251*. While the chassis was overloaded, it was nevertheless an effective antitank weapon.

resulting explosion. Feig was able to escape the suicidal ambush unharmed.

Feig then ordered his companies into the town. He directed an all-round defensive posture be established. Later on, at night, a T-34 appeared in the sector of the 7th Company. It was destroyed by a tank hunter/killer team. Things became increasingly disquieting. Contact was lost with both the regiment and the sister battalion of *Hauptmann* Hübner.

The next morning, Feig ordered the road to the regimental headquarters elements to be cleared. He soon received an alarming report: "Twenty enemy tanks advancing south, 2 kilometers east of Gnilez."

Feig saw the tanks for himself a short while later. He determined they were headed in the direction of the regimental headquarters. He had his radio operator send a message to the tank regiment.

Then, all of a sudden, the tanks turned directly for Gnilez. They approached ever closer, and the men feverishly worked to improve their defensive positions. Then the battalion opened up with its initial defensive volley. One of the T-34's went up in flames. A second one exploded a few seconds later. The remaining tanks replied with their main guns and machine guns, before disappearing into a depression. *Leutnant* Kunz, who had remained up front despite his wounding, directed the fires of his antitank guns. A few enemy tanks were able to penetrate into the defensive position. The heavy weaponry of the 8th Company dispatched them.

Soviet infantry followed, and some entered the defensive perimeter. Close combat ensued. *MG 42's* barked, and hand grenades detonated with sharp cracks. A wall of the house the headquarters was in collapsed thunderously. It was a struggle for life and death. By the afternoon, 14 T-34's had been knocked out. The enemy fought with unparalleled bravery. He was literally bled white. Feig's men also suffered heavily. In the end, the enemy had enough and withdrew. *Leutnant* Kunz would later receive the Knight's Cross to the Iron Cross for his actions.

The battalion then received orders to capture several enemy soldiers for intelligence purposes. While making his rounds, Feig saw two Soviets running in front of Demmler's platoon, the scene of some of the heaviest fighting. Feig grabbed two soldiers with automatic weapons and drove off in the direction of the running Soviets. In all the excitement, Feig forgot that he had not been carrying any weapons. Katzmann, Feig's driver, soon caught up with the gasping Soviet, who stopped and remained quiet. The staff car continued on, while Feig and another soldier guarded the first Soviet.

The *Major* told the soldier to keep an eye on the enemy soldier. Feig then turned in the direction of his bouncing *Kübelwagen* to follow its progress in chasing down the second man. The next thing he knew, he heard a dull thud and a cry. Then, almost simultaneously, he felt a knife bore into his back with great force. Feig collapsed to the ground. The Soviet, who had stabbed the two men, bolted off. The stricken *Panzergrenadier* fired a burst in the direction of the fleeing Soviet, who then collapsed to the ground.

Katzmann returned with the second man. The wounded climbed aboard and Feig was immediately taken to a field hospital, where he was then evacuated to Germany. The knife had penetrated 7 centimeters into Feig's back. *Hauptmann* Mertens, the commander of the 8th Company, assumed acting command of the battalion.

Feig convalesced in the homeland and returned to the front on 21 January 1944. Upon his return, he was given command of the regiment's 1st Battalion. The *1. Panzer-Division* was in defensive positions in a line running Maly–Kustowzy–Pagiorzy. In the meantime, *Generalleutnant* Koll had assumed command of the division.

On 13 February 1944, *Major* Feig's battalion and elements of *Panzergrenadier-Regiment 1* relieved *Gruppe von Pogrell* in Tschichowka. The next day, the division formed *Gruppe Feig* in Risino. When Feig reported to the division operations officer, *Oberstleutnant* von Zitzewitz briefed him as follows: "Clear the route to the Lissjanka Bridgehead; bring logistics forward to *Kampfgruppe Frank.*"

In addition to his battalion, Feig received the reinforced *II./Panzergrenadier-Regiment 1*, as well as the *SPW* companies of that regiment's 1st Battalion. In completing the *Kampfgruppe*, he received tank, anti-armor, artillery and engineer support.

The division commander went on the attack with Feig. The advance to Lissjanka succeeded, and the *Kampfgruppe* there could be resupplied. The next day, Feig established a blocking position to secure his previous day's gains. The battalion was then in almost uninterrupted combat for several days.

On 16 March 1944, Feig was given command of the regiment. Employed as the rearguard for the withdrawal of the *XXIV. Panzer-Korps*, Feig's men defended Gustyn on 1 April 1944. It was there that the acting commander of the division, *Oberst* Marcks, appeared at Feig's command post and issued an order to attack and take the important road hub at Jezierzany. He was ordered to move out at 1300 hours.

The first attack by *Kampfgruppe Frank* had failed. It was imperative to take the village if the crossings over the Seret at Ulaszkowce were to be secured. The men arrived shortly after midnight. Shouting the German battle cry and led by their *Major*, the men launched their attack.[7] The northern part of Jezierzany was filled with the sounds of fighting. Houses went up in smoke.

Dismounting in a raging snowstorm, the regiment continued its attack on foot. The enemy's infantry and armor attempted in vain to eject the *Panzergrenadiere* from the village.

When the division was directed to continue the attack north, *Kampfgruppe Feig* was expeditiously relieved in Jezierzany. Shortly after midnight on 4 April 1944, it prepared to attack again. It turned out to be the blackest day of the regiment. Strong enemy infantry forces allowed the *Panzergrenadiere* to approach to within a few meters before opening up with a murderous fire from all directions. The 1st Battalion, out front, lost some 100 men. The left thigh of *Major* Feig was shattered by a rifle round. Placed on a shelter half, *Major* Feig was evacuated under extremely heavy fire by his messengers.

That wound proved to be the one that kept him off the battlefield for the rest of the war. On 23 May 1944, in a hospital in Germany, he received the German Cross in Gold. He was promoted to *Oberstleutnant* on 1 June 1944, receiving the Close Combat Clasp on the 29th.

After his convalescence, Feig was assigned to the officer-candidate school in Weimar for future officers of the *1. Panzer-Division* and the *7. Panzer-Division*. At the end of the war, he was taken captive by the

---

7. Author's Note: Feig's original order read as follows:
   Panzergrenadier-Regiment 113 attacks Jezierzany on foot. The *I./113* on the right; headquarters *113* in the middle; *II./113* on the left. Echelon right and far to the rear.
   Stark [commander of the reinforced heavy company] guards the force. After dismounting, vehicles follow on radio order. No firing until penetration. No lights; no talking. When the enemy is clearly identified—on him with a Hurra! as from a 1000 throats.

Americans and released in 1947. Feig entered civilian life and also proved successful there, passing away in Wiesbaden on 12 February 1970 after a well-deserved retirement.

A later model KV-I, with the longer 76-mm gun, knocked out by close-combat means. Note the dead crewmember on the mudguard beside the rear deck.

Johannes "Hannes" Grimminger

CHAPTER 5

Major "Hannes" Grimminger

SOLDIER TO THE END

The sun rose, blood red, in the east that morning of 30 June 1941. *Leutnant* Johannes Grimminger had sent *Feldwebel* Binder on patrol at 0100 hours. As it turned light, the young officer went forward to his outposts and then headed to Barmaki to reconnoiter.

On the ridgeline that he reached was an abandoned Soviet fast tank, which was being employed by the Germans against its former owners.

Grimminger watched as the 6th Company moved out after sunrise to expand the security belt around Rowno by some 5 kilometers. *Oberleutnant* Abel, the acting company commander, had moved forward in a borrowed armored car to conduct reconnaissance.

Grimminger, whose men were resting that day, decided to follow the 6th Company with his men, after the enemy forces in front of the abandoned tank had been driven back. Grimminger's men moved out at full speed, reaching Abel's company after only 2 kilometers.

"What's going on, Wirth?" Grimminger asked his comrade from the 6th.

"It's bad, Hannes! Up front, in no-man's-land, is *Oberleutnant* Abel. He's been wounded. I'm rounding up forces to get him."

For a few seconds, Grimminger reflected back on the social get-together spent among the officer families before the division had marched east. He especially remembered the wife of *Oberleutnant* Abel. What if he . . . He didn't dare to finish his train of thought.

"Wamsler," he said to his driver, "we're moving forward!"

They took off in the motorcycle-sidecar combination all by themselves. A short while later, they ran into the battalion commander.

Oberstleutnant Bräuchle stopped them. He grabbed Grimminger, who had been the battalion liaison officer until only recently, by the arm.

"Abel is about 1,200 meters in front of us. We'll get him out, Grimminger. I'm putting you in charge of the 6th. I want you to attack along the left side of the road."

"I'll get the company up here as fast as possible, *Herr Oberstleutnant!*"

Wamsler had already turned the motorcycle around. Soon they were racing back the same way they had come.

Leutnant Wirth came racing towards him with the first few vehicles of the company. He also had some machine-gun sections with him.

Grimminger quickly issued orders: "The company advances on line left of the road!"

The grenadiers advanced under the blazing sun, which had already risen high in the sky. After moving some 600 meters, the men started to receive fire from the grain fields. He had his men continue to advance. Grimminger immediately moved forward. Hunched over, he heard machine-gun rounds whizzing past his head. One of the machine-gun sections accompanying him returned fire. The enemy pulled back, and Grimminger's men covered the 1,200 meters without taking any casualties. They had surprised the Red Army men with their advance.

Grimminger had his men halt when they reached a large farm complex. He had patrols sent out with instructions to immediately report any enemy contact.

The farm buildings seemed surrounded by endless fields of grain. Soon, Grimminger started receiving reports that large groups of Soviets were headed directly for the farmstead.

"All-round defense! All machine guns prepare to fire! Do not open fire until I give orders!"

"Up front, *Herr Leutnant!*" Wamsler called out excitedly.

Large groups of Red Army men appeared in the fields about 500 meters out. They were working their way towards the farm buildings in quick leaps and bounds. Grimminger ordered his men to open fire; he also fired, using a rifle. The reports from the guns echoed loudly in the courtyard of the farmstead. Binder's machine guns contributed mightily to the racket. Off to the right, echeloned somewhat to the rear, there were two more machine guns firing. Looking farther in that direction, Grimminger could see the company commander's vehicle. The Soviets were advancing there and forcing the Germans back. He ordered his machine guns to put down some flanking fires on the advancing Soviets.

The machine guns swung in that direction; riflemen also joined in.

Some of the Soviets then turned towards the 6th, attempting their own flanking maneuver. The men of the 6th started receiving fire from both the front and the right flank.

A messenger showed up, coming from the left: "The 3rd Battalion is pulling back to the outer defenses of Rowno due to massed enemy attacks."

Grimminger started directing fires to the left. But the fires of the 6th were being dissipated. What he could afford to employ on the left flank could not hold up the enemy forces pushing back the 3rd Battalion. The 6th started receiving fire from three directions at that point.

"Here they come, *Herr Leutnant!*" The Soviets were charging the farmstead from the front.

Grimminger order Binder to have his machine guns set grazing fires at one meter through the grain fields, firing from left to right.

Unteroffizier Binder had no time to repeat the order; he simply nodded. The machine guns let loose a few seconds later and mowed down the grain and anyone advancing upright through it. The enemy had closed to within about 80 meters. Grimminger switched from a rifle to a submachine gun. He could see the brown waves roaring towards him, jumping up and down through the greenish-gold grain stalks and firing.

Grimminger fired three bursts, depressed the release and inserted a new magazine. The Soviets were about 40 meters away before the last of them succumbed to the withering German fire.

The officer looked at his wristwatch and determined it was 1500 hours. They had been subjected to the massive fires of the Soviets for nearly 45 minutes. He turned towards Wamsler: "Give me the flare gun and a handful of white star clusters."

Wamsler handed over the weapon and the pyrotechnic ammunition, and Grimminger fired into the clear, blue skies.

"The enemy's attacking again, *Herr Leutnant!*"

"Green pyro!"

The signal indicating an attacking enemy was fired into the air.

"Where in the hell is the battalion?" one of the platoon leaders called out in anger.

"It's probably fixed in place just like we are," Grimminger responded, attempting to calm down the excited men. "As soon as it's possible, it'll attack."

It was swelteringly hot, but the Soviets continued to attack.

"We're out of ammunition for our machine guns," Binder called out. A minute later, Scheurmann, a platoon leader, also reported a shortage of ammunition.

Grimminger knew what that would mean in case of another attack. He acted immediately. He ordered the company to deploy back to the large farmhouse 500 meters farther to the rear. Firing a final burst, Grimminger and some other men forming the rearguard also headed back.

"I don't think we can defend here!" one of the gasping platoon leaders sputtered, as all of them had reassembled in the new position. Grimminger reorganized his small force and was also able to integrate two mortars and two machine guns from the 8th Company into his defensive planning. They had taken up positions behind the farmhouse after being separated from their own company. Grimminger had his men train on the potato field. They did not have to wait for long before the Soviets started advancing again. Grimminger ordered his men to open fire.

The mortar shells started impacting in the potato fields. The shrapnel forced the attacking Soviets to ground. The last remaining machine-gun ammunition was fired. The enemy, attacking in five-fold superiority, was turned back only after he had closed to within 50 meters. The Soviets pulled back into the former positions of the 6th Company.

Off to the right, the men could hear other machine guns and infantry guns firing. Grimminger prepared a message for the battalion: "Enemy stopped. We're holding the road!"

As the company messenger took off, Grimminger looked at his watch. It was 1630 hours. The 8th Company started to come forward. Its men were integrated into the improvised defensive position.

Grimminger asked the company commander for a platoon of men to reconnoiter forward and recover the wounded. A short while later, the men made their way through the grain fields as it was turning dark. They were able to recover an abandoned antitank gun, which Grimminger had sent to the rear. A short while later, Grimminger reached the vehicle of the company commander. He got into the armored car and moved it away from the curve in the road, where it had been ambushed. He then forced himself to look at his dead comrade, the man with whom he had fought together in France. *Oberleutnant* Abel had been hit three times: once in the upper left arm, once in the shoulder and, finally, just above the heart. He then looked at the other dead men. There were several other officers as well as a machine-gun team. All had met their death in the lines in front of the rest. Johannes Grimminger turned ashen,.

A prime mover from the regiment's heavy company recovered the armored car. It also took back the dead. The men of the 6th and the 8th covered the recovery measures.

It wasn't until after midnight, after Grimminger had walked the lines one more time, that he finally found a foxhole and attempted to go to sleep. Fortunately, the night passed peacefully; the enemy appeared to have had enough for the day. As it turned first light, Grimminger was up and about again, trying to rally his men. They were still somewhat shell shocked from their first combat experience in the Soviet campaign.

Towards evening, he assembled the company, over which he had been given formal command after the death of Abel, in the fruit orchard behind the command post. *Leutnant* Hofacker arrived from the battalion; he was to take over Grimminger's 1st Platoon. With the exception of those pulling guard, the entire company gathered at the gravesite of its fallen commander. Grimminger had no easy time of it in giving the eulogy for the fallen commander and the other dead comrades.

The next day, the 6th Company received another tough mission. At the request of Grimminger, the battalion had granted permission for the company to recover its remaining dead. The battalion provided infantry guns and mortars in support. The men headed out to conduct their unpleasant task.

Together with *Unteroffizier* Duffner, who had already brought back a number of wounded to safety during the night of 30 June/1 July, Grimminger headed out. They recovered 15 dead men. Farther out to the front, there had to be even more. It was decided to wait until night had fallen to try to get them.

Under the cover of night, the remaining men were recovered and all were accounted for. Many of the men who went forward with Grimminger broke down upon seeing the terrible scenes. Later on, Grimminger wrote home:

> Recovering those mutilated comrades was a stress test for mind and body that only a few passed. I was among the dead men, coming in contact with them, handling them with care and love, removing their personal belongings, breaking their identity disks in two and removing their pay books.
>
> The smell of decomposition was horrible.
>
> But when my people saw me, they pulled themselves together. We placed the comrades in a freshly dug grave, covered them with shelter halves and took our leave of them.
>
> We presented arms with two rifles, covered the graves and stood silently by that hallowed ground, until I gave the sign to start heading back.
>
> It was the hardest day for our company.

✠

Johannes Grimminger was born a twin in Schwäbisch Gmünd on 6 June 1914. Two months after their birth, the father, a silversmith by trade, was drafted into service in the First World War.

His twin sister died on 10 February 1919, a shock to the young child that he never forgot. As he attended grade school, Hannes, as he was called by his school friends and family, showed a penchant for illustration. Physically, he was not very strong. It had been assumed for a long time that Johannes would become the craftsman in the family. He left school and started an apprenticeship as a silversmith. In competitions conducted in Saarbrücken in April 1935, he was the top competitor in all of Germany in metal- and silversmithing.

On 31 October 1936, he was drafted into the Army. He served for two years in the *6./Infanterie-Regiment 119* of the *25. Infanterie-Division*, which he would later rejoin in the war. Grimminger was promoted to *Unteroffizier* on 2 July 1938. Four weeks later, he discovered that he had been selected to attend the officer-candidate course at Döberitz on 15 August. While in attendance, he became acquainted with one

2426283032343638404244464850525456586062646668707274767880828486889092949698100

Major Bräuchle, the 2nd Battalion attacked the *Fort de la Malmaison* and took it. One day later, on his 26th birthday, *Leutnant* Grimminger was shot in the right arm while attacking with his platoon. Later on, he received the Iron Cross, First Class, for that action. His wounding also signaled the end of his participation in the fighting in France; he was air-evacuated to a German military hospital in Trier.

On 16 June 1940, *Oberstleutnant* Grasser became the first soldier of the division to be awarded the Knight's Cross to the Iron Cross. By 26 September 1940, *Leutnant* Grimminger had recovered enough from his wounds that he participated in the march of his regiment to its garrison at Schwäbisch Gmünd as part of its homecoming from France. Despite rumors of potential employment in the Middle East, the division found itself headed towards the Soviet frontier in June 1941. By then, it had been reorganized and redesignated as the *25. Infanterie-Division (mot.)*—as from 15 November 1940.

✠

The *25. Infanterie-Division* was not employed until 27 June 1941, when it was became part of the second attack wave against the Soviet Union. It crossed the Bug on an engineer pontoon bridge at the frontier town of Uscilug in the area around Wijganowice (near Lublin) in the withering summer heat. It marched past burned-down farmsteads, tank wrecks and the graves of soldiers along the road as it headed in the direction of Luck on 28 June. Rowno was the division's next objective, and the lead elements of the division entered the city around 1000 hours on 29 June. The battalion bivouacked in a park in the eastern portion of the city. Grimminger was installed as a platoon leader again, after having served well as a liaison officer. After the death of *Oberleutnant* Abel, as detailed at the beginning of this section, Grimminger continued in acting command of the company as it advanced into the southern Ukraine in a series of exhaustive and intense fights. Always at the front of his men, he was continuously demonstrating courage, a sense of duty and a spirit of self-sacrifice. Moved to the center sector of the Eastern Front, the division participated in the assault on Moscow in that ill-fated winter of 1941/1942, fighting as far east as Tula and Riasan. For six of his most difficult operations, all of which would have individually made him eligible for the Iron Cross, First Class, Grimminger became one of the first soldiers of the division to receive the newly created award, the German Cross in Gold, on 29 January 1942.

During the subsequent withdrawals outside of Moscow, Grasser summoned Grimminger to be his regimental liaison officer. He was confronted with a new set of demands in that position, all of which he mastered well. In addition to his regular duties, he was also entrusted with the establishment of several military cemeteries. It was thanks to him that a number of families were able to receive photographs of the final resting places of their next-of-kin.

On 1 March 1942, he was summoned to the division command post, where he was informed that he had been promoted to *Oberleutnant* for bravery in the face of the enemy. Grimminger then saw action in the fighting around Kirjekowo–Orel and, in 1943, at Orscha–Dubrowno. He participated in the fighting to take the industrial region at Kriwoj-Rog, the encirclement of Marshal Budjenny's field army east of Kiev and the advance on Kharkov. He returned to command the 6th Company. On 1 March 1943, he was promoted ahead of his peers to *Hauptmann*, again for bravery in the face of the enemy.

At the beginning of 1944, Grimminger was entrusted with running the field army's Grenadier Combat Academy at Dubrowno. At the academy, he was responsible for the training of hundreds of officers, who benefitted from his experiences in conducting the merciless fighting that was the hallmark of the campaign in the East. He ran the academy until the spring of 1944, when a bout of malaria forced him into the military hospital at Dubrowno. At the end of May, Grimminger was allowed to take home leave to convalesce. He under went a "cure treatment" in Freudenstadt, which he was able to spend with a comrade from his regiment, Laufer.

While on home leave, Grimminger discovered the catastrophe that had befallen the Eastern Front in the form of the collapse of *Heeresgruppe Mitte.*[5] He returned to the front, only to discover that his division, which had been reorganized and redesignated as the *25. Panzergrenadier-Division* on 23 June 1943, had been encircled in the area between Minsk and Beresina.

On 3 July, he wrote home:

---

5. Editor's Note: A catastrophe for the *Wehrmacht* that came to be known as the "Destruction of Army Group Center."

The fighting is very difficult. Cannot rejoin my division; have made myself available at the place where the greatest chance of breaking through to my division exists and where I can therefore be of the most use.

The situation will probably dictate that you will not receive any mail from me for a long time; don't be worried about me because of that.

My obligation now is to help my comrades and my dear brother in any way possible.

Over the next few days, *Hauptmann* Grimminger tried to reach his division. On 3 July, the Soviets captured Minsk. A few soldiers made it back through the Soviet encirclement; replacements came forward from Germany. Grimminger assembled those men around him and led the replacement battalion for the division. He told his men that they would try to hold back the enemy for as long as possible. On 8 July, the few men under Grimminger's command joined forces with the relief effort poised to try to hack out the encircled German forces.

✠

The morning of 8 July dawned wanly in the East, as *Hauptmann* Grimminger gave the order to attack. The *SPW's* rolled out. Two assault guns were attached to his force; they were in the lead. The two towed antitank guns attached to him followed the *SPW's*. They moved in the direction of the enemy forces feeling their way forward.

The enemy force consisted of elements of General Rotmistrow's 5th Guards Tank Army, which had taken Minsk and were then pressing forward. Minsk had previously been the headquarters of *Generalfeldmarschall* Model's forces.

A Soviet tank division was advancing, and one of its attack wedges struck Grimminger's small *Kampfgruppe*.

"Tanks ahead, *Herr Hauptmann!*"

Grimminger took immediate action: "Move into the depression over there . . . both of the antitank gun set up on the upper edges . . . have the assault guns report to me!"

With tracks rattling, the assault guns moved to Grimminger's position in the depression. He ordered the gun commanders to take up positions close by, since they had clear fields of fire on the enemy approach route along the road from there. Grimminger then turned his attention to the positioning of his *Panzergrenadiere.*

A short while later, the enemy tanks closed in. Both of the antitank guns opened fire. Grimminger had positioned himself forward, to the right of the road. He observed the two tanks that had left the road go up in flames. The rest of them continued to advance along the road. It was a group of at least 30 armored vehicles: a few T-34's, some SU assault guns and a number of troop transporters. The next few rounds set the Soviet troop transporters on fire. Red Army men jumped off, only to be caught up in bursts of fire from the machine guns, which then opened up.

"They're coming through over there!" someone yelled out to Grimminger.

"Hold your fire and take cover!" Grimminger ordered his headquarters section.

The T-34's roared past the hiding men, reaching the edge of the depression. Then all hell broke loose. The two assault guns fired at 400 meters, and each of their rounds was a direct, devastating hit. Six . . . seven . . . eight T-34's were in flames at the edge of the depression. The rest of the Soviet forces turned and sought their salvation in flight. The two assault guns, which advanced to the edge of the depression, then proceeded to knock out two more T-34's before the last of the enemy armored vehicles disappeared into the woods.

"We need to stay here, *Herr Hauptmann,*" *Leutnant* Pötter said.

"That's what we're going to do. We'll hold the road until the hole in the lines further to the rear has been plugged."

The next few days demanded the utmost of everyone in the *Kampfgruppe.* Thanks to the example of Grimminger, the "old hands" and the green recruits were soon a band of brothers. He reorganized his defenses in the ideal terrain. It was a bottleneck: the enemy's tanks could not leave the road network without getting stuck in the marshland.

Despite that, the enemy attacked constantly. Strong armored and infantry forces attempted to break through so as to envelop the Germans farther to the rear.

"Here they come again, *Herr Hauptmann!*" *Leutnant* Pötter announced after the first attack wave had been turned back and the burning wrecks of knocked-out T-34's were left abandoned by the enemy on the battlefield. The Soviets attacked down the road, at least a regiment of them.

"Fire!" Grimminger commanded, when the enemy had approached to within 200 meters.

The *MG 42's* began to hammer away. The Soviets took the German defenders under fire with heavy machine guns, a brigade's worth of mortars and Stalin organs.

Grimminger fired at a squad of Soviets with his submachine gun. They had appeared out of nowhere in a ditch about 40 meters in front of him. The men to his sides were throwing hand grenades. Muzzle flashes could be seen from the trenches. Hand grenades came flying through the air. One of them landed barely 2 meters from Grimminger's feet.

Fast as lightning, Grimminger dove for the floor of the trench. The bursting hand grenade sprayed the area with shrapnel. It was a close call. Grimminger reloaded, rose and saw Soviets coming out of the vegetation in front of him.

Stalin organ rockets screamed through the air, passing close by overhead, only to explode relatively harmlessly a short distance to the rear. Nonetheless, the concussion from the explosions pressed the men flat against the walls of their trenches and on the ground.

The *MG 42's* started to rattle anew. Arcs of tracers raced from the flanks of the Soviets to their interior, and extracted a fearsome toll. What remained of the latest wave of attackers collapsed under the combined effects of submachine guns and hand grenades.

On that 19th of July, the Soviets attacked seven times. They were turned back that same number. One of the antitank guns and one of the assault guns were knocked out by the enemy tanks. The remaining heavy weapons were able to turn the tide, however. A penetration on the right side of the position was sealed off and cleared up by an immediate counterattack launched by Grimminger's reserves, a platoon of *Panzergrenadiere*, all armed with captured Soviet submachine guns. During the immediate counterattack, Grimminger was wounded for the second time. Despite that, he remained with his men, because he knew how much they needed him. The men held out, even though they knew that the Soviets had already gone past them on both sides on the other side of the marshland.

Grimminger's radio operator reported to him that evening: "*Herr Hauptmann*, the front has been closed behind us. We have been ordered to pull back to the new main line of resistance."

That meant that Grimminger's hopes of freeing up his encircled division were dashed. But he was comforted by the knowledge that his efforts there had enabled other groups of determined soldiers the opportunity to break out.

The news of the impending withdrawal spread like wildfire. *Leutnant* Ebelein told his commander that he would at least have the chance to allow his wounds to properly heal. That night, the men disengaged from the enemy. On the way back to the main line of resistance, they encountered other enemy elements that had already made it well past them. After a short engagement, the enemy threat was eliminated. A short while later, the *Kampfgruppe* was passed through the German lines.

Grimminger was taken to the main dressing station. He had been weakened from loss of blood, but he was happy to know that things had turned out well for his *Kampfgruppe*. On 11 August, he was sent back to Germany along with the rest of his men. His battalion was disbanded in Gmünd, and Grimminger was reassigned to the *21. Panzer-Division* in the west. On 23 August 1944, he was notified that he had been awarded the Knight's Cross to the Iron Cross for his defensive actions along the Minsk road. Ten days later, he was fighting in the west. During the intense fighting from 27 to 29 September in the area around Antrepiérre, Grimminger was so badly wounded in the right hand that he had to be evacuated to Germany on 1 October. At the hospital, he was awarded the Wound Badge in Silver.

Nine days later, he was headed back to the Western Front. He was given acting command of the division's armored reconnaissance battalion, only to be given command of the *II./Panzergrenadier-Regiment 192* a few days after that. Grimminger's battalion always seemed to be in the thick of things; he could always be seen moving from one hot spot to another in his command *SPW*. Whenever the enemy captured a few meters of ground, he would launch his reserves and drive him back.

When an American regiment had to be attacked in order to clear a path across a bridge, Grimminger moved out ahead of his men. He conducted his reconnaissance and then led his men under extremely heavy enemy fire across the railway bridge. When the *Panzergrenadiere* hesitated to enter the volcano of fire, Grimminger went across the bridge three times to spur his individual sections on.

When the Americans pressed hotly on their heels, Grimminger remained with his rearguards. They succeeded in holding off the U.S. forces long enough for the entire regiment to gain some distance from the enemy. On one occasion, he relieved one of his encircled companies with a small force consisting of a single tank and two *SPW's*. The Americans then commenced to launch psychological warfare against Grimminger's battalion, making promises of very good treatment if it would deliver him to them.

On 24 October, a *Panzergrenadier*, Emil Klingler, was captured by the Americans. When he refused to reveal where the battalion command post was, he was beaten. Later on, he said to the author: "Even if they had beaten us to death, we would have never betrayed our Hannes."

At the beginning of November, the regiment was in the Voges Mountains. The enemy attacked constantly. The regimental commander was wounded, and *Hauptmann* Grimminger assumed acting command on 9 November at St. Beniot. He acquitted himself well until the newly designated commander could arrive a few days later and he resumed command of his battalion on 17 November.

From 25 to 30 November, Grimminger was in constant combat with his battalion in the area around Saarlautern. He was wounded by shrapnel while in the front lines on 30 November. He was wounded in his eyes as well and was evacuated to the eye clinic in Würzburg on 1 December.

After being treated, he went on convalescent leave and spent the time with his parents until 2 February 1945. One day before departing for the Eastern Front, Grimminger discovered he had been promoted to *Major* for bravery in the face of the enemy. On 9 February, the division loaded on trains for the Eastern Front, heading for the Lauban area of Upper Silesia (present-day Czech Republic).

It was there that *Major* Grimminger would save the division in a difficult situation. It was 18 February and the regimental command post was in Klix. The commander turned to his regimental operations noncommissioned officer, *Stabsfeldwebel* Ditzel, and told him to assemble all of the classified documents and see whether he could make his way to the rear. The Soviets were already in the vicinity of Halbau, not far from Klix. Ditzel and his clerks loaded out their vehicles. As they started to take off, they were already starting to receive submachine-gun fire from the Soviets. It looked as though the regimental headquarters might be wiped out.

Suddenly, *Major* Grimminger and his ready reserves appeared. In short order, his men had hacked out the encircled men and enabled them to move back. The regimental commander was nowhere to be found, however. He had gone forward to check on his men. *Major* Grimminger reconnoitered and, in the process, discovered the Soviets had already blocked the road to Halbau, the only withdrawal route available to the division. He ran into *Major* Brand, the commander of the divisional reconnaissance battalion: "Brand, we need to open up the road. I'll take the lead, if you advance on the other side of the road."

Grimminger headed off towards the enemy and soon started to receive fire. The armored vehicles advancing on both sides of the road replied and continued to attack. They ran into the enemy's main body. Grimminger's *SPW* was hit, immobilized and caught fire. He ordered his men to dismount and follow him.

Machine guns blazed . . . demolitions went up . . . Red Army transport vehicles went up in flames. . . . ammunition exploded. The determined officers cleared a path through the chaos that had erupted. They chased off the strong Soviet advance guard; nine tanks went up in flames. After the dust had settled, they saw that they had been successful. The route to Halbau was open. The rest of the division, as well as the remnants of two other battered divisions, were able to make their way through the corridor that had been carved out, thus escaping destruction or captivity.

Later that evening, Grimminger went to his command post. He had prevented a catastrophe of the first magnitude by his decisive and bold action. The commanding general recommended him for the Oak Leaves to the Knight's Cross to the Iron Cross, since his actions had contributed decisively to the outcome of the fighting. The division succeeded in holding the Soviets along the Neiße for a while. Grimminger wrote about it in a letter home written on 25 February:

> I assumed command of the regiment a week ago. Open all doors
> for our countrymen who have had to leave their homeland in

the face of the Red Army. Pray for our people. May God not
withhold his mercy from them.

Grimminger was evacuated to the homeland once again and sent
to to the eye clinic in Würzburg. On 5 March, he wrote his parents:

Dear Parents,
My general has sent me here, since my eye is no longer
cooperating. A small follow-up operation today; I hope to be
able to visit you in a week.

On 11 March, Grimminger became the 776th member of the
German Armed Forces to be awarded the Oak Leaves.

During a short stay in Hof (Bavaria), he wrote what would be his
final words to his young wife, whom he had maried on 21 March. Early
on the morning of 6 April, he assumed command of the regiment
again in Greifenberg, southeast of Görlitz–Lauban. On 10 April,
the regiment was moved to the area southeast of Kottbus. Late in
the afternoon of 16 April, the regiment received orders. As always,
Grimminger carefully briefed his men and the attached tanks. He
then headed out to conduct reconnaissance. He got caught in a salvo
of fire from a Soviet mortar brigade and was mortally wounded.

His comrades evacuated him to the rear. In the course of the
subsequent withdrawals, they took his remains as far as Drebkau
(Niederlausitz). They did not want their Hannes buried somewhere
where his final resting place would remain unknown. Towards
midnight on 19 April, Johannes Grimminger and 14 of his comrades
were given the final honors in the palatial park at Drebkau. Chaplain
Tarnow-Schwerin, the division's chaplain, presided over the ceremony.

Following the war, in 1952, the parents of that exemplary officer
were not permitted by the East Germans to visit his final resting place
in Drebkau. A short while later, the East German authorities moved all
of the remains from there to a collective cemetery in Halbe (District of
Königswusterhausen).

Later on, one of his former soldiers paid him a fitting tribute:

In the Federal Republic of Germany, the military wants to
create a new type of leader. Now, whenever I think about

what type of person should be a German officer, a man to whom I would entrust my own son, then I wish it could be someone like *Major* Johannes Grimminger.

A photo from the early advance in the Soviet Union with a typical scene: A knocked-out Soviet tank beside the main axis of advance—in this case, a BT-5.

Hans-Joachim Kahler

CHAPTER 6

Generalmajor Joachim Kahler

PANZERGRENADIER **IN THREE DIVISIONS**

While the southern pincers of Operation "Zitadelle" attacked north from the area between Fastov and Bjelgorod on 4 July 1943, *Gruppe Weiß* of *Generaloberst* Walter Model remained in its staging areas behind the broad arc of the main line of resistance in the Orel Bend.

On the morning of 5 July, hundreds of *Stukas* and horizontal bombers flew above the *9. Armee* towards the south.

The members of the *4. Panzer-Division* discovered that the northern pincer of the attack had started at 0615 hours that morning. The armored division was positioned behind the attack waves of the *6. Infanterie-Division.*

Towards noon, the tanks of the division and the mechanized infantry of the division's *Panzergrenadier-Regiment 33* and *Panzergrenadier-Regiment 12* moved towards their attack positions, a giant fruit orchard. From there, the barren terrain stretched out to the east towards the dominating high ground of Hill 274 at Olchowatka. The gently rising terrain was crisscrossed by a number of marshy defiles, many running along the direction of attack.

Major Joachim Kahler, who assumed acting command of *Panzergrenadier-Regiment 33* after the wounding of *Oberst Dr.* Mauss on 12 May 1943, discovered that the attacks of the infantry regiments of the *6. Infanterie-Division* in front had bogged down. *Generalleutnant* Großmann's[1] grenadiers were stuck in front of Hill 274. The *4. Panzer-Division* was ordered to move out to attack through the infantry division early in the morning of 7 July. At midnight, Kahler heard the following

---

1. Author's Note: Großmann was a competent and capable commander, having been awarded the Knight's Cross to the Iron Cross on 23 August 1941 as an *Oberst* and commander of *Infanterie-Regiment 84.* On 4 September 1943, he became the 292nd member of the German Armed Forces to be honored with the Oak Leaves to the Knight's Cross. He was still commander of the *6. Infanterie-Division* at the time of the award.

on the radio: " . . . the largest battle of materiel of the war south of Orel
. . . gigantic employment of tanks and artillery on both sides . . . "

Hauptmann Mitteldorf, the logistics officer of the *4. Panzer-Division*,
sent all of his supply columns forward during the night. *Major* Kahler
finally got his formal attack order:

> *Panzergrenadier-Regiment 33*, reinforced by the *2./* and *5./Pan-
> zer-Aufklärungs-Abteilung 4*, attacks the enemy on Hill 274 and
> ejects him. *Panzer-Regiment 35* and the *Tiger* battalion support
> the attack and take up the pursuit.

The fight could begin.

✠

The *Panzergrenadiere* advanced dismounted. Up ahead, nearly 2
kilometers away, *Major* Kahler could see the mighty hill, from which
the enemy was firing uninterruptedly.

Artillery shells hammered into the ground all around them. The
first mechanized infantrymen went to ground. A powerful artillery
salvo fell on the *2./Panzer-Aufklärungs-Abteilung 4*, killing all officers,
save *Oberleutnant* Weidner.

"*Herr Major*, it's impossible to advance!" one of the officers called
out.

"We cannot afford to bog down!" he replied.

Major Kahler thrust himself up, ran through the vortex of bursting
rounds and artillery shells, which seemed to have covered the terrain
in front with thick fog, from which the flames of the explosions jutted
out without interruption.

The men of the 1st Battalion followed the field-grade officer and
reached the intermediate objective: the final marshy defile in front of
the objective.

Enemy machine-gun fire pelted the men and forced them to ground
again. First crawling, then exploiting the concealment provided by the
dense vegetation, *Major* Kahler reached the men of the 2nd Battalion.

"Seventh Company, follow me! Everyone else, provide cover!"

While the men providing cover sought out targets, *Major* Kahler
led the 7th Company in a wide arc, headed into the marshy defile and

rolled up the enemy from the flanks. One machine-gun nest after the other was taken out until the defile had been cleared.

"Let's go . . . hit the hill!"

The men gasped for breath as they ascended the high ground and tried to dodge the enemy's fires. Despite the murderous fire, the tall figure of the commander could always be seen leading at the front. Despite all their efforts, however, they could not wrest the hilltop from the enemy. *Major* Kahler considered his options and decided to try to get around to the right, which was the location of the village of Teploje. He ran over to the 2nd Battalion, which was closest to the village.

"We're attacking Teploje!"

Kahler ran at the head of the 2nd Battalion towards the enemy in Teploje. He felt himself becoming ever more exhausted with each stride, but he persevered and held out. Teploje was palpably close. Perhaps they could do it . . .

The grenadiers reached the edge of the village, helped along by the covering fires provided by the 1st Battalion. They fought house-to-house in bitterly conducted close combat. Kahler's submachine gun was heard with ever greater frequency. After what seemed like an eternity, Teploje was in German hands.

He then ordered the men to attack the main objective, the hill, off to their left. He relayed to the 1st Battalion that it was to attack frontally.

A new attack started. Once again, the men were rallied forward by the dashing example of their acting commander. The attack succeeded. The men cleared the hilltop and the surrounding defiles of the enemy. The men had reached their objective, but at tremendous cost. *Generalleutnant* von Saucken, the division commander, was wounded in Teploje. His aide-de-camp was killed. The division's operations officer, *Oberstleutnant* Lutz, and *Hauptmann* Schmidt, the acting commander of *Panzer-Aufklärungs-Abteilung 4*, were killed. *Major* Kahler had also been wounded—shrapnel to the head—but he continued to lead his force.

The Soviets then counterattacked the hill, which had only about 100 *Panzergrenadiere* defending it. The men were able to defend until midnight, when the superior Soviet force turned them out. *Major* Kahler pulled back with his men to Teploje. The trench strength of *Panzergrenadier-Regiment 33* averaged 15 men per company.

The fighting for Teploje lasted for three days. The enemy fired down on the village from the hill with dug-in T-34's. The Soviet artillery also fired without letting up, coupled with mortars. The inferno was aided and abetted by the screaming hiss of rockets, which landed 30 to 40 at a time in a small area.

During the morning of 10 July, *Leutnant* Sachse, the liaison officer for *Panzer-Aufklärungs-Abteilung 4*, received orders to report to *Major* Kahler's regiment to coordinate operations. He moved through the enemy fires on a motorcycle with a sidecar towards the regimental command post, which was right behind the front lines. Enemy antitank guns and tank main guns fired at him. When Sachse reached the command post, he was greeted by *Hauptmann* Hertl, the regiment's adjutant. *Major* Kahler had just left for the division. He and his men had turned back a Soviet attack an hour before, helped by the division's tanks and a handful of attached *Tigers*. While Sachse was still being briefed by Hertl Kahler returned. His cap sat crookedly across his bandaged head.

"*Leutnant Sachse* reports to the regiment as liaison officer from the reconnaissance battalion, *Herr Major*!"

"Thanks, Sachse!" Kahler greeted the officer, whom he already knew, shaking his hand. "Müller's company has been attached to me. Go get it and guide it in here."

Leutnant Sachse dutifully took off, but was unable to locate the company. When he sheepishly returned to the regimental command post, *Oberleutnant* Müller was sitting in *Major* Kahler's foxhole, which had a shelter half over it. The men were soon contentedly eating some cold pea soup in the spartan shelter, which measured about two meters by two meters. Sachse later recounted his experience:

We had a strange sense of security, as if there wasn't a shelter half above us but a concrete roof. The *Major* was a portrait of calm. He was completely dedicated to conducting the fight, and it was due to him and his complete disregard for the hellish circumstances surrounding us that the illusion of a safe harbor succeeded. Even the screeching sounds of the firing of weapons from the close-support aircraft that were attacking at the time were unable to shake the spell that the deliberate, calm and professional manner of the *Major* had cast over us.

Underneath his head dressing he was already calculating his next measures, while there was the devil to pay outside.

Reports arrived. Liaison officers arrived, and the *Major* had nothing to offer them except his unflappable calm, his clear recommendations and his orders.

But that mattered more than a lack of materiel or replacements. We hoped nothing would happen to our *Major.*

The Soviets continued to attack again and again, always with seemingly fresh forces. The *Panzergrenadiere* eventually had to pull back, meter by meter. They pulled back, dug in again and continued the fight.

Major Kahler seemed to be everywhere at once. When he wasn't up front with his men, he was headed to the division headquarters to try to obtain additional forces. It was during one of those visits that he received the news that electrified everyone: four armored divisions had to be pulled out of the Kursk offensive to counter the Soviet attacks in the Bolchow area that had succeeded in penetrating the German front.

For the *4. Panzer-Division,* that meant that it would hold its positions until the following night, when it would pull back 5 kilometers. Kahler issued the corresponding orders: "The new main line of resistance is north of Ssamodurowka. The regimental command post is located at the edge of the defile at Ssaborowka. We will move back in bounds, covering one another . . . Sachse, notify *Rittmeister* Bettag! . . . Thomsen, get the command post ready to move!"

As was frequently the case, *Panzergrenadier-Regiment 33* formed the division's rearguard. As it turned night, elements moved back over the 60-ton bridge that had been erected across the mighty defile that spanned the Ssamodurowka. The ripening fields—hemp, sunflowers, grain and buckwheat—provided some additional concealment for the men. It was not until the following morning that Kahler saw the Soviets, who had given pursuit. He was able to pull his regiment back almost entirely without casualties.

The Soviets started following up with a vengeance, however. Tanks raced forward and fighter-bombers attacked from the sky. Hordes of infantry began to arrive and cross the defile towards the evening. The German artillery took them under fire. Infantry guns and mortars joined the fray, which stopped any effort to cross the defile cold.

Kahler then had to pull back his *Kampfgruppe* another 12 kilometers. By 16 July, he had conducted four withdrawal operations. Even in the most difficult of situations, he remained the master of the situation by virtue of his unflappable calm, his clear manner in issuing orders and his extraordinary fearlessness. Despite the wound to his head, he remained with his troops. On 16 July, when the Soviets attacked again with strong armored forces, it was Kahler who was up front with his forces and who rallied them in the defense. He had to commit his last remaining reserves. By the skin of their teeth, they pulled it off and were even able to push the Soviets back a bit.

Since Kahler was largely on his own during those engagements, it must be he who is credited with stopping any Soviet breakthrough in the divisional sector. On 18 July, Kahler was put back in charge of his former formation, *Panzer-Aufklärungs-Abteilung 4*. He formed a *Kampfgruppe* with the reconnaissance battalion, being augmented by the *1./Panzer-Pionier-Bataillon 79* of *Oberleutnant* Berlitz, a battery of self-propelled guns under *Hauptmann* Winterling and a tank company under the acting command of *Leutnant* Gsell.

Kampfgruppe Kahler set up shop at the airfield southwest of Orel. There it received considerable reinforcement in the form of a towed battalion of 8.8-centimeter antitank guns. Kahler was ordered to report to the command post of the *9. Panzer-Division* at Snamenskoje, 40 kilometers northwest of Orel. On 19 July, Kahler's forces were integrated with that division's reconnaissance battalion—*Panzer-Aufklärungs-Abteilung 9*—that then formed *Kampfgruppe Oberst Schmahl.*

Major Kahler and his force were sent forward, occupying Kaschtscheikowa, Sujewka, Nisina and Hill 233.3 (near Mywrino). Kahler's moves came as a surprise to the enemy and were successful.

During the night of 20/21 July, the Soviets attacked with tanks. In the fighting for Hill 233.3, *Oberleutnant* Weidner of the battalion's heavy company was badly wounded, dying a short while later. *Oberleutnant* Luther assumed command of the company, and it had to evacuate the high ground two days later under the enormous pressure. *Oberleutnant* Sachse covered the withdrawal with two self-propelled 8.8-centimeter *Flak* that he commandeered and employed against the advancing Soviets.

On 24 July, *Major* Kahler was able to enjoy a respite from enemy attacks long enough to present well deserved awards to his men at the command post. One day later, the *Kampfgruppe* was hastily transferred to the Karatschow area to deal with another enemy penetration there. On 26 July, after a preparation by *Stukas*, the *Kampfgruppe* moved out in the direction of Pyrjatinka, which was taken. A short while later, however, the attack bogged down in some woods at Warki.

The *Kampfgruppe* pulled back to Pyrjatinka, which then received a salvo of Stalin organ rockets the next day. Kahler's command post received a direct hit. *Feldwebel* Motten, the headquarters company section leader was killed, as was *Oberleutnant* Haas. *Feldwebel* Meister, the platoon leader of the infantry gun platoon in the battalion's heavy company, was badly wounded. *Major* Kahler emerged unscathed and rallied his shaken men to continue the fight.

The *Kampfgruppe* fought in the area around Krassnyi and Pachbar until 6 August. An enemy penetration at Krassnyi–Roschta was sealed off and eliminated; several other enemy attacks were turned back. Finally, Kahler was given permission to pull back. He was then informed that he would be given command of *Panzergrenadier-Regiment 5* of the *12. Panzer-Division*. As a result of his exemplary performance of duty and success in a difficult situation, he was promoted to *Oberstleutnant* ahead of his peers on 1 September 1943.

✠

Hans-Joachim Kahler was born in Moerchingen in the Alsace region on 21 March 1908. He was born into an officer family, the son of an *Oberst*.

He was graduated from the *Gymnasium* in Hanover and entered military service immediately thereafter, becoming an officer candidate in *Reiter-Regiment 14*, a horse cavalry regiment, in Ludwigslust on 1 April 1927. On 1 April 1932, he was commissioned as a *Leutnant* and designated as a troop commander. By 1934, he was an *Oberleutnant* and regimental adjutant. He was considered among the best riders in the German Army. He attended a number of tournaments, garnering prizes and show finishes, as well as suffering a number of falls. In 1938, he was promoted to *Rittmeister*.

In Poland, he served as the commander of the regiment's advance guard. He received the Iron Cross, Second Class, on 3 July 1940 in France. In 1941, he became the adjutant of the *12. Panzer-Division*, earning the Iron Cross, First Class, as the acting commander of *Panzerjäger-Abteilung 2* of the division.

After being promoted to *Major* on 1 January 1942, Kahler was given a new command: *Kradschützen-Bataillon 34* of the *4. Panzer-Division*. The motorcycle battalion was later reorganized and redesignated as the division's reconnaissance battalion. In 1942, Kahler and his men were in the thick of things as part of the division's operations in the central sector of the Eastern Front.

In the spring of 1943, Kahler participated in the most important operation he had conducted up to that point in the war. On 14 March, he helped retake Seredina-Buda and Ssewsk. His motorcyclists were employed between two important rail lines and had to advance against a well-defended locality. Since it was the linchpin of the enemy's defenses, it was packed with heavy weapons. He succeeded in getting a company right up to the outermost buildings of the village, whereupon he and his men infiltrated into its western portion. The men approached the two bridges over the Sjew and took them. The remaining companies of battalion closed up. *Major* Kahler then continued the advance, with each house having to be taken individually. Whenever the attack threatened to bog down, it was *Major* Kahler who appeared to rally the men and issue new orders. They eliminated the enemy forces in their path and opened the gates for the remaining forces of the division to move on and take the city of Ssewsk.

For his success and the success of his men, *Major* Kahler was awarded the Knight's Cross to the Iron Cross on 14 April 1943.

On 1 April, Kahler was given acting command of *Panzergrenadier-Regiment 12*, replacing *Oberst* von der Damerau, who had gone on home leave. He remained in that temporary assignment until 26 April. He then assumed acting command of *Panzer-Aufklärungs-Abteilung 4* again for several weeks.

✠

Following *Zitadelle* and the fighting around Orel, Kahler was given command of *Panzergrenadier-Regiment 5*, replacing *Oberst* Dietrich von Müller, who had commanded the regiment since it was formed prior to the war.[2] Those were no easy shoes to fill for a newcomer, even one as experienced and capable as Kahler.

On 23 August, the regiment was committed into the area around Rushnoje. *Major* Kahler's orders: "Hold open the bridge over the Iwot north of Martschichina Buda and form a bridgehead there, including the named locality."

When Kahler's advance guard arrived there during the morning of 30 August, the *7. Infanterie-Division*, which was defending in that sector, had already sustained heavy losses. *Oberleutnant* Wendland's *6./Panzergrenadier-Regiment 5* attacked from the march into the flank of the attacking Soviet forces, which had just launched their advance. Wendland was mortally wounded in the assault; *Leutnant* Trautwein assumed acting command. He was also wounded and could no longer fight. *Feldwebel* Albrecht took charge of the company, since no more officers were left. Thanks to his obstinacy, the rest of the 2nd Battalion was able to establish a new main line of resistance along the Iwot that evening. By then, the 1st Battalion had also closed into sector and joined its sister battalion on the left.

Kahler, who was promoted to *Oberstleutnant* ahead of his peers on 1 September, worked with the commander of the *7. Infanterie-Division, Generalleutnant* von Rappard, to stabilize the situation and accomplish his mission, which was to establish a bridgehead across the river. The 1st Company of *Oberleutnant* Thormann was directed to cross the river and establish a foothold on the far bank, enabling the forces of the *7. Infanterie-Division* remaining there to be relieved.

Thormann's company was then subjected to enormous pressure by the Soviets, who concentrated all of their fires on the single company. It took numerous casualties when hit by a barrage of rocket fire. *Oberstleutnant* Kahler was forced to pull that company back across the river, and the bridge was blown up by the engineers.

---

2. Author's Note: Von Müller received the Knight's Cross to the Iron Cross on 3 May 1942, when the regiment was *Schützen-Regiment 5 (mot.)*. For his successful fighting around Orel, he was awarded the Oak Leaves on 16 August 1943, the 272nd member of the German Armed Forces to be so honored. After leaving command, he became an instructor at a number of military academies, including a battalion commander course, until he was later given command of the *16. Panzer-Division*. Serving as the Division Commander, he became the 134th officer of the German Armed Forces to be awarded the Oak Leaves to the Swords on 20 February 1945. After the capitulation in May 1945, he spent 10 years in Soviet captivity.

In subsequent operations as part of the general withdrawal known as *Operation Spätlese,*[3] the division, as part of the *LVI. Panzer-Korps,* which had seven other divisions allocated to it, pulled back across the Dessna on both sides of Nowgorod Ssewersk. During the night of 6/7 September, Kahler's regiment crossed the river and occupied new positions directly along the river to the north of the city. The mighty torrent, which ran between 800 and 1,000 meters wide, became the new main line of resistance.

The Soviet offensive seemed inexorable, however, and they soon established a bridgehead on the far side near Drobyschewo. Kahler was ordered to eliminate the Soviet bridgehead by the commanding general, *Generalleutnant* Hoßbach, but his force proved inadequate for the task. The regiment was configured as a *Kampfgruppe* and then served as a rearguard for the corps for the subsequent withdrawals. The withdrawal route led along the Nowgorod Ssewersk–Tschernigow road to the west. It was not until 17 September that Kahler's men were also able to disengage from the enemy and pull back in the direction of Tschernigow.

Generalmajor Freiherr von Bodenhausen, the commander of the *12. Panzer-Division,* arrived at Kahler's command post in Tschernigow on 20 September to be briefed on the situation. Before Kahler could render a report, the general was privy to an incoming report that seemingly shocked him. *Oberleutnant* Kalau, the regimental adjutant, had just established contact with the adjutant of the battalion in the front lines, asking him the situation.

"Shitty!" The sound of *Leutnant* Lenzing's voice could be heard through the receiver, echoing as far as the general. The general was not happy: "That's no situation report! Kahler, go up front immediately and get briefed properly on the situation. Then report to me."

Oberstleutnant Kahler headed up front as ordered, moving through enemy artillery fire. He saw that the enemy had broken through at Towstoles. He returned and rendered a "proper" report to the general. The general ordered Kahler to conduct an immediate counterattack to retake Towstoles and eliminate the enemy forces that had broken through there. To that end, his *Kampfgruppe* was to be reinforced by the *SPW* battalion of *Panzergrenadier-Regiment 304* of the *2. Panzer-Division,* which was also in the sector.

---

3. Translator's Note: "Late Vintage."

Kahler reorganized his forces to conduct the attack. *Kampfgruppe Kahler* moved out, the *SPW* battalion in the lead and flanked by self-propelled 8.8-centimeter antitank guns—known as the *Nashorn*, the Rhinoceros—to either flank. Tank main gun rounds hissed above the regimental commander's *SPW*. He had his men move faster. They could see Towstoles: "Attack . . . get in there!"

The enemy antitank-gun positions were destroyed after perhaps a dozen rounds from the accompanying *Nashorn* main guns. The *Panzergrenadiere* dismounted and cleared the village, led by their commander. The men continued their assault, rolling up the flank of the enemy force that had broken through. Thanks to his men, Kahler had achieved another decisive success. By sealing off and eliminating the enemy's penetration, Kahler had prevented the enemy from prematurely interdicting the Tschernigow–Repki–Gomel road and forcing the German divisions east of the Dnjepr into the pathless marshland.

Generalmajor Lübbe, the commander of the *2. Panzer-Division*, in whose sector Kahler had attacked, recommended him for the Oak Leaves to the Knight's Cross to the Iron Cross. That recommendation was approved by the *Führer*, and Kahler later became the 355th recipient of the high award on 17 December 1943.

Kahler's achievement did not go unnoticed by the Soviets. They were determined to eliminate *Kampfgruppe Kahler*, which was interfering with their offensive plans. Subjected to incessant attack, Kahler's men held out for 13 days before they were finally given the order to cross the Dnjepr. In those 13 days, Kahler's men had paid a terrible price: 188 dead.

Kampfgruppe Kahler received no respite when it withdrew. It was employed in the so-called "wet triangle" that existed between the Dnjepr and the Pripjet. In order to upset the Soviet offensive planning, Kahler was again ordered to attack. *Panzergrenadier-Regiment 5* was ordered to take the villages of Possud and Possudowo.

When the regiment moved out of the vegetation to attack, it was greeted by heavy defensive fires from the Soviets. The acting commander of the 1st Company, *Leutnant* von Hagen, was killed with a round to the head. The company started to waver upon the loss of its commander. *Oberstleutnant* Kahler was soon on the scene. He brought tanks with him, reorganized the force and ensured that there was no pulling back.

Leutnant Trautwein, a friend of the deceased von Hagen, took over the company. The attack picked up steam again, inspired by the examples set by Kahler and Trautwein. Possud was assaulted and taken. It was directed for the attack to be continued the next day. The attack was delayed when the 2-centimeter automatic *Flak* did not arrive on time. If that disturbed the unflappable Kahler, he did not show it. The subsequent attack was unable to gain ground, however.

At the end of October, the *12. Panzer-Division* moved back to the area around Lojew on the Dnjepr. On 1 November, the men felt the full brunt of the offensive launched by the 2nd White Russian Front. Again it was *Oberstleutnant* Kahler and his officers who helped maintain discipline and prevent any signs of dissolution. While the *Panzergrenadiere* stayed the course in their foxholes under the punishing Soviet artillery preparation, Kahler brought the antitank forces forward. The fighting for the so-called "Bear Position" started.

In the armored engagements that followed, the self-propelled antitank guns succeeded in knocking out many Soviet tanks. They were at an advantage in defensive fighting. Soon there were some 60 burning and smoldering T-34's and KV variants on the battlefield. By the end of the day, there were more than 100. A few of the T-34's made it through, but they were eliminated by the *Panzergrenadiere* in close combat. Stripped of their accompanying infantry, they were virtually helpless in the defensive network of the German lines.

The Soviets then launched their second wave, which was even bigger than the first. The *2./Panzergrenadier-Regiment 5* was overrun by 14 enemy tanks. Only the accompanying infantry could be stripped away. The Soviet tanks continued pressing on; they wanted to reach their objective and cause the German position along the mighty river to fall.

The 1st Company of Kahler's regiment was also overrun. The men were forced out of their positions and forced to seek cover further to the rear. Despite those setbacks, the rest of the regiment was able to stop the Soviet assault. For example, *Feldwebel* Horst Jäger destroyed five enemy tanks with Molotov cocktails and hand grenades. At the last minute, *Leutnant* Eichler showed up with four tanks and three 8.8-centimeter *Flak*. Within a short time, the area in front of and within the German lines was a tank cemetery consisting of an additional 54 knocked-out tanks. Many of them burned; some simply remained motionless on the battlefield, thick clouds of smoke drifting skyward from turrets positioned at all sorts of unusual angles.

In all, some 184 Soviet armored vehicles were destroyed in the sector of *Panzergrenadier-Regiment 5* on that 10 November 1943. Once again, the great success was not achieved without great cost: 231 men of the regiment were killed, wounded or were reported missing.

The next day, the Soviets continued their assault, losing another 95 armored vehicles. Orders were received shortly thereafter, for the German forces to pull back. It took until 22 November before Kahler's men were out of the lines.

The Soviets attacked again on 1 December. At the time of the attack, Kahler was with his 9th Company. *Gefreiter* Friedel Berger, a forward observer from the regiment's infantry guns, was up forward with the men. The *Gefreiter* observed Soviet forces attacking across the frozen-over Ipa on the left. He started to send a fire mission, when he was interrupted by *Leutnant* Brunow, the acting company commander, who was listening in on the conversation on the field telephone: "Berger, that can't possibly be right!"

Oberstleutnant Kahler, who had just been in that area, knew better: "Let him fire. He's right!"

The artillery fired a salvo, and their shells landed right on target, stopping the enemy attack. Later on, Kahler had Berger report to him at the regimental command post. He gave him some hard candy and filled out a homeland leave form. In closing, he told the soldier: "Berger, that's the only thing I have I can give to you at the moment!"

A few days later, *Unteroffizier* Dahler and 10 men succeeded in entering a village occupied by the enemy and defended by antitank guns and antitank rifles. Although successful, Dahler was wounded. Before he knew what was going on, his regimental commander was at his side, awarding him the Iron Cross, First Class.

The regiment spent Christmas without its commander. He was award the Oak Leaves to the Knight's Cross to the Iron Cross on 17 December, being the 355th member of the German Armed Forces to be so honored. To receive his high award, he was summoned to the *Führer* Headquarters to personally receive the award from the hands of Adolf Hitler.

Following his award, Kahler was able to enjoy home leave. On 1 January 1944, he was promoted to *Oberst*.

Returning to the Soviet Union, he found his division had been moved to the northern sector of the Eastern Front in the area of Lugau–Pleskau. He participated in the offensive operations southeast of Luga and the subsequent fighting east of Lake Pleskau from 9 to 20 February. On 20 February, the *12. Panzer-Division* was mentioned in the German Armed Forces Daily report for its successful role in the fighting there.

The division was moved to the Idriza area on 2 March. Soviet divisions had broken through there. Once again, his *Panzergrenadiere* distinguished themselves. *Oberst* Kahler was able to recommend two of his best for the Knight's Cross: *Oberleutnant* Fritz Feller of the 1st Company and *Hauptmann* Friedrich-Karl Krützmann, the commander of the 1st Battalion.

When the enemy attacked the hill at Maximzewo after an intense artillery preparation on 14 March, it was *Obergefreiter* Strehlau who threw himself down with his machine gun and took up the fight with the attacking Soviet infantry from his forward outpost. A young *Panzergrenadier* from Litzmannstadt later crawled over to assist him. The Soviet infantry started to waver under the withering fire of the "one-man" army; only the tanks continued roaring up the hill. The thick haze from gunpowder prevented the Soviet tankers from identifying the lone German machine-gun position.

Strehlau manned his post until German tanks arrived. The 22-year-old son of a farmer from Western Prussia had distinguished himself, and it wasn't the first time. Kahler later recommended him for the Knight's Cross to the Iron Cross for his bravery and decisiveness in engaging the enemy. Strehlau later received the award on 9 June 1944.

During that time, a neighboring hill, manned by men of the regiment's sister formation, *Panzergrenadier-Regiment 25*, was lost. A company of the *II./Panzergrenadier-Regiment 5* received orders to move out in an immediate counterattack in the evening and retake Hill 187.2. The attack bogged down when the men, exposed on the open hillside under a full moon and on the snow, were exposed to murderous defensive fires. The acting company commander explained the situation to his regimental commander. *Oberst* Kahler pulled the men back and personally directed the subsequent attack. He had motorcycle infantry advance from the south, while the 5th Company came in from the west and the north. The supporting tanks were to advance as the situation dictated.

The attack from the north, eventually supported by the tanks, proved decisive. The Soviets fled from their positions on the mountain. *Generaloberst* Model, the commander in chief in the north, was in the division command post at the time and praised the success of the attack.

Kahler continued to lead the regiment into the summer of 1944. With 16 Knight's Cross and 2 Oak Leaves recipients, it was one of the most successful *Panzergrenadier* regiments of the German Army. After being in command for 10 months, he was given a new assignment in July 1944 as commander of the *Führer-Grenadier-Brigade*.[4]

Kahler led the brigade during the ill-fated Ardennes offensive. It was initially held back as the German Armed Forces operational reserve for the offensive, along with its sister formation, the *Führer-Begleit-Brigade*. When the brigade was eventually committed, Kahler's *SPW* received a direct hit on 20 December. He was badly wounded and evacuated to the main dressing station. The war was over for him. In the hospital, he discovered that he had been promoted to *Generalmajor* on 31 January 1945, although he would never command at that rank. At the age of 37, he was one of the youngest German generals. He passed away on Hamburg on 14 January 2000.

Kahler being awarded the Knight's Cross. The adjutant general of the *4. Panzer-Division*, *Major* Korte, presents him with the high award. *Oberst* Betzel, the last commander of the division, who was killed in the street fighting for Danzig, congratulates him.

---

4. Translator's Note: This was an offshoot formation of the famous and elite *Panzer-Grenadier-Division "Großdeutschland."* It was formed primarily from members of the guard elements around the *Führer* Headquarters, augmented from personnel levies against the division proper.

Generalleutnant Hasso von Manteuffel seen while the division commander of the elite Army formation *Panzergrenadier-Division "Großdeutschland."* To his left is *Oberst* Oldwig von Natzmer, the division's operations officer.

CHAPTER 7

General der Panzertruppen Hasso von Manteuffel

COMMANDER OF THE *7. PANZER-DIVISION* AND *PANZERGRENADIER-DIVISION "GROSSDEUTSCHLAND"*; COMMANDER IN CHIEF OF THE *5. PANZER-ARMEE* AND THE *3. PANZER-ARMEE*

The attack elements of the *7. Panzer-Division* moved out. It was the evening of 3 October 1941. The mission that *Oberst* von Manteuffel had received from the division commander, *Generalmajor Freiherr[1]* von Funck, read: "Form a bridgehead on the far side of the Dnjepr at Gluschkowo. After all of *Schützen-Regiment 6* has crossed, continue the advance along the Gluschkowo–Obljezy–Kamenjetz–Wjasma road and break open the enemy lines."

Despite the evening haze, the bridge could be made out from the assembly area on the slight rise. Leading the armored elements was the *SPW[2]* of von Manteuffel.

As the *Kampfgruppe* left the protective concealment of the woods, the Soviets on the far side of the river opened fire. The first rounds from the *Ratschbumm* impacted into the earth in front of the attacking armored vehicles.

"Fire!"

The main guns of the tanks began to fire almost simultaneously. One pocket of resistance after the other was eliminated. One enemy round almost grazed the side of von Manteuffel's vehicle.

"On to the bridge!" the commander ordered over the radio.

The driver stepped on the gas and passed the lead tank. Von Manteuffel was leading his men from the front. He directed the battle by radio from his *SPW*. Soviets appeared in front. The machine guns on

---

1. Translator's Note: *Freiherr* is a term of nobility, equivalent to Baron.
2. Editor's Note: Semi-tracked armored personnel carrier, in this instance a command version.

143

the *SPW* began to rattle. The bridge was reached and vibrated under the weight of the half-track. A hard blow struck the superstructure of the vehicle and knocked it sideways. The crew, stunned, stopped for a moment to check out the damage.

Fortunately, there was still enough room on the bridge to pass. The tank battalion commander's tank soon took up the lead. The armored vehicles on the near bank provided covering fires while they waited their turn to cross. Mortars could be heard firing from the enemy side of the river. Von Manteuffel's *SPW* was not damaged enough to be out of the fight, and the vehicle continued on its way across the bridge.

"Faster!" the *Kampfgruppe* commander ordered. Soon, he was on the far bank with the tanks. The enemy was firing at them from three sides. One of the tanks was immobilized when its track was shot off. The crew was able to dismount in time before the next round hammered home. The steel colossus soon went up in flames.

The commander's *SPW* pressed forward towards the Soviet's main line of resistance, 500 meters to the east. A message was sent to the division: "Bridge at Gluschkowo taken by surprise. Bridgehead expanded to 500 meters."

By the morning of 5 October, the entire *Schützen-Regiment 6* had crossed over to the far side of the river. Towards noon, von Manteuffel summoned his company commanders. He told them: "We'll move out at 1400 hours, break open the enemy positions and advance on both sides of the main road. As soon as we have broken through, we will continue on and interdict the retreat route of the enemy."

The regiment moved out at the designated time. *Oberleutnant* Bergmann, a company commander on the left flank, gave his men the signal to attack. At the same time, the rocket launchers put down a thick bank of smoke.

The first assault yielded the Germans only 30 meters. The Soviets then started firing with mortars. The shells exploded with dull roars. The men moved out again.

Stukas appeared above the riflemen. The designated recognition-signal pyrotechnics were fired. The machines tipped over and howled earthward. The Soviet positions were literally plowed up by the precision targeting.

"Move out!" the company commanders called out after the last of the *Stukas* started climbing and heading west.

Von Manteuffel's men continued their assault. They reached a wire obstacle, and the men cut their way through. Close combat ensued along the entire sector. The men advanced, meter-by-meter. Von Manteuffel showed up in Bergmann's attack sector. The young company commander was wielding a captured Soviet rifle with a telescopic sight. Von Manteuffel exhorted the men: "Just a few hundred meters, men, and we'll have it behind us!"

The men, spurred on by their commander and the example he set, moved out and took the last of the Soviet positions. The vehicles for the men made their way forward during the night. After a short rest, the men mounted up again and headed east.

"The direction of march is Wjasma!" Von Manteuffel radioed his lead elements.

The regiment stormed forward, as if on a gigantic hunt. By then, the division commander kept on feeding other divisional elements to von Manteuffel's *Kampfgruppe*. Von Manteuffel seemed to be everywhere at once. The *Kampfgruppe* took the main road on occasion; other times, it moved cross-country. Its objective was the Minsk–Moscow highway at Wjasma.

At twilight on 6 October, the broad band of the highway could suddenly be seen in the distance. Von Manteuffel's *SPW* advanced across it to the other side and stopped. He was the first one to set foot on the highway. As he was making his way back to his vehicle, a salvo of heavy artillery shells landed at the place he had stood only seconds previously.

The *Kampfgruppe* set up for the defense. The heavy weapons of the division closed up. The men had finished the loop in encircling the enemy in what was to become known as the Wjasma–Briansk Pocket.

Generalfeldmarschall von Brauchitsch, the Army chief of staff, had the following telegram sent to the division:

> My special recognition to the capable *7. Panzer-Division*, which has contributed significantly in the encirclement of the enemy for the third time this campaign by its advance on Wjasma.

The men of *Schützen-Regiment 6* of the *7. Panzer-Division* and its commander, *Oberst* von Manteuffel, had achieved a significant victory.

✠

Hasso von Manteuffel was born on 14 January 1897 as the third of three children of *Hauptmann a.D.* Eccard von Manteuffel in Potsdam. On his father's side, there was a long line of officers, including some general officers. He attended the *Viktoria-Gymnasium* in Potsdam for a short while, followed by entrance into the Corps of Cadets at Naumburg in 1908. In 1911, he was transferred to the main officer academy at Berlin-Lichterfelde, whereupon he was formally accepted into the army in 1916, after receiving his college-preparatory degree.

Von Manteuffel was assigned to the 5th Squadron of the Zieten Hussars, which was attached to the *6. Infanterie-Division* for reconnaissance purposes.

On 14 October 1916, the young *Leutnant* was wounded during the fighting along the Somme and was evacuated to the reserve military hospital at Münster in Westphalia. He was released in January 1917 and went back to the field. Until the end of the war, he served as a liaison officer in the headquarters of the *6. Infanterie-Division.*

Following the war, von Manteuffel served in *Freikorps von Oven,* one of many paramilitary organizations that sprung up by disaffected veterans that fought both for and against the fledgling Weimar regime. *Freikorps von Oven* operated in Bavaria and was pro-government. Later on, von Manteuffel was accepted into the postwar 100,000-man army. He was assigned to *Kavallerie-Regiment 23* in Rathenow on the Havel, where he served as both a company officer and liaison officer.

In the course of a reorganization, *Kavallerie-Regiment 23* formed the nucleus of *Reiter-Regiment 3,* and von Manteuffel became the adjutant of the latter regiment. After promotion to *Oberleutnant,* von Manteuffel requested a transfer to the "Technical Squadron" on 1 February 1930. That company-level unit was the precursor of what would become the heavy-weapons company of every German cavalry and infantry regiment.

During that period, he also made a name for himself in riding tournaments. On 2 January 1931, he was awarded the Rider Badge in Gold, the highest award of its sort for horsemanship.

The commander of *Reiter-Regiment 17* in Bamberg eventually requested von Manteuffel be assigned to his formation, where he became a troop commander. In 1935, the regiment provided two troops to Eisenach to help form *Kradschützen-Bataillon 2.* Von Manteuffel was transferred there along with his troop. The motorcycle battalion was part of the newly forming *2. Panzer-Division*.

Subsequent to that, von Manteuffel conducted numerous officer-candidate courses for men of the division. On 1 January 1936, he was transferred to the Armor School—*Panzertruppenschule*—at Wünsdorf as an instructor. Von Manteuffel helped infuse the old "rider *esprit de corps*" into the fledgling *Panzertruppe*. Von Manteuffel was the very picture of a German cavalry officer: small, tough, unmistakable facial features and the nose of a hawk.

At the request of *Oberst* Guderian, von Manteuffel was transferred to the Inspector General's office for the *Panzertruppe* on 1 February 1937. He joined the staff section concerned with motorization issues for the infantry; correspondingly, he can be considered one of the founders of mechanized infantry in the German Army.

After serving in that capacity, he returned to the main offices of the Inspector General, where he was responsible for writing the regulations concerning the employment and operations of combined arms within an armored division.

On 1 February 1939, he was transferred back to the Armor School in Potsdam-Krampnitz, where he assumed duties as the head of the instructional department there. Von Manteuffel, promoted to *Oberstleutnant* before the start of the war, remained there until the start of hostilities with the Soviet Union.

He requested a transfer to the field army, which was granted. Initially, he was given command of a rifle battalion of *Schützen-Regiment 6* of the *7. Panzer-Division*, which had gained famed as the "Ghost Division" under *Generalmajor* Rommel in France.

When *Oberst* von Unger was killed on 21 August 1941 outside a patch of woods east of the Duchowtschina–Beloij road, von Manteuffel assumed command of the regiment. He would command the regiment to the gates of Moscow.

During the night of 6/7 October 1941, the first snows fell. The next day, the snow squalls were so heavy that the divisional artillery had to call off observed firing, since observation was impossible. The riflemen and motorcycle infantry fought against the forces desperately trying to break out of the Wjasma Pocket. Von Manteuffel said at the time:

> What took place here in terms of working together and cohesiveness, where everyone offered his services and helped, even those who had been in action for days and were completely overwhelmed, is something that can only be grasped by those who experienced it. It is the epitome of comradeship, as we understand it—that is the *7. Panzer-Division!*[3]

On 13 and 14 October, the division was pulled out of the line; the fighting for the pocket was over. In all, the enemy lost 663,000 personnel—a number that only includes prisoners taken—1,242 armored vehicles and 5,412 artillery pieces.

After a few days of rest, the division resumed its advance. It reached the area around Karmanowa on 8 November, marching through sudden downpours and knee-deep muck and mud. That was followed by the onset of freezing weather. At Sobzow, the division crossed the headwaters of the Volga.

Oberst von Manteuffel was given command of a *Kampfgruppe* consisting of his regiments, elements of *Schützen-Regiment 7*; the division's reconnaissance battalion, *Aufklärungs-Abteilung 37 (mot)*; parts of the tank regiment, *Panzer-Regiment 25*; and the divisional engineers, *Pionier-Bataillon 58 (mot)*.

Kampfgruppe Manteuffel took Dorina on 16 November and continued its assault early the next day. By noon, it had reached Koslowa, south of the Volga–Wolschjkoje reservoir (southeast of Kalinin). That evening, it took Fofanowa and Sawidowskaja in attacks. At that point, the battle group was positioned along the Kalinin–Klin–Moscow rail line. On 23 November, the *Kampfgruppe* was relieved by the *36. Infanterie-Division (mot.)* and sent to the sector of the division's *Panzer-Regiment 25* along the northern outskirts of Klin.

By the evening of 27 November, the battle group had reached the Astrezowo–Jakolewo area, 4 kilometers northwest of the bridge over the Moscow–Volga Canal at Jachroma. Von Manteuffel described the action to take the bridge by surprise in the divisional history:

---

3. Author's Note: This statement was heard by a *Feldwebel* of the division, who noted it in his diary.

After crossing the major road that led south from Rogatschew, we did not use the roads and trails that were marked on the map to advance on the bridge at Jachroma.

A prerequisite for the intended *coup de main* on the bridge was a stealthy approach through the expansive tracts of woods and an avoidance of the (populated) localities.

The battle group advanced along iced-over trails and deeply snow-covered fields to the southeast. The regimental engineer platoon, which was attached to the lead element, had to cut paths through the expansive woods with chain saws, so that the SPW's and tanks could get through, the dismounted personnel moving to the sides of the powerful assault detachment in the lead. A compass served to orient us.

Towards evening, about an hour after it had turned dark, the lead elements, including the commander of the *Kampfgruppe*,[4] reached Astrezowo. It was forbidden to exit the woods in the direction of Jachroma in order to preserve the element of surprise.

The leader of the *Kampfgruppe*, accompanied by a small escort, made his way to a slight rise to reconnoiter. From there, he and his escorts could see the city and the bridge over the canal, north of the city. The officers, noncommissioned officers and enlisted personnel implored me to take the bridge by surprise that very evening.

With a heavy heart, I decided not to do that. Instead, I planned a surprise attack for the next day when all of the vehicles of the *Kampfgruppe* had had a chance to close up and provide adequate fire cover for the attacking elements . . .

I asked for volunteers for assaulting the bridge and crossing it. Everyone volunteered; no one wanted to be left behind. From those who volunteered, *Oberleutnant* Rudi Reineck was chosen.

At 0200 hours on 28 November, the handpicked assault company moved out of Astrezowo. The Soviet sentries on this side of the canal were silently overpowered. Then *Oberleutnant*

---

4. Translator's Note: As is typical in many German narratives of this sort, the author refers to himself in the third person.

Reineck was the first one to race across the bridge ahead of his men. It seemed the plan had worked completely.

Finally, the enemy began to commit reserves, but *Hauptmann* Schroeder, whose tanks rolled across the bridge, gave fire support. On the east side of the canal, the riflemen attacked the steeply rising band of high ground in front of them. They assaulted with hand grenades and cold steel. The first foxholes of the Russians were reached.

Just as the riflemen were attacking along the east bank, an enemy armored train advanced along the railway line, which paralleled the east bank. At the same time, several T-34's advanced along the canal road towards our riflemen. The tank company of Knight's Cross recipient *Oberleutnant* Ohrloff[5] eliminated the enemy armored train and knocked out three T-34's. The riflemen wrested a bridgehead position on the east slope from the enemy.

In the course of taking the canal bridge, a Soviet officer was taken prisoner, who had all of the written orders and map positions of the enemy forces on that side of the canal. Despite the success of his venture, von Manteuffel was disappointed to learn that the field army did not have any combat elements available to exploit the success and conduct a decisive assault on the Soviet capital. Worse, the senior command ordered the bridgehead position to be evacuated on 29 November, after it had been hit by freshly introduced Siberian divisions that day. Von Funck later wrote:

When the commanding general told me that he had no forces at all to exploit the great victory at Jachroma and he forwarded the order from higher headquarters to evacuate the bridgehead that had just been won with much sweat and blood, it seemed a bad omen indicating the turn of the campaign and, as a result, the entire war.

Over the next few days, *Kampfgruppe Manteuffel* was in the thick of the defensive fighting. On 6 December 1941, the Soviets launched

5. Author's Note: *Oberleutnant* Horst Ohrloff, the company commander of the *1./Panzer-Regiment 25*, was awarded the Knight's Cross on 27 July 1941.

their major counteroffensive that would not end until it was stopped in January 1942 along the Königsberg Line.

He received the Knight's Cross to the Iron Cross on 31 December. His recommendation had read, in part: "... for his judicious leadership of his battle group and his exemplary, brave behavior."

Von Manteuffel was influential in ensuring that *Oberleutnant* Rudi Reineck also received the high award. Unfortunately, the terrific officer was unable to wear the award, since he died in a field hospital on 20 January 1942 as the result of wounds sustained in combat.

At the beginning of May 1942, the division was pulled out of the line and sent to France for reconstitution. Von Manteuffel showed his remarkable talents for training during the reconstitution. On 15 July 1942, when *Oberst* Lungerhausen left the division to assume a command in Africa, von Manteuffel assumed command of *Schützen-Brigade 7*, the headquarters element for the two rifle regiments of the division. On 15 November, von Manteuffel also left the division to assume command in the Tunisian area of operations. He repeatedly flew to Africa to get oriented on the unique aspects of that theater of war. In January 1943, he assumed command of the division that simply bore his name at that point: *Division "Manteuffel."* The *ad hoc* division consisted of elements of an armored division, the remnants of *Oberst* Ramcke's paratrooper brigade and newly formed elements from the homeland. Later on, he also received an Italian regiment of *Bersaglieri.*

Von Manteuffel showed his unique talents in that theater of war as well. Within a short period of time, he had molded the hastily assembled division into a powerful combat formation. In February 1943, the division underwent its baptism of fire. Von Manteuffel had his forces attack so as to improve their positions in the Tebessa area. Von Manteuffel, who had been promoted to *Generalmajor* on 1 May 1943, was able to gain 12 kilometers on the right wing southwest of Cape Serrat. His main effort, which attacked into the bottleneck north of the Djebel Abiod, entered the enemy positions and advanced as far as St. Temara. Two days later, the division reached Hill 199.

The division held positions there until 28 March, when the enemy broke through the position on both sides of main road after the *Bersaglieri* regiment had been wiped out. The division had to pull back to the east in a sudden downpour. The fighting over the next three days saw the division withdraw, step-by-step, to a line running 20 kilometers east of Cape Serrat–St. Jeffna–St. de Nair.

The enemy did not attack again until 11 April. Despite an eight-fold superiority in numbers and a large contingent of armor in support, they were held. As was typical of him, von Manteuffel raced around the battlefield, appearing at the hot spots of the engagements. In the midst of the fighting, he arranged a 4-hour truce with the Americans so that the dead and wounded could be recovered. Von Manteuffel was sharply rebuked by his superiors for his actions, but he did not let it bother him, as was shown in an incident a few days later, when he sent an emissary to the Americans to inquire about the status of a member of his division who had fallen into the hands of the enemy, wounded, during a patrol. He found out that the officer was still alive and being treated by medical authorities.

On 27 April, the enemy attacked the right wing and center of the division, just north of Jeffna. The enemy forces were turned back. Three days later, he attempted to break through with fresh forces 6 kilometers south of the coast. A gap was created in the German lines, and the situation became more critical the next day, since von Manteuffel had no more forces at his disposal to close the gap. On 3 May, Mateur was lost. Three days later, *Generalmajor* von Manteuffel collapsed, completely exhausted and seriously ill. He was evacuated from Africa on one of the last hospital ships leaving for Europe.

The actions of *Division "Manteuffel"* in Africa were praised by a certain *Monsieur* Roederer in Alan Moorehead's African trilogy:

> *General* von Manteuffel acted properly and in an engaging manner to the very end. We had breakfast together every morning, and I was almost sorry to see him leave.
>
> The Germans paid for everything during the four months they stayed here and caused less damage in that time as your forces have on a single morning.[6]

---

6. Translator's Note: This passage was reverse-translated into English from the German. Consequently, it may not correspond exactly with the original version, written in English.

After he had recovered, von Manteuffel was summoned to the *Führer* Headquarters, where he discovered he was to replace *Generalleutnant Freiherr* von Funck in command of the *7. Panzer-Division*. He assumed command of the division on 16 August 1943. He joined his division in the Achtyrka area, where it was engaged in heavy defensive fighting.

Five days after assuming command, von Manteuffel was wounded in the shoulder and back by a Soviet fighter-bomber attack. He sustained a total of 20 shrapnel wounds. It appeared that his command was over, but he refused to give up. He had his wounds dressed, and he continued to lead his division.

Together with the highly decorated commander of *Panzer-Regiment 25*, Diamonds recipient *Oberstleutnant* Schulz,[7] von Manteuffel mastered many a crisis situation. On a few occasions, the division had to be resupplied from the air. The German Armed Forces diary report for 8 October contained the following commentary on the division:

> The *7. Panzer-Division*, under the command of *Generalmajor* von Manteuffel, has distinguished itself along the center portion of the Dnjepr through its dashing attacks and tough defense.

The division, which had been pulled out of the line for a battlefield reconstitution, was alerted in Kiev on 3 November. The enemy had torn open a 10-kilometer gap in the German lines north of the city. On 3 and 4 November, the division conducted a series of immediate counterattacks, only to pull back to the west bank of the Irpen on 5 November. During the night of 5/6 November, Kiev was evacuated. The enemy then advanced in the direction of Shitomir, with the city falling into Soviet hands a short time later. The *4. Panzer-Armee* was in danger of being cut off.

---

7. Translator's Note: Adalbert Schulz, born on 20 December 1913 in Berlin, received the Knight's Cross on 29 September 1940 as a *Hauptmann* and commander of the *1./Panzer-Regiment 25*. He then received the Oak Leaves to the Knight's Cross on 31 December 1941. He was still a *Hauptmann* but was in command of the *I./Panzer-Regiment 25* by then. He was the 47th recipient of the German Armed Forces to be so honored. He became the 33rd recipient of the Swords to the Oak Leaves as regimental commander on 6 August 1943. As an *Oberst*, he became the 9th recipient of the Diamonds to the Oak Leaves on 14 December 1944. He eventually fell in the Soviet Union on 28 January 1944 as the commander of the *7. Panzer-Division*.

Heeresgruppe Süd then assembled an attack force south of the line Fastov–Shitomir. It was intended for the force to shatter the Soviet advance and wrest back the initiative. One of the divisions in the attack force was the *7. Panzer-Division*, which moved out on 14 November. It moved past Iwniza, advanced to the northwest on 15 November in the direction of the Kiev–Shitomir road, reaching the Teterow bend, 4 kilometers northeast of Shitomir. It accomplished all that without having any formations to its flanks; they were simply unable to keep up the attack pace of the *7. Panzer-Division*. On 16 November, Lewkoff, 12 kilometers east of Shitomir, was taken. The enemy forces in Shitomir were encircled.

Von Manteuffel later wrote about the operation, considered by many to be the masterwork of the *7. Panzer-Division*:

I attempted to enter Shitomir all day on 18 November but was unable to find a weak spot in the enemy's defenses . . .

About an hour before it turned dark, I received a radio message: "Net call . . . Manteuffel is requested to go to Schulz's location immediately!"

That was unusual and I feared something untoward had occurred, even though I had seen *Oberstleutnant* Schulz just two hours previously at my command post.

When I arrived at *Oberstleutnant* Schulz's location, he informed me that in the course of a local advance on Shitomir, he had run into an antitank-gun crew that was completely drunk and overpowered it.

That information was a signal for me to immediately take action. I sent out a "net call" that everyone was to immediately move out to attack the city and follow me and *Gepanzerte Gruppe Schulz*. I sent out another radio message: "Our Christmas presents are waiting for us in Shitomir!"

We—Schulz with his six tanks and me with my *SPW* and a *Panzergrenadier* battalion with about 100 men—advanced in the darkness, meter-by-meter, towards the city. Schulz was at the head of his tanks. In exemplary teamwork between the individual tanks and the *Panzergrenadiere*, our group advanced, block-by-block.

Having moved out at 1700 hours, we broke the enemy's resistance at 0300 hours on 19 November and could start mopping up the city.

The relentless momentum of the *Panzergrenadiere* and the tank crews remained one of my strongest impressions of the entire war.

Schulz and I were on foot with the lead elements, and I remember even today how Schulz kept on shaking my hand, overwhelmed by everything that each individual man had accomplished.

On 20 November, the following was announced during the Armed Forces Daily Report:

General Balck [the commanding general] was of the opinion that a bold move on the part of the tried-and-true *7. Panzer-Division* was of decisive importance for the entire battle . . .

The mission of that division, which was advancing along an open flank, demanded great skill, adaptability and energy. It is led by *Generalmajor* von Manteuffel, an officer who possesses those qualities in abundance. In addition, he had the personal courage and *élan* that were necessary to rally his men in such a difficult situation.

On 23 November 1943, von Manteuffel received the Oak Leaves to the Knight's Cross to the Iron Cross "for his circumspect, bold and decisive leadership and his extraordinarily brave behavior in the face of the enemy." Von Manteuffel was summoned to the *Führer* Headquarters once more. It was there that he discovered he was to receive a new command, that of *Panzergrenadier-Division "Großdeutschland,"* an elite and extremely well-equipped formation that was frequently employed as a "fire brigade" at the hot spots of the Eastern Front. On 26 November, *Oberst* Schulz assumed acting command of the *7. Panzer-Division.*

On 22 February 1944, von Manteuffel also received the Swords to the Oak Leaves after a decisive defensive victory. He was the 50th officer of the German armed forces to be so honored. During the withdrawal to the Bug at the beginning of March, von Manteuffel's division was in great demand. He was able to hold up the Soviet offensive with his forces. The farthest Soviet advance was limited to 5 kilometers. Despite fighting in deep muck and mud, the division help prevent an envelopment of the field-army group. On 14 March, the Armed Forces Daily Report announced:

> In the southern sector of the Eastern Front, our forces continue to distinguish themselves in the face of the numerically superior enemy forces through their exemplary obstinacy and unshakeable offensive spirit. Over the last few days, for instance, *Panzergrenadier-Division "Großdeutschland"* under the command of *Generalleutnant* von Manteuffel . . . has especially distinguished itself.

On 31 March, the division headquarters reached Kishinew. The lead elements of the division occupied positions in Cornesti, east of Jassy. The Soviets immediately attacked with strong armored forces. They wanted to take the road to Jassy. At the same time, a violent snowstorm commenced. Despite these challenges, the division held out.

Early on 10 April 1944, the division moved out from Jassy to interdict enemy attack spearheads that were advancing between Jassy and Sereth. The immediate counterattack was so successful, that von Manteuffel had the attack continued to Targul Frumos, just east of the Sereth, with powerful reconnaissance forces.

The continued attack was able to cut off the enemy's spearheads, and the division was able to establish a defensive position on both sides of Targul Frumos. The Armed Forces Daily Report announced the following on 25 April 1944:

> The Russians moved out with strong forces to attack north of Jassy. Their attack failed in the face of the stubborn resistance of the German forces. During that fighting, an assault gun element from *Panzergrenadier-Division "Großdeutschland"* under the command of *Oberleutnant* Diddens especially distinguished itself.[8]

---

8. Author's Note: During this round of fighting, many members of the division stood out by their actions. Among them was *Oberst* Horst Niemack, the commander of

Generalleutnant von Manteuffel then prepared for the defensive fight he knew he would soon have on his hands. His planning and execution of the mobile defense at Targul Frumos has since gone into the annals of military history as a textbook case for conducting a defense by an armored division.

The Soviets started their offensive on 2 May 1944 by employing some 20 divisions. On the first day of fighting, the division's tanks, assault guns and *Flak* knocked out around 250 enemy armored vehicles, including several of the newly introduced heavy tank, the *Josef Stalin*. A breakthrough by the Soviets was prevented. The Soviets stopped attacking in the sector of the division.

Later on, von Manteuffel commented on the division's efforts: "The success was thanks to the sense of duty and bravery of the individual *Panzergrenadiere*, fusiliers and tankers, regardless of rank, and the other men of the division."

The German Armed Forces Daily Report announced the following on 8 May 1944:

> The defensive fighting that had started on 26 April between Pruth and Moldau has come to a tentative close. The desired breakthrough of the Soviets failed in the face of the determined and dogged defense of the German forces . . .
>
> During that fighting, *Panzergrenadier-Division "Großdeutschland,"* under the command of *Generalleutnant* von Manteuffel, especially distinguished itself.

The fact that von Manteuffel was again able to hold up the Soviets at Jassy was also thanks to the leadership of the general. In the middle of June, the division left that area of operations and reached a battlefield reconstitution area 100 kilometers south of Jassy. The division received new equipment, and it soon became even better equipped with the latest of weaponry than it had before.

In the middle of July, the Soviets had also launched a major offensive. By 21 July, it had already reached Ponewitsch, some 150

---

one of the division's mechanized regiments, *Füsilier-Regiment "Großdeutschland."* He became the 69th officer of the German Armed Forces to receive the Swords to the Oak Leaves. For his actions, *Oberleutnant* Dido Diddens received the Oak Leaves to the Knight's Cross on 15 June 1944.

kilometers west of Dünaburg. On 29 July, the enemy was positioned along the Gulf of Riga at Tukkum. The Soviets had effectively separated *Heeresgruppe Nord* from the rest of the German forces on the Eastern Front.

The individual elements of von Manteuffel's division were raced north by rail. While still en route, the Soviets started attacking west north of Wilkowischken. They broke through the thin German lines in their first effort. They then advanced on Wirballen and soon had lead elements at the eastern borders of the *Reich*.

The formations of the division were immediately committed to operations from the railhead. They advanced to the northeast in an effort to stop the Soviet advance.

On 9 August 1944, all of the division was in position. Von Manteuffel had his division move out without any type of preparatory fires. By evening of the first day of the attack, the Soviets had been ejected from Wilkowischken. The division then received a new mission: "Reestablish contact with *Heeresgruppe Nord* in conjunction with the other divisions and armored formations."

The attack started with an advance across the Venta to Kursenai. Elements of *Panzer-Füsilier-Regiment "Großdeutschland"* crossed the river and entered the city. The division finished taking the city the next day. The attack on Schaulen then started, but it was stopped on orders from higher headquarters during the night of 19/20 August. The division was directed to attack farther north in the direction of Doblen. It moved out, but the attack bogged down 8 kilometers from its objective; the enemy forces were just too strong.

About that time, von Manteuffel was summoned back to the *Führer* Headquarters. There he was designated the commander in chief of the *5. Panzer-Armee*, skipping corps command. He was also simultaneously promoted to *General der Panzertruppen*. He was one of the youngest field-army commanders.

The *5. Panzer-Armee* was selected to play a central role in the upcoming Ardennes offensive, more familiar to American readers as the Battle of the Bulge. On 3 November, von Manteuffel was summoned to *Generalfeldmarschall* Model's headquarters, where the upcoming offensive was discussed. He later wrote:

After the recognizable let-up in enemy pressure ever since the beginning of October, Hitler saw a new opportunity, vastly overestimated by him, to provide the war in the west with a decisive turning point. He pursued the thought of a far-reaching offensive with the greatest of energy, to which he subordinated the rest of the conduct of the war in the west. Hitler considered it certain that what had not been possible in front of the *Westwall* had to then be done by an attack from out of the *Westwall* . . .

Without bringing in the commanders in chief in the West or seeking their advice, he established the foundation for the offensive in September/October with the German Armed Forces High Command–West. The area of the front around the Eifel was selected as the attack area, and Antwerp was established as the objective.

In his briefing at the headquarters of the German Armed Forces High Command–West, *Generaloberst* Jodl stated that the supreme commander considered the sector Monschau–Echternach to be the most suitable for the attack. He calculated that a fast breakthrough could be achieved by the German forces as long as complete secrecy was maintained.

At the conclusion of the briefing, Jodl designated 25 November as the start date for the offensive. The Chief of the German Armed Forces Command Staff then outlined the missions for the field armies to be employed, including von Manteuffel's *5. Panzer-Armee*. It was to cross the Meuse between Amay and Namur and prevent the interference of enemy reserves in the flanks and rear of the *6. SS-Armee* that might come from the west. Von Manteuffel was allocated seven divisions, including four armored divisions.

Von Manteuffel stated that he could probably achieve the mission set for him, if the assurances that had been made to him by the Armed Forces High Command were met. He believed the earliest start date for the offensive could be the middle of December. He then stated his reservations, which caused Jodl to react vehemently. He insisted on the middle of November as the start date for the offensive.

In the discussion that followed, *Generalfeldmarschall* von Rundstedt, *Generalfeldmarschall* Model and *General der Panzertruppen* von Manteuffel agreed to present Hitler with an alternative plan. Von Manteuffel worked up a so-called "small solution." Hitler rejected the plan and insisted on his original concept, but he did delay the start of the offensive. The generals then tried again to persuade Hitler to change his plan. Von Manteuffel went to Berlin to be with Model on 2 December, when they were allowed to brief the *Führer.* Model briefed Hitler for five hours on his perceived shortcomings of the original plan. Once again, the men were rebuked. The offensive was set for the morning of 16 December.

The Ardennes offensive started at 0500 hours on 16 December 1944 along 100 kilometers of frontage between Monschau and Echternach. The *5. Panzer-Armee* had 40 kilometers of the front. Von Manteuffel personally directed his forces across the bridge over the Our. By 21 December, his formations had advanced as far as St. Hubert. But Bastogne, the thorn in the side of the Germans in the sector of the *6. SS-Armee,* continued to hold out. Von Manteuffel's *2. Panzer-Division* reached Dinant, 5 kilometers east of the Meuse, on 24 December. But all hopes of a successful conclusion of the mission in the sector of the *5. Panzer-Armee* disappeared when the spearheads of the *2. Panzer-Division* were cut off and eliminated after running out of fuel. Von Manteuffel's forces had to go over to the defensive.

The energetic general skillfully conducted the withdrawal of his forces over the next three weeks. He had three vehicles shot out from under him. The fact that the *5. Panzer-Armee* was able to be extracted was largely thanks to the leadership of its commander in chief. Eventually, the field army assembled west of the Rhine and established a cohesive defensive front. On 18 February 1945, von Manteuffel received the Diamonds to the Oak Leaves. He was the 24th of a total of 27 recipients of that award.

At the beginning of March, he was given command of the *3. Panzer-Armee*, which reported to *Heeresgruppe Weichsel.* He succeeded in establishing a cohesive defensive front west of the Oder River. He was able to turn back all Soviet attacks in his sector until the middle of April 1945.

On 16 April, the Soviets launched a major offensive south of the *3. Panzer-Armee.* During the last week of April, the Soviets turned north against the unprotected southern wing of the *3. Panzer-Armee.* While being attacked from that direction, the Soviets then attacked von Manteuffel's forces frontally across the Oder. He exhorted his men:

"Stay in contact with your neighbors. Go back, hand-in-hand. If you do that, the Russians won't dare attack you!"

On 29 April, *Generaloberst* Heinrici, the commander in chief of *Heeresgruppe Weichsel*, was relieved of his post. Von Manteuffel was informed that he was to assume command of the field-army group. He refused to do so, sending Keitel an open telegram in which he stated "that I have to turn down command of the field-army group, taking into consideration that *Generaloberst* Heinrici was relieved of his post, as well as the manner in which it was done." Von Manteuffel also sent forces to Heinrici's headquarters to ensure that nothing happened to him.

Von Manteuffel continued in command of the *3. Panzer-Armee* until 2 May 1945. He led it back to the demarcation line in the British sector. Not a single element of his field army fell into Soviet hands. As the result of skillful negotiations on his part, his soldiers were allowed back across the demarcation line along the Elbe.

The fighting was over.

Over the course of his career, he received officer evaluation reports such as these:

Magnificent leader in every aspect; great professional talent with a well-developed sense for what is essential.

And:

There is no mission that he does not accomplish in a terrific manner. He always distinguishes himself through exemplary bravery; never rested and a bold go-getter in leading his men forcefully forward . . . A troop leader, whom you can depend on in every situation and an especially striking, charismatic leader.

Hasso von Manteuffel passed away in Austria on 24 September 1978.

A heavily camouflaged late-model *Sd.Kfz. 251 Ausf. D*. Enemy air superiority on all fronts dictated that all vehicles had to be concealed as much as possible. Long gone were the days when German combat vehicles displayed large swastika flags as a means of recognition by *Luftwaffe* units.

Another shot of *Generalleutnant* Manteuffel with *Oberst* Natzmer.

Manteuffel presides over an orders conference.

A drawing of Georg Michael by the famous war artist Wolfgang Willrich. In the upper righthand corner is the unit insignia of the *24. Panzer-Regiment*.

CHAPTER 8

Major Georg Michael

"THE FIRST CAVALRYMEN HAVE VORONEZH IN SIGHT!"
Reserve *Oberleutnant* Georg Michael had gathered his troop's platoon leaders around him: "Men, things will get hot soon! The code word for the attack has just arrived."

The *6./Schützen-Regiment 26* was part of the *24. Panzer-Division*. The division had been the venerable *1. Kavallerie-Division* prior to its reorganization and redesignation as an armored division. This element was only a part of the forces advancing toward the great bend of the Don. German Army High Command Directive No. 47, issued on 5 April 1942, called for the conquest of the Caucasus and beyond.

In a movement lasting three weeks, the *24. Panzer-Division* had traveled from France through Upper Silesia to Kiev, and from there to Kursk. On 27 June 1942, it had occupied an assembly area near Schtschigri.

"And what are we doing in all this, *Herr Oberleutnant?*" *Oberwachtmeister* Brackebusch asked one of the platoon leaders.[1]

"At dawn tomorrow, our squadron [*II./Schützen-Regiment 26*] will attack the enemy in Truchatschewka from our assembly area, here in Ssemenowka. It will be supported by fires from all available heavy weapons. Its first objective will be the southern entrance to Truchatschewka—here—and its second the north slope of Hill 247.7 north of Petrischtschewa. That would be this point."

Georg Michael folded the map and continued:

"The 6th Troop will advance on the squadron's right. We have to be on our toes at the first road we will cross. There is a Russian bunker there. We move out at 2000 hours. Brackebusch's platoon will take point, followed by the heavy machine-gun platoon with a demolition team. Reconnaissance-in-force ahead of the advance, deployed in

---

1. Translator's Note: In keeping with its lineage, many of the formations of the division as well as the ranks of its soldiers retained traditional cavalry terms.

depth, with Hilmer's heavy machine-gun section on the right and Lichte's section on the left. That is all. Get ready!"

✠

Michael's troop moved out at 2000 hours. Covers were placed on the load-bearing equipment to prevent rattling. Twilight was falling quickly as the men advanced. The riflemen passed a *Nebelwerfer* battery, that was also moving up. Michael greeted the men from the rocket-launcher crews. A *Ju 52* circled above.

"What's that old bird up to, *Herr Oberleutnant?*" *Leutnant* Keiler asked. He led the reserve platoon.

"It's making noise so that the Ivans don't hear us too soon."

Suddenly, there was a howling sound from the direction of the Russian lines. The noise intensified, becoming a cacophony of high-pitched screams, and then four salvoes of sixteen rockets each fell close in front of the troop.

The men took cover in time. *Oberwachtmeister* Brackebusch crawled over to the troop commander.

"Have they spotted us?" he asked, obviously unsettled.

"Definitely not! We'll wait to see if the barrage is repeated."

Everything remained quiet. At about 2200 hours, the men reached the attack position and dug in.

Oberleutnant Michael walked down the line to see if the holes were deep enough. "Try to get some sleep, people!" he told them. He took the opportunity to get some rest himself, and soon he was fast asleep.

At 0145 hours, *Gefreiter* Gehring woke his commanding officer. "It's time, sir."

Georg Michael sat up. Yawning, he rubbed his eyes. Then he walked over to Brackebusch's platoon.

The *Oberwachtmeister* greeted him: "Good morning, *Herr Oberleutnant!* Now we wait to see what happens."

At 0200 hours, the German artillery opened fire on the enemy positions. High above, shells whistled through the sky. The soldiers around Michael were filled with elation: "They're right on target!"

Indeed, it looked as if the heavy shells were landing right in the midst of the enemy positions.

The barrage had been going on for 19 minutes when the *Nebelwerfer* opened fire. Smoking and hissing, fireballs zoomed over the assembly area. The Germans were lying flat in their holes, when the rockets fell on the enemy, but *Oberleutnant* Michael and his men still felt the blast from the exploding projectiles. It felt as though each explosion lifted him off the ground.

Then, in the blink of an eye, the artillery fire stopped.

"6th Troop—get up—move forward!"

The men got up and rushed forward. They reached the enemy's barbed wire and openings were cut. Georg Michael jumped to his feet and moved ahead. Suddenly, he saw flashes of gunfire to his left and right. Something struck him hard in the thigh and he fell to the ground.

"Get up!" he told himself. "You can't let your men go on alone!"

He got to his feet. As he ran, he fired his submachine gun at an enemy heavy machine gun and silenced it.

Together with Brackebusch and the others, he jumped into the first enemy trench. He saw the bodies of dead Russians lying on the ground. The concussion from the exploding rockets had torn apart their lungs. A few survivors raised their arms. They had already thrown away their weapons. The first Russian line had been taken.

A runner then arrived and informed the commander there were about a large number of Russians behind the troop. In the darkness, they may have mistaken the Germans for their own.

Oberleutnant Michael did not hesitate for a moment. He ordered his men to turn around and engage the enemy from the rear. Most of the Soviet soldiers soon surrendered. One soldier, however, suddenly reached for a hand grenade hidden in his tunic. Fortunately for the Germans, they noticed this in time and took cover. Several others preferred death to captivity and shot themselves before the Germans could disarm them. Although many of the men had been in combat since the start of the war, they had never seen anything quite like that.

Breathing heavily after the new action, *Oberleutnant* Michael leaned against the wall of the Russian trench. "Medic, over here!"

Obergefreiter Gettkant bandaged his commanding officer's wounded thigh.

"You must go back to the aid station, *Herr Oberleutnant!* That bullet has to come out!"

"Nonsense, Gettkant, get me a stick."

The men fashioned a passable crutch from broken trench framing. Then the sound of aircraft engines began to fill the air.

"Look at that! The whole *Luftwaffe* has shown up!"

Three hundred aircraft—close-support aircraft, dive-bombers and fighters—appeared over the front. The *Stukas* rolled over and dove on the second Russian line. They dropped their bombs and then climbed away.

Thick black columns of smoke rose into the sky. The close-support aircraft dropped their bombs and then strafed the enemy trenches with machine guns and cannon.

Soviet troops got up and began to run. Their earth-brown backs were clearly visible.

"Troop, follow me! Keiler, bring up the rear as reserve."

Michael beckoned to *Leutnant* Keiler. Supported by his stick, he hobbled ahead of his men. They reached the second Russian line and eliminated pockets of resistance that flared up here and there.

A runner rushed back to Keiler's platoon: "Reserve platoon to assume the lead!"

"Forward, men!" the *Leutnant* shouted. "We can't keep the boss waiting."

A steady stream of German aircraft flew overhead. The forces on the ground fired flares and laid out identification panels to show their location.

The Germans advanced deeper into enemy territory.

During a brief respite behind a captured Russian antitank gun, Keiler turned to his commanding officer: "You should stay behind, *Herr Oberleutnant.*"

"Nonsense, Keiler, I'm going with you."

And so, undeterred by the bullets whizzing about him, Michael limped along at the head of his troop. At about 0900 hours, by which time it had become very hot, the *6./Schützen-Regiment 26* had reached the area of the Soviet division command post. The men had fought their way 20 kilometers into enemy-held territory. The Tim River soon came in sight.

German armored vehicles rumbled up from the rear and received a jubilant welcome. In the first armored personnel carrier behind the leading tanks was the division commander, *Generalmajor Ritter* von

Hauenschild. The Knight's Cross at his throat glittered in the sunshine. He had received the decoration on 25 August 1941 for actions while serving as commander of the *4. Panzer-Brigade.*

"How's the advance going, Michael?" he asked.

"Good, *Herr General!*"

The tanks rushed ahead to the bridge across the Tim, seizing the crossing before the Russians could blow it up. German pioneers removed the detonators.

The trucks sent in behind the tanks arrived. The riflemen climbed aboard and set off after the tanks, moving toward the Kschen River.

The advance continued all day and through the night, until dawn on 29 June. It began to rain. The division received orders from the corps to go over to the defensive where it stood. Michael's troop had lost 2 men killed and 11 wounded. The troop had captured seven guns and taken more than 100 prisoners.

✠

Georg Michael was born in Hamburg on 10 February 1917. He attended college preparatory school and then a National Socialist academy at Plön. On 1 October 1936, joined the *1. Kavallerie-Brigade.* The German Army was modernizing its force, replacing horse cavalry units with motorized ones. Based in East Prussia, the brigade was the last horse-cavalry formation.

Michael took part in the fighting in Poland as a *Wachtmeister* and platoon leader in the *1./Reiter-Regiment 2.* He participated in the fighting at Dylewo, and the attack on Warsaw. The cavalry brigade formed part of the screen around the Polish capital until 21 September.

After the Polish campaign, the brigade was reorganized as the *1. Kavallerie-Division.* Two cavalry regiments were formed, *Reiter-Regiment 21* and *Reiter-Regiment 22.* On 30 March 1940, Georg Michael was promoted to reserve *Leutnant* and given a platoon in the *6./Reiter-Regiment 22.*

When the campaign in the west began, the *1. Kavallerie-Division* was given the mission of breaching the Dutch border fortifications and occupying all of northern Holland. At this time, the division was commanded by *Generalmajor* Feldt. It was a battle for roads and bridges. By 20 May 1940, the cavalry regiments had covered a total of 700 kilometers.

On 25 May 1940, *Leutnant* Georg Michael was awarded the Iron Cross, Second Class.

Three days later, the division was ordered to proceed with all dispatch into the area around Amiens for employment at the front. After a march of 500 kilometers, it reached the Somme on the evening of 6 June.

Attached directly to the headquarters of the *4. Armee*, the division was ordered on 7 June to establish a bridgehead on the far side of the Poix River in the area of Femachon and clear the *Foret d'Ailly*, which was still held by the enemy.

On the morning of 7 June, the *6./Reiter-Regiment 22* crossed the Somme along with the rest of the *1. Kavallerie-Division*. The cavalry then charged across the Poix, causing the enemy to break and run. Six hundred prisoners were taken. The division formed two pursuit elements and set off after the fleeing enemy.

Attacks by enemy tanks halted them only briefly, and 28 of the 30 enemy tanks were knocked out by antitank guns or mines.

At dawn on 14 June, Michael led a combat patrol across the Seine. There was no fighting there, however. The enemy had already withdrawn.

The pursuit continued south of the Seine, past Chartres to the west. Shortly after noon on 17 June, the lead elements led by Michael came upon a battalion of French colonial troops marching down a road.

The young officer immediately ordered his men to spread out and surround the enemy unit. He personally took prisoner the French major leading the battalion.

Leutnant Michael was recommended for the Knight's Cross for this feat. The recommendation read:

Through his extremely bold and fearless actions, *Leutnant* Michael of the *6./Reiter-Regiment 22* captured an entire Negro battalion without loss. The enemy troops would surely have deployed across the line of march of the 2nd Squadron, and it would likely have required a long and costly action to dislodge them. Michael's initiative and his bold, energetic action achieved a unique success for the squadron, which suffered no losses, and for the *1. Kavallerie-Division,* engaged in ruthless pursuit of the enemy.

Leutnant Michael knew nothing of this recommendation. He and his platoon continued their vigorous advance and helped capture the bridge at Le Port Boulet on the evening of 20 June. The next day, they assaulted the bridge at Chanon, capturing 40 officers and 200 men of the Saumur cavalry school.

Georg Michael was later awarded the Iron Cross, First Class, for this feat (27 June 1940). It was followed on 19 January 1941 by the Knight's Cross.

✠

At the beginning of the campaign in Russia in 1941, *Oberleutnant* Michael was the acting commander of the *6./Reiter-Regiment 22.* *Leutnant* Köhler and *Leutnant* Schenk were his platoon leaders. The *1. Kavallerie-Division* was ordered to guard the right flank of *Panzergruppe 2* (Guderian). In the terrible heat of the Russian summer, the breakthrough to the Dnjepr placed great demands on horses and riders.

The regiment reached Siniawka, 478 kilometers from where the advance began. On 6 July, it reached the Bobruisk bridgehead. There, the cavalrymen guarded the corps' southern flank. On 17 July, the division was attached to the *XII. Armee-Korps* for the defensive fighting at Stary Bychow.

Three enemy divisions assaulted the German bridgehead at Stary Bychow on the Dnjepr. Over four days, the Soviets attacked 19 times. *Oberleutnant* Michael and his troop successfully defended their sector in the defensive front.

This successful defensive action was followed by an advance on Snowsk and the fighting along the Ssudost River. After crossing the Desna, the division was deployed at Pogar on the Ssudost, where it relieved the *18. Panzer-Division.* Once the Briansk Pocket had been closed, the division was ordered to advance east across the Ssudost and clear the encirclement area. On 23 August 1941, *Generalmajor* Feldt was awarded the Knight's Cross for his division's accomplishments to date.

Starting on 20 October, the division assembled in the Gomel area. Then it was sent back to Germany. The cavalry division's history ended at this point, because it was reorganized as an armored division and redesignated as the *24. Panzer-Division*. Its new commanding officer was *Generalmajor Ritter* von Hauenschild. The old and new elements of the division were integrated at French training areas. On 10 May 1942, the division began its second long journey to the Eastern Front. As previously related, its second tour of duty there began on 28 June 1942.

RETURN TO RUSSIA

On 10 May 1942, the *24. Panzer-Division* entrained in Brittany and began the long journey back to the Eastern Front. The division passed through Holland, Germany and the conquered territories leading up to the Eastern Front. It then traveled parallel to the front toward Kursk, where it detrained and moved into a staging area 20 kilometers behind the front lines.

The division was subsequently inserted into the front lines of the *XXXXVIII. Panzer-Korps*, joining *Infanterie-Division "Großdeutschland"* and the *16. Infanterie-Division (mot.)*. The new armored division found itself in the vanguard of preparations for the new German offensive.

Directive No. 47 of the German Army High Command listed three main objectives for the offensive in the southern sector:

1. Destroy the Soviet forces in the great bend of the Don.

2. Capture the oil-producing regions in the Caucasus.

3. Conquer the Caucasus.

To accomplish those intentions, the summer offensive was to be divided into four phases:

1. The left wing of Army Group South was to attack from the area of Kursk, reach the Don on both sides of Voronezh and occupy the city.

2. The motorized formations of the left wing, essentially the *4. Panzer-Armee*, were to then advance along the Don toward the great bend in the river. The *4. Panzer-Armee* was to move at right angles to the infantry's line of advance and encircle the enemy forces between the

Don and the Donets. This was to be done in conjunction with forces of the *6. Armee*, which were to advance from the Kharkov area.

3. Continuing along the Don and coming from the north, the motorized forces were to encircle the enemy forces in the great bend of the river together with elements attacking up the Don towards Stalingrad from the Taganrog–Rostov area.

4. Both pincers would then secure the fourth phase—the advance by Army Group South toward the Caucasus.

✠

For the planned summer offensive, Army Group South had the following large formations under its command: *2. Armee* (Kursk); Hungarian 2nd Army (Kursk); *4. Panzer-Armee* (Kharkov); *6. Armee* (southeast of Kharkov); *1. Panzer-Armee* (Stalino); and *17. Armee* (southeast of Stalino).

Back-up forces behind the *17. Armee* and the *1. Panzer-Armee* were the Italian Expeditionary Corps, consisting of the XXXV Corps (later the Italian 8th Army), and the Romanian 3rd Army.

Bad weather forced several postponements, but the offensive was given the green light for the attack on the night of 27/28 June 1942.

1942 IN THE SOUTHERN SOVIET UNION

Of course, *Oberleutnant* Michael's men were not the only ones to see action that day. Let us turn to another element of the division that was experiencing its baptism of fire as a motorized unit within an armored division, the *2./Kradschützen-Abteilung 4*. Here is a firsthand account by a former reconnaissance soldier—*Fahnenjunker-Wachtmeister* (officer candidate) von Senger und Etterlin—in the troop equipped with light half-tracks:

> The motorized rifle regiments attacked. The dull growl of the artillery started up. With a devilish howl, the rockets from the rocket-launcher [battalion] flew over us towards the enemy in a shallow arc.
>
> We stood up on the vehicles to take in this spectacle better. Cover was not necessary. Finally, we were sent forward. The troop formed up, platoon after platoon in march order. It

rolled behind the endless columns of tanks over the bridge at Ssmenkowka through the recently taken Russian positions and in the direction of the Tim. A bombing and strafing attack was made by close-support aircraft en route. I have the first casualty. A machine gunner had jumped out of the safety of the armored vehicle in order to be able to engage the aircraft better. He got hit in the knee with an explosive round.

Our advance moved faster and faster. We broke through the enemy's main line of resistance. On the way, the riflemen, who were fighting dismounted, jumped into our vehicles to advance faster.

The enemy position that we overran did not appear to have been fortified all too strongly. There was a small traffic jam at the Tim; the tanks had taken the bridge intact, however, and immediately crossed it. We had the riflemen dismount so we could move forward faster. We moved unstoppably forwards through the glowing hot fields, through the hilly terrain— forward to the east. Everything seemed to happen as fast as lightning. There was a second line of enemy defenses behind the Kschen. The enemy offered considerable resistance in the grain fields, from fortifications that were almost invisible to the eye. Using a narrow frontage, the tank battalion we were attached to broke through and let us clear the enemy trenches.

Practicing extended formations then paid extensive dividends to us. Steered by the invisible reins of the radio, the platoons and sections moved in an exemplary fashion, supporting one another and helping each other forward. My platoon moved in the forward-most line to the left of the 2nd Platoon. We unhinged several trench lines and bunkers and then advanced rapidly through the grain field past Rubinowka, which was burning.

The attack on Jefrossinowka then took place; we followed the tanks. It started to turn dusk. The tracer rounds from the tanks hissed into the village. Somewhere, a Russian ammunition stockpile exploded. Using a short but fast approach, we entered the village. We passed the tanks at this point. With me in the lead, we moved along the village main street. My squads moved to the right and left of me through the gardens. All of the buildings were burning.

Going around a corner, we were suddenly confronted with a Russian gun. Next to it was the limber and, sitting on the limber, were the cannoneers—all dead. The horses were also dead.

We advanced as far as the end of the village. We saw a few Russian trucks disappear in the distance, clouds of dust trailing them. I chased after them with my antitank vehicle; it was able to set the last truck alight.

For the first time in the campaign, we formed the famous tank "hedgehog" in the vicinity of the village. The tanks and the armored personnel carriers formed a large circle and oriented in all directions. The supply vehicles and the mess trucks gradually arrived and went into the middle. We were far out ahead of the division and discovered that we had almost captured a Russian field-army headquarters.

It started to rain during the night. It was not until quite late at night that we received some warm soup, which we ate under the small lamp in the cozy closeness of our armored vehicle. Outside, the rain fell on our cover.

✠

After the crossing of the Tim and the Kschen, orders had been issued for the attack on Voronezh. A *Kampfgruppe* was formed under the command of *Oberst* Maximilian von Edelsheim, the commander of *Schützen-Regiment 26*. Elements of the division's tank regiment, *Panzer-Regiment 24*, were attached.

The *Kampfgruppe* advanced rapidly. On the evening of 3 July, it was divided into two assault groups. The group on the right was ordered to seize the ferry crossing at Rudkino, while the other group was sent against the bridge at Voronezh.

Von Edelsheim issued final instructions to his two groups. When he went to the group on the left, he talked to his commanders. He had specific instructions for *Oberleutnant* Michael: "Listen to me, Michael! You follow the lead elements across the bridge, while they are clearing the town, continue on through the woods in the direction of Voronezh."

✠

"Get a move on!" *Oberleutnant* Michael ordered. "Quicker . . . the bridge is just beyond the bend!"

The men of the troop had dismounted. *Stukas* had bombed a Russian supply column, blasting it to bits. In addition, the bridge had been damaged and was only passable on foot.

As the men crossed the bridge, they could hear the sound of fighting from the town. The three other troops were busy clearing it. Russian aircraft approached.

"Look out! Take cover!"

The soldiers took cover in ditches and shell holes near the bridge. The Russian close-support aircraft swooped very low. Flames spurted from their noses.

The *Oberleutnant* pressed himself against the ground. Bullets struck the ground all around, but no one was hit.

"Come on men, get moving!"

They stormed forward. Siberian snipers fired from hedges, huts and trees. Then the Germans came to the edge of a sand pit. From above, Michael saw the Soviets stabbing a German soldier.

He gave the order to attack and rushed down the slope under heavy enemy fire. Firing as he ran, Michael emptied his magazine. Behind him and on both sides, his riflemen fired from the hip. The Russians took cover. Those who resisted were killed.

It was 1000 hours when Michael's men took over the point position.

"Stay alert! The Russians may be hiding in the woods."

Step-by-step, they combed the forest. *Oberleutnant* Michael was at the head of his men. The woods started to narrow out. Michael spotted two enemy antitank guns in an open field.

"Mortars and heavy machine guns into position!" After they had assumed hasty firing position, they opened fire.

After the first few rounds, the two Russian guns also opened fire. They had a clear view of the wood line where the Germans were. Shells exploded and a few men were wounded. It looked like the advance might bog down.

Oberleutnant Michael then took a platoon of men, bypassed the antitank positions and attacked them from the rear. The threat was soon eliminated. Michael then had the surviving Russians explain how the guns worked in order to get a better idea of their design and effectiveness.

The German wounded and the Russian prisoners were taken to the rear. Michael, however, marched on through the woods and into uncertainty. The troop reached a clearing. The men saw the city in front of them.

Michael had a radio message sent to *Oberst* von Edelsheim: "The first German cavalrymen have Voronezh in sight!"

The reply: "I'm sending you the 5th (*5./Schützen-Regiment 26*). It will join you from the left."

A short while later, Michael's troop came under fire. The Russians had moved two heavy antiaircraft guns into the tip of a patch of woods in front of the Germans.

"We're going to get them!" Michael directed his men through the underbrush.

They had almost reached the two guns when they came under rifle and mortar fire from all sides.

"The entire forest is full of Russians, *Herr Oberleutnant!*"

"Don't worry, the 5th will be here soon," the *Oberleutnant* stated flatly. He was trying to put a calm face on a ticklish situation.

Much to Michael's relief, the other troop arrived soon afterward. It had been brought forward by *Major* von Heyden.

"Dig in!" he ordered. "The Russians might send in tanks. They'll easily knock down this stuff."

The men began digging. Shadowy forms were sighted advancing on their position. The Russians didn't fire, though. Instead, they also began digging in, about 100 meters from the German foxholes.

Major von Heyden turned to the commander of the *6./Schützen-Regiment 26.* "What do you think, Michael? Shouldn't we attack?"

"By all means!" replied the *Oberleutnant.*

Five minutes later, the riflemen charged, firing their weapons. The Russians jumped out of their positions and ran away. Several approaching tanks also turned around and headed back in the direction of Voronezh. The Germans counted 27 T-34's.

By this time, the *7./Schützen-Regiment 26* had also arrived. The *Major* had an all-round defense established.

The Germans dug in at the tip of a finger of woods next to Voronezh airfield. A Soviet Rata fighter began taking off from the nearby runway. As the aircraft lifted off, *Oberwachtmeister* Dose shot it down with his machine gun. He later fired on an enemy bomber as it was starting up and set it on fire.

As dusk fell, 16 T-34's approached from Voronezh proper. *Oberleutnant* Michael let them approach until he could see the tank commanders standing in their turrets. Using a sniper scope, he hit several, and the rest disappeared inside their vehicles. Unsettled by the sudden and unexpected loss of several tank commanders, the attackers turned away without firing a round.

After a relatively quiet night, the three troops came under heavy fire from all directions the next morning. The Russians even had men in the treetops. The Germans began taking casualties. Three members of the 3rd Platoon were killed near *Oberleutnant* Michael.

"It's a battalion of Russians, *Herr Oberleutnant!*"

"Let them approach to within 200 meters!"

When the order was given to open fire, the Germans decimated the attacking Russians. Then Michael began receiving reports from all his platoons that ammunition was running low.

"Hold your fire until they're 30 meters away!" He ordered.

The Russians charged the German positions again, this time with tank support. One enemy tank became stuck 30 meters from the command post. *Obergefreiter* Pelz raised his heavy antitank rifle and put seven holes in its hide.

After the T-34's withdrew to refuel and rearm, *Oberwachtmeister* Dose moved forward in a captured armored car and overran the dug-in Russians. When they returned, Dose took out one tank with a *Teller* antitank mine. *Wachtmeister* Rasch destroyed a second, also with an antitank mine.

The Russians attacked yet again, shouting their battle cry as they stormed toward the German line. Georg Michael had his troop firmly in hand, however.

"Hold on, men. Make every shot count!"

Once again, the attackers were repulsed.

At about 1200 hours, a shout went up from the relief troop as it fought its way to the front. Leading the way was *Oberst* von Edelsheim himself.

"Put down some smoke!" Michael ordered.

Under cover of smoke, the forward units withdrew to the line held by the relief troop. Georg Michael saw the regimental commander. Edelsheim had two bandoliers slung over his shoulders. He had taken them from the body of a fallen machine gunner. Tears ran down his cheeks as the survivors of the *6./Schützen-Regiment 26* filed past. With them, they carried the bodies of many fallen comrades.

The troop had lost 55 men killed or wounded, but it attacked again at 1800 hours with supporting fire from *Nebelwerfer* batteries. The men shouted as they charged the enemy positions, and the Russians were driven back. Once again, the riflemen dug in.

The next morning, *Schützen-Regiment 21*, the sister regiment, fought its way into the southern part of Voronezh. The next day, the entire division entered the city, sealing its fate. The German radio issued a special bulletin announcing the fall of Voronezh. After 10 days of fierce fighting, the *24. Panzer-Division* had reached its objective.

The pursuit of the enemy began. As the corps' spearhead, the division had orders to push as far as possible into the great bend of the Don and cut off the Russians' avenue of retreat.

Meschkow was taken on 16 June, and the division was ordered to seize a bridgehead across the Don at Zymljanskaja.

After a daring night movement, the advance guard reached the Don. Just five vehicles arrived at the river—all the rest had broken down along the way.

The Russians had established a strong bridgehead in the bend of the Don near Kalatsch to cover the withdrawal of their forces towards Stalingrad. Instead of resuming its advance south to the Caucasus, the *24. Panzer-Division* was diverted toward this Russian bridgehead. Its new march route led straight to Stalingrad.

Early on 26 July, *Oberleutnant* Michael and his troop launched a night attack in the direction of Nishnij Tschirskaja and the bridge over the Don there. The objective was 30 kilometers away.

"Mount up!" Michael ordered.

The troop advanced in trucks among German tanks, overrunning weakly held enemy positions. Then artillery and rocket fire began raining down on the riflemen.

The tanks remained under heavy fire until 1500 hours. Two hours later, Michael was ordered to make his way to the Tschir River, following a depression that led all the way to the river. Once there, he was to cross over and establish a bridgehead.

Standing, Georg Michael issued his orders with iron calmness. When a mortar round fell barely five meters away, everyone around him dropped to the ground. Michael didn't even flinch. A second round fell, and Michael merely brushed the dust from his sleeve before hopping into the nearest hole.

The men stared at their commanding officer, eyes wide.

The *Oberleutnant* concluded his orders with the words: "We attack at dusk!"

✠

Dusk fell. At Michael's command, the men left cover and made for the depression. They reached it without being fired on. Then, however, the Soviets came out to meet them. Michael's men charged into them with a battle cry on their lips. Once the initial group of Soviets had been dispatched, Michael summoned his platoon leaders.

"*Leutnant* von Arnim, take your platoon to the top of the depression and cover from there. Once there, the advance will continue."

Seconds later, shells began impacting among the attackers.

"Tank, mortar and rifle fire coming from a factory, *Herr Oberleutnant!*" the young *Leutnant* reported down to his commander.

"We'll carry on down here until we're even with the factory. Then I'll send in an assault team."

Ten men slipped into the building and captured 25 Soviets. Three tanks escaped, not desiring to take on infantry in a factory area all by themselves.

By the time the rest of the troop had arrived, the prisoners were being interrogated. They said that the town ahead was called Nishnij Tschirskaja and was heavily defended.

"We're going through the city!" Michael decided. "No firing, no talking. The Russians will take us for their own people."

In the town there was an eerie silence. Sleeping Russians lay by the sides of the road. If one woke up and tried to speak to them, the jig would be up.

But Georg Michael had nerves of steel. He went to the head of the column. When one of the Russian sentries spoke to him, he pointed down at the river without speaking. The Russian let him pass.

Messengers ran past him. Enemy tanks and trucks rumbled by. The Germans reached the Tschir without a shot being fired. Several men felt their way toward the river. They returned and reported that there was no crossing there.

"To the right!"

Then the squad leader saw 15 Russians fording the river.

"Follow them!" the *Obergefreiter* ordered.

They found a submerged path and waded across to the other shore. When they reached the riverbank, they were met by rifle and machine-gun fire.

Oberleutnant Michael heard the gunfire and was concerned. He raised his arm. The entire troop waded across the Tschir. On the other side, the men came upon two antitank guns and eliminated the crews. They advanced 200 meters before fierce enemy fire forced them to take cover.

"Dig in!" Michael ordered. Then he contacted the squadron by radio.

"Hold the bridgehead! We're sending tanks!" That was both a promise and an order.

Half an hour later, four tanks rolled through the town. After receiving directions to the river, they crossed the Tschir and significantly reinforced the hastily established bridgehead.

Under interrogation, prisoners had revealed that the main bridge over the Don was only five kilometers away.

Michael consulted with the officer commanding the tanks. "We should press ahead, what do you think?"

"You're running late, as far as I'm concerned," he replied.

✠

Towards midnight, the small force moved out, with the tanks forming an armored spearhead. A wide road led through forest, straight to the bridge. The tanks moved down the road single file, while the riflemen walked in the ditches on both sides.

About one kilometer into the forest they came under fire from three sides. The Soviets were using tracer exclusively, and yellow lances of flame pierced the darkness.

The tanks traversed their turrets, two orienting right and two orienting left. They began firing high-explosive rounds into the forest towards the enemy's positions. Then they began advancing in bounds. The tanks would move forward 50 meters, halt and wait for the riflemen to catch up. Once there, they would move forward again.

A T-34 appeared on the road ahead. The lead German tank opened fire and the T-34 burst into flames. Another Soviet tank approached. It suffered the same fate as the first. Then a third T-34 suddenly appeared in front of *Stabswachtmeister* Brackebusch. He quickly took it out with a hand-grenade bundle.

Glancing at his watch, Michael saw that it was 0400 hours He could already see the far edge of the wood line.

"Take up positions at the edge of the woods! 1st and 2nd to the left of the road . . . 3rd to the right!"

The platoons came under heavy fire as they carried out these movements. *Leutnant* Reschke was wounded. *Wachtmeister* Rasch took over the 3rd Platoon and led it into positions at the edge of the woods above the Don.

The terrain fell away sharply to the riverbank. Hundreds of Russians were trying to swim across the river. Reschke opened fire on the fleeing soldiers with his machine gun.

The Russians succeeded in blowing a 30-meter section of the bridge before the German tanks arrived.

In 32 hours of combat, Michael's troop—once 150 men strong—had destroyed three Russian regiments at the cost of 53 men. Once again, it had showed itself to be one of the most steadfast troops in the regiment.

It had achieved its objective, reaching the Tschir and Don Rivers.

CONTINUED OPERATIONS

On 6 August, the *24. Panzer-Division* received orders from the commanding general of the *XXIV. Panzer-Korps* to attack from out of the bridgehead of the *297. Infanterie-Division* the next morning. It was to advance 35 kilometers deep into the enemy pocket west of Kalatsch, link up with the *XIV. Panzer-Korps* to the north and then close the ring around the enemy to the east.

The *24. Panzer-Division* was still on the south bank of the Tschir. It had to cover 30 kilometers to reach the area of operations. Under the command of the *Panzer-Regiment*, the entire attack force reached the assembly area during the night.

The first objective was the group of enemy positions on Hill 89.3. These were eliminated, and the enemy put to flight. Immediate counterattacks by enemy tanks were repulsed and several were destroyed.

The division forced a breakthrough and rolled across the steppe in several parallel columns. It reached its objective of the day, the commanding Hill 184.2 southwest of Kalatsch. Initially involved were *Panzergrenadier-Regiment 21* (*Oberstleutnant* Vollrath von Hellermann), the *II./Panzergrenadier-Regiment 26* and the *III./Panzer-Regiment 24* (*Major* Hild-Wilfried von Winterfeld). The overall operation was led by *Oberst* Gustav-Adolf von Nostitz-Wallwitz, who had received the German Cross in Gold on 1 December 1941 as commander of *Reitendes Artillerie-Regiment 1* (1st Horse Artillery Regiment) of the *1. Kavallerie-Division.*

His orders read: "Strike out to the east in a wide arc, advance north through Kumowka on the Don toward Kalatsch and link up there with the *16. Panzer-Division.*"

The tanks advanced quickly, although several were lost to concealed antitank guns. The following non-attributed firsthand account describes the role of the *II./Panzergrenadier-Regiment 26, Oberleutnant* Michael's squadron, in the action:

Ten kilometers outside of the train station at Tschir we were suddenly in the middle of the burning steppes. Communications with the tanks had been lost. The Russians had advanced between us and were positioned in the dry steppe grass. We jumped down from the vehicles, ran through the enemy fire and immediately overran the first Russian line. We were then employed against a grain field. We received fire from a heavy machine gun from the flank and I saw how Michael flipped around twice and hit the ground.

When I ran over to him to help, he yelled at me to ensure the attack kept going. He could dress his wound himself!

He had been hit in the upper thigh. In the end, he was taken to a hospital in Germany. *Stabswachtmeister* Brackebusch assumed acting command of the troop.

I was unable to advance because the heavy machine gun was holding me in check. I had to dig in. The regimental commander, *Oberst* von Edelsheim, came to me in his half-track. I explained the situation to him. He then took up position behind the [half-track's] machine gun and advanced by himself, overrunning the enemy machine gun.

Then I started to receive fire from the front from a heavy machine gun. When I wanted to employ my two machine guns against it, I noticed that machine gunner 1, *Gefreiter* Jüdes, had been killed. He had been shot in the neck and was instantly killed so quickly that no one in the section had noticed it.

I was able to take out the enemy heavy machine gun with my machine guns. The Russians had received reinforcements, however, so that an advance was out of the question for us. We then dug in while we were lying on the ground and exchanged some lively fire with our friends from the other side.

In the meantime, the reserve tank troop had rolled up from the rear and established itself behind us to provide covering fire. Our vehicles rolled up to about 400 meters behind us and we received orders to mount up. Running, we reached the vehicles individually, while the tanks pinned down the Russians with their main guns.

I grabbed a motorcycle with a sidecar and went up front one more time to recover Jüdes, which I succeeded in doing despite the heavy mortar fire of the Russians. We then took off at speed towards the north in order to follow our armored elements.

Other motorized and horse-drawn columns were also moving to the right and left of us. Looking through our field glasses, we saw that they were all Russians, who were being continuously attacked by our aircraft.

Rittmeister Jankowski assumed command of the troop.

In the evening, after a breakthrough of 90 kilometers, we reached some high ground, where the entire division set up an all-round defense.

The Armed Forces High Command issued a special bulletin to announce this victory and count the booty taken in the battle of Kalatsch. The division alone had destroyed or captured 38 aircraft, knocked out 81—mainly heavy—tanks, disabled 110 antitank guns, and destroyed 8 antiaircraft guns, 197 mortars and 148 antitank rifles. It also accounted for a railroad train loaded with ammunition.

7,760 Red Army soldiers, including more than 150 officers, surrendered to the *24. Panzer-Division.*

Oberleutnant Michael could not celebrate in the victory, however. His wound had taken him out of the fighting, an event that probably saved his life.

STALINGRAD

While *Oberleutnant* Georg Michael was in the hospital in Germany, the *24. Panzer-Division* was playing a vital role in the fighting that resulted in the breakthrough to Stalingrad.

The destruction of the Kalatsch bridgehead was not complete until the Red Army withdrew its Stalingrad Front to the east bank of the Don, which was completed on 23 August.

On 23 August, the *XIV. Panzer-Korps* of the *6. Armee* crossed the Don and reached the Volga north of Stalingrad.

The *24. Panzer-Division,* which had been allocated to the *4. Panzer-Armee* since 12 August, rolled across the Romanian bridge over the Don at Potemskinskaja and into the Kalmuck Steppe. It subsequently joined the spearhead units of the *6. Armee:* the *14. Panzer-Division* and the *29. Infanterie-Division (mot.),* as part of the *XXXXVIII. Panzer-Korps.* Its objective was to attack along the Kotelnikowo–Stalingrad rail line to the southern part of Stalingrad.

The advance proceeded rapidly, and the corps launched its attack on 20 August on the southern defense line. Its objective was to advance along Jergeni Hill to Krasnoarmeisk in the bend of the Volga.

Oberst Gustav-Adolf Riebel, the commander of *Panzer-Regiment 24*, was killed in fierce fighting against waves of Russian tanks and rifle elements at Hill 118, 15 kilometers south of Krasnoarmeisk.

The battle continued with unimaginable ferocity. The Red Army had been ordered not to move one step back.

Oberst Wilhelm von Lengerke was killed in action on 26 August after leading his *Panzergrenadier-Regiment 21* to the Volga at the southern edge of Stalingrad. He had received the Knight's Cross on 31 August 1941 as commander of the *I./Reiter-Regiment 1*.

The *6. Armee*, with the *4. Panzer-Armee* on its right flank, began the final drive to the Volga on 3 September. Several of the main Russian fortifications were taken in bitter fighting. The attack was halted when it got to the military facilities, where the Russians had dug in a large number of heavy tanks. The tanks were shielded by an in-depth system of bunkers.

The attack on the city began on 11 September. The *24. Panzer-Division* fought with its the left wing on the Zaritza and its right wing at the railway line. Although the station was taken, the grain silo remained in enemy hands. On 16 September, the *6. Armee* assumed command of all forces in the city. All subsequent fighting took place within the city, a role for which armored divisions were ill suited.

The German determination to take the city on the Volga was based on its propaganda value rather than military necessity. The city had no operational value to the campaign, and what transpired there in the months that followed was a tragedy. The battle of Stalingrad became a wearying struggle in cellars, shell holes, sewer systems and factory buildings, ultimately sapping the strength of the *24. Panzer-Division* and resulting in its virtual annihilation.

GEORG MICHAEL AND THE CHAOS

Georg Michael returned to his unit in time for the counterattack against the Russian offensive. The objective was to retake the crossings over the Don at Kalatsch and prevent the enemy attack force from linking up with the IV Mechanized Corps. The attack was poorly planned and failed to achieve the desired results. The *14. Panzer-Division* became isolated and suffered heavy losses. Those elements available from both the *16. Panzer-Division* and the *24. Panzer-Division* were committed singly with little effective coordination between them. Other elements were drawn into these chaotic conditions. *Oberleutnant* Michael was given command of an alert unit, where he was wounded on 18 January. He was flown out of the battlefield on 23 January, where he convalesced at the Stalino military hospital. While there, he wrote down some of his experiences after the attempts to rescue his comrades of the *24. Panzer-Division* and, by extension, the *6. Armee*, had failed:

1. The Encirclement

The possibility of a Russian breakthrough through the Rumanian lines along the salt lakes in the Kalmuck Steppe was anticipated as early as October, as can be gathered from the different orders and evidence. The villages in the northern Kalmuck Steppe south of the Stalingrad–Kalatsch main supply route as far as Aksai and up to the Myschkowa were suitable for a strongpoint defense primarily due to their position in the terrain, in some cases their well-constructed new field fortifications and the already existing Russian field fortifications, their access to water and their supplies of wood. Vehicles and equipment that were not needed on the Volga Front had been stored there. In accordance with a corps order at the beginning of November, all of the localities were to be immediately and energetically fortified, with a target date for defensive preparedness by the middle of November.

The field fortifications already there were overhauled, and new ones were constructed for heavy weapons and especially for the defense of buildings within localities. The locality of Iwanowka on the Myschkowka can be used to demonstrate the defensive options in the Kalmuck Steppe. It is illustrative of many others.

In the holding area of *Panzergrenadier-Regiment 26* at Iwanowka there were approximately the following [personnel and equipment] at the time of the Russian breakthrough through the Rumanian positions:

500 soldiers
80 Russian volunteers
200 trucks and personnel carriers
1 heavy infantry gun (without rotating sight)
1 light infantry gun

2 5-centimeter antitank guns

50 light machine guns

2 armored personnel carriers with 7.5-centimeter main guns

The work of improving the positions had almost been completed. The Myschkowa, to the south, presented a difficult obstacle for tracked vehicles with its steep backs; to the west and east was a Russian tank ditch that was still partially mined. The only place that presented a danger from armored vehicles was a route north that rose towards Businowka that was 2 kilometers wide and flat. Many bunkers had been strengthened with steel and concrete beams and two observation posts had been set up. Five half-tracks were kept in a specially built heated holding area, ready to conduct immediate counterattacks at any time.

Stocks of rations were available. The inventory of small-arms ammunition was sufficient; the ammunition for heavy weapons was limited. The strongpoint of Iwanowka, like many other villages, would have been able to hold out against a medium-sized enemy attack for a longer period of time.

All of the vehicles had been dug in, and the personnel were housed in mortar-proof underground bunkers. The landline and radio communications between and among the different parts of the village had been secured and tested through alerts. Buildings were torn down to reduce the danger of fire spreading—if they had not already been torn down—using the assistance of the village populace. Fuel was available to move the vehicles to the west side of the Don. All equipment, ammunition, weapons and even old uniform items had already been loaded [on them]. It should be mentioned, however, that displacing the vehicles to the west would have led to the loss of the drivers, who had been included in the trench-strength figures, and would have considerably reduced the combat power of the strongpoint.

Despite the considerable defensive capabilities of all of these localities, they were handed over to the enemy without a fight, in some cases ordered to do so and, in some cases, as a result of the large-scale mood of panic.

Holding the strong-points would have enabled a deliberate withdrawal of all logistics elements from the area Tinguta–Abganerowo–Aksai to the west. As a result, in an atmosphere of ill discipline and panic:

1. Rumanian formations that were pulling back—some of them in good order and, as was the case with some horse troops, still willing to fight—could not be halted or collected.

2. Rations, fuel, ammunition and equipment dumps were not, or only insufficiently, destroyed.

3. Not the slightest effort was made to hold up the enemy, even though all of the localities were almost completely manned, in some cases with more than 1,000 personnel capable of fighting, who had sufficient small arms and ammunition.

As a result, the advance guards of the Red Army marched down the roads to the Don without meeting any resistance. Only in Marinowka, which housed a field hospital, did the garrison mount a determined and successful defense.

2. Destruction of Equipment and Ammunition

During the evacuation of the area between the Don and the Volga, it was shockingly evident that the logistics elements were incapable of saving what was necessary for combat and destroying that which was of use to the enemy.

a) No villages were burned down or systematically destroyed.

b) For all practical purposes, the fuel dumps were the only areas that were always blown up. Vehicles frequently had to be left behind because of a lack of fuel, while fuel dumps nearby were being destroyed. The lift capacity of the columns moving back was usually taken up with plundered items and personal items. Most of the trucks were empty. In any event, no one made the effort to take along the important elements of the storage facilities. If someone attempted to stop civilian officials, the only thought for many was to save their personal baggage.

In some cases, one saw a real mania for destruction, which usually occurred at those places where one should have come

to the simplest of tactical conclusions that it was precisely in
that place that it was unnecessary. For example, clothing issue
points were burned down again and again instead of handing
out the felt boots and the winter uniform articles to the troops
moving through the area.

In conclusion, there were substantial and essential
foodstuffs, equipment, weapons, vehicles and munitions that
were either unnecessarily destroyed, not evacuated or left for
the enemy.

3. The Withdrawal Movements

The day we were encircled I went from the south out of the
Kalmuck Steppe into the city [of Stalingrad]. Several things
were worthy of note:

a) The Romanians left their weapons and vehicles behind
and, in their place, drove large heads of cattle with them.

b) Many R0manian officers abandoned their men and took
off in their vehicles.

c) The good discipline of the Romanian [horse] cavalry
troops, who took care of their horses as they rode and,
in some cases, also posted rearguards. They availed
themselves to German officers to fight and, when given
combat missions, executed these with a sense of duty
and obligation.

d) The good convoy discipline of the German columns
that were pulling back. Only the leaders were excited.

e) The panicky manner of the civilian officials who came
from the "front." When they heard that the Russians were
coming with tanks and cavalry, they drove everyone crazy
with their overloaded vehicles, which they clung to like
bunches of grapes in some instances. When questioned,
none had any real contact with combat operations and
had concluded from the sound of fighting and a few
soldiers on horseback that there were large tank and
cavalry [forces].

f) There were no outposts anywhere. People were packing
and burning like mad in the localities. There was not a
single listening post at the entrance to the localities.

g) The behavior of the signals switchboards was exemplary.

h) The maintenance company did not make their maintenance vehicles inoperable.

i) At locations of traffic jams (e.g. at collapsed bridges), the drivers often left their vehicles where they were, went up front (without weapons!!) and attempted to get a ride there.

j) Any and all type of desire to fight and defend was missing.

✠

While this was happening, the fighting at Stalingrad entered its final phase. While much of the division was lost in the final fighting and ultimate surrender within the northern part of the Stalingrad pocket, considerable elements managed to escape the encirclement. During the first three months of 1943, these elements were gathered together and transported by rail to France, where the division was reconstituted. *Oberleutnant* Michael was one of the fortunate survivors.

THE DIVISION IS RECONSTITUTED IN FRANCE—ITALIAN INTERLUDE—RETURN TO THE SOVIET UNION

The first elements of the *24. Panzer-Division* began arriving in its reconstitution staging area in France on 26 February 1943. The division was reconstituted and reorganized there, the most important change being a greater complement of more powerful armored vehicles. In theory, *Panzer-Regiment 24* retained three battalions. In reality, however, it only had two, one equipped with *Panzer IV's* armed with the long-barreled 7.5-centimeter main gun and one battalion with assault guns. The third battalion, with *Panthers*, was only formed later. It never returned to the regiment, however.

The *I./Panzergrenadier-Regiment 26* became fully armored, as did the division's reconnaissance battalion, which was reorganized and redesignated as *Panzer-Aufklärungs-Abteilung 24*.

The *II./Panzergrenadier-Regiment 26* and *Panzergrenadier-Regiment 21* remained unarmored and moved its soldiers to the battlefield on trucks. The division's antitank battalion, *Panzerjäger-Abteilung 40*, was not reconstituted. Georg Michael, who had been promoted to *Hauptmann* in the meantime, was given command of the *II./Panzergrenadier-Regiment 26*.

✠

By the end of August 1943, the division was again fully operational. That same month, it was transferred to Italy in response to the change of government there.

The division suffered no casualties during this deployment. It was initially employed to secure Florence, before assuming coastal defense duties in the Pisa, Livorno and Cecina sectors. The division was also responsible for disarming and arresting members of the Italian Army.

A total of 96,741 soldiers were disarmed, including a large contingent of about 37,000 British, Serbian and Greek soldiers. Large numbers of weapons were also seized, including 344 aircraft. The division seized Padua and advanced step-by-step into the northern part of the country. In early October, the division left Italy to return to Russia.

✠

There, after the failure of Operation Citadel, the Soviets had launched their own offensive on 8 August 1943. Its objective was Kharkov. The Red Army established a large bridgehead across the Dnjepr between Krementschug and Dnjepropetrowsk. It threatened the mining center of Kriwoi Rog and the rear of the new *6. Armee*, which still held a bridgehead east of the Dnjepr and Nikopol. The bridgehead had been declared a fortified location.

The division was transported by rail by way of Vienna, Krakow and Winniza to Uman. The first elements detrained there on 17 October. The entire division did not reach the area of operations until 27 October.

The last major period of operations by the division in which Georg Michael took part began under the command of the *XXXX. Panzer-Korps* in the Alexandrija area.

On 28 October the *XXXX. Panzer-Korps* attacked a force of attacking enemy infantry supported by three waves of tanks. This was the division's first operation, and it helped the *1. Panzer-Armee*, which was under heavy pressure near Kriwoi Rog, to stop the enemy's westward advance.

WITH *HAUPTMANN* GEORG MICHAEL UNTIL HIS DEATH

Ever since the evening of 4 November, the main body of the *24. Panzer-Division* was located in the area of the Nikopol bridgehead. At first, the enemy remained quiet and brought up forces from the rear area into the area around the bridgehead. The only village he had been able to take was Rogatschik, which was located on the boundary between the *XXXIX. Armee-Korps* and the *IX. Armee-Korps.*

The division received the order to seal off this penetration and restore the main line of resistance.

On 5 November, reconnaissance was conducted in the area of the intended attack and contact was established with both of the divisions on the boundary (*17. Infanterie-Division* and *79. Infanterie-Division*). The latter was doubly important because of its relatively heavy concentrations of divisional artillery, which the *24. Panzer-Division* desired to use in support.

The division occupied its staging areas during the night of 5/6 November. The terrain was devoid of cover, which was almost universally typical of the Ukraine. It moved out to attack at 0545 hours on 6 November. Because the morning dawned with clear skies for the first time in some time and sun was already above the horizon, the attack of the armored group was held up, since its route took it directly to the east. With the tanks being blinded, the group would have taken unnecessary losses at that hour.

When the attack resumed, the penetration of the enemy's main lines occurred without difficulty. The lefthand *Kampfgruppe*—the reinforced *Panzergrenadier-Regiment 21*—ejected large enemy forces in front of Hill 81.4 and gained ground as far as the southern entrance to the village of Werch Rogatschik, where the enemy resistance stiffened. The armored group was able to penetrate almost without resistance, and it rolled up the Malaja Saphoniska defile heading north. It hit an enemy division in the flank as it was attempting to pull back towards the southeast. The armored group was able to eliminate all of its artillery and heavy weapons.

Clearing the area that had been recaptured and destroying the captured enemy equipment took some time. While this was taking place, the lefthand *Kampfgruppe* was pulled back from the southern part of the village. It was then reorganized and recommitted, along with the division reserve, Georg Michael's *II./Panzergrenadier-Regiment 26*.

Around 1500 hours, the reinforced *Panzergrenadier-Regiment 21* reached the area around the fork in the road with its lead elements. At the same time, the *II./Panzergrenadier-Regiment 26*, which had been committed to the right, had also pulled even with it sister regiment.

Hauptmann Michael spurred his men on: "Forward, men, we have to get into that god-forsaken hole!"

Machine-gun fire from the right then forced the men to take cover. Georg Michael led the *5./Panzergrenadier-Regiment 26* to the left, into the wake of the advancing sister regiment. When 150 meters behind the enemy pocket of resistance, he turned his force to the right. He came upon another enemy position, taking it from the rear and flank.

Firing their submachine guns and lobbing hand grenades, Michael's men overwhelmed the enemy position. Then, looking in the direction of his battalion, he saw two or three Maxim machine guns. Using hand signals, Michael directed a machine-gun squad against each of the enemy nests.

Michael raised his arm, and he and the three squads charged the enemy machine-gun nests. The Russians tried to swing their guns around, but it was too late. Machine-gun fire and grenades silenced the enemy guns. Michael fired a white flare, which indicated their forward position.

The battalion rushed forward to Michael's position, after which he sent the *7./Panzergrenadier-Regiment 26* forward as the lead element. The battalion then resumed its advance. As usual, Michael accompanied the lead company.

They passed through the town and, with fighting still going on at the northeast end, dug in as ordered.

The advance resumed on the morning of 7 November. Whenever resistance slowed the advance, supporting forces were brought in to get it moving again. The last resistance was broken in the town, and the infantry divisions were then free to reoccupy the former main line of resistance.

The next objective was Wessely-Nesamoshnik. The Russians had achieved a penetration against the *79. Infanterie-Division* there. The

258. Infanterie-Division was to its north, but both formations were well below strength and exhausted.

The *24. Panzer-Division* formed two *Kampfgruppen* for its attack. *Panzergrenadier-Regiment 26* formed the core elements of *Kampfgruppe "H,"* which was led by the regiment's acting commander, *Major* Hans Wilhelm von Heyden. The *Kampfgruppe* also had two *Ferdinand* tank-destroyer companies in support as well as a battalion of divisional artillery.

Kampfgruppe "M" was led by *Oberst* Müller-Hillebrand, the commanding officer of *Panzer-Regiment 24*. In addition to a tank battalion, this *Kampfgruppe* also had the divisional reconnaissance squadron, a troop of flamethrower tanks and a battalion of artillery in support.

In his command tank, the division commander first drove to *Kampfgruppe "M."* At 0900 hours he personally issued the following order:

> Powerful enemy tank forces, about 100 T-34's, have broken through west of the Beloserka Defile and are advancing toward the artillery positions of the divisions in position there. A large force of enemy infantry with tanks in support is attacking our forces, attempting to seal off the area of penetration in the Wessely-Nesamoshnik area.
>
> I intend to hold the enemy forces that have broken through *Kampfgruppe "H,"* by employing it across the enemy's front. The main effort will fall on the attached tank-destroyer battalion. Stopping them will prevent the enemy from advancing on Snamenka. Once these enemy groups have been halted, *Kampfgruppe "M"* will attack the enemy's deep flank in the area north of Wesselyj-Nesamoshnik. The objective is to first pinch off the enemy spearhead, then attack the Beloserka Defile and restore the main line of resistance.

Once the division commander had finished with his instructions to Müller-Hillebrand, he moved on to *Kampfgruppe "H."*

At around 1100 hours, both of the *Kampfgruppen* had established enemy contact: *Kampfgruppe "M"* around Point 76.9 and *Kampfgruppe "H"* two kilometers northwest of Point 72.7.

The division commander issued the following order to the commander of the *II./Panzergrenadier-Regiment 26*: "Michael, you are to seal off the area there. Let none of them get through!"

"None will get through here, *Herr General!*" the *Rittmeister*—the cavalry equivalent of *Hauptmann*—promised. Then he immediately marched his battalion in the direction of Hill 72.2.

As the battalion approached the hill, it drove straight into the flank of a Russian battle group making ready to seize the hill before attacking the gorge. Dusk was already falling and the Red Army soldiers forming the rearguard were visible only as silhouettes.

Michael directed the men of his lead company: "Position yourself just to the left of that torn-apart tree! Steiner, take your machine-gun section and set up there and separate the rest of them from the people in front. Steinbrinck, take your section and start with the last group on the left. We'll swing from left to right and from right to left and meet in the middle."

Michael gave a hand signal and the machine guns opened fire. They mowed down the enemy, working their respective ways into the center.

"Müller, move your platoon forward. Try to make contact with the end of the Russian forces."

Georg Michael went forward to join the platoon, passing the Russians mowed down by the machine guns.

By then, it was completely dark and several times the advancing platoon passed Russians moving the other way. Each time, the Russians spoke to them and Michael responded with a hand signal indicating that they were moving toward the front. The Russians let them pass.

When Michael and his men came under fire from Hill 72.2, they moved to the left and took cover.

Three minutes later, a group of Russians appeared from behind. They had slipped in between the main German force and Michael's *Panzergrenadiere*. A Russian officer came straight toward Michael. Ten meters from the German, he stopped suddenly, realizing there were Germans in front of him, and raised his weapon. Michael fired, and apparently hit the man's weapon, which was knocked from his hands. The Russian jumped at Michael, whose weapon was knocked out of his hands. They grappled for a while, before Michael was able to knock the Russian unconscious.

One of the *Panzergrenadiere* came running. They picked up the officer and Michael gestured to the rear. "Take him back for questioning!" was all he said.

Michael fired the recognition signal and resumed the advance. From the hill, a company attacked the defenders. Hand grenades and submachine guns were used to eliminate the enemy.

"That was just in time," a *Leutnant* whom Michael did not recognize gasped.

"What about contact?" the *Rittmeister* asked.

"Lost, and we couldn't send out a patrol."

"Very well, we'll do it. Bülles, take your squad and scout to the east and southeast. Report any enemy. Move out at once!"

The *Unteroffizier* with the Iron Cross, First Class, nodded to his old comrade and waved to his squad, which had made itself comfortable in the enemy's defensive positions on the hill.

The patrol moved out. Georg Michael directed his men into the defense area while he waited for the results of the patrol.

An hour and a half later, Bülles and his men returned.

"Contact established. No enemy left in our main line of resistance, *Herr Rittmeister*."

During the night, Georg Michael received orders from division to leave the position and advance to the southeast. Aerial reconnaissance had reported heavy vehicle traffic there heading toward Nowo Petrowka and Nesamoshnik.

When dawn came, the *II./Panzergrenadier-Regiment 26* under *Rittmeister* Michael had found a perfect ambush position from which it could halt enemy supply traffic and fight off Russian attacks.

Barely 10 minutes later, the men heard the sound of approaching tanks. The *Rittmeister* gave the order to ready the defenses. He had a platoon emplace two hasty minefields about 100 to 150 meters in front of his positions.

At the last second, six assault guns of *Sturmgeschütz-Abteilung 278* arrived. The lead assault gun approached Michael's command post. The gun commander, *Hauptmann* Johannes Stier, a towering figure, left the vehicle and walked toward Michael. He gave a sharp whistle when he saw who it was.

"Things are soon going to be going full tilt here, eh, Georg?"

"Hannes, I am relieved to have you here!" Michael had twice been in action with his comrade from the "fast" artillery.

"The corps [*XXXX. Armee-Korps*] has placed us in direct support," Stier said.

"Then have a look for the best positions. I think it would be best if you took Ivan from both flanks."

Hauptmann Stier split his force in two and sent three assault guns right and three left. By then, the first enemy tanks were becoming visible in the pale moonlight. They advanced in a huge wave. Russian infantry advanced behind the tanks, while some rode on the vehicles.

From the left and right, the six assault guns opened fire at the six or seven KV-I's and KV-II's leading the armored wedge. All were knocked out barely 100 meters from the positions of the *Panzergrenadiere*. The *MG 42's* opened fire on the following infantry. Though heavily outnumbered in men and armored vehicles, *Rittmeister* Michael and *Hauptmann* Stier succeeded in repulsing the enemy, inflicting heavy losses.

After this success, the assault guns were sent elsewhere. But the Russians attacked again and Michael let the tanks overrun his position. The enemy thought he had broken through and prepared to exploit his success. At this point, *Rittmeister* Michael ordered his men to open fire on the infantry that had been following the tanks at some distance.

All of the battalion's *MG 42's* opened up on the enemy attack force. There was an unbelievable massacre. When the Soviet tankers realized they no longer had any infantry following them, they turned back, only to be received by Michael's tank-killing teams and the combined fires of *Hauptmann* Stier's assault guns, which had been summoned back.

Georg Michael and some men personally attacked one of the T-34's. While his men gave covering fire with submachine guns, Michael climbed onto the tank. He dropped a bundled charge on the rear deck and jumped off the vehicle. The resulting explosion from the 3-kilogram charge ignited the tank's fuel tank and set it alight.

Other tank-killing squads set upon the Russian tanks. The surviving tanks turned east and disappeared. The engagement was over.

An hour later, the division commander arrived, accompanied by the *Kampfgruppe* commander. By then, the *II./Panzergrenadier-Regiment 26* had moved back into the old combat-outpost line and was ready to meet the next attack.

Georg Michael was asked to walk the battlefield with the commanding officer and report on what had happened there. The knocked-out tanks were inspected to see if any could be put to use. What intrigued the divisional commander the most were the hundreds of enemy dead in the battalion's sector.

"And you did all of this with your *MG 42's* and no heavy weapons?" he asked the *Rittmeister*.

"The heavy weapons, our assault guns, stopped the enemy tanks. But this here is our handiwork. Nothing's too much for an *MG 42*."

✠

Kampfgruppe "M" had fought with equal success. It was a graphic demonstration of what a division at full strength in men and equipment could do, even in 1943.

In the words of the division commander, it was "an example of how flexible command can allow even numerically inferior armored *Kampfgruppen* to achieve considerable success in a defensive role when working together with *Panzergrenadiere*."

In the subsequent fighting in that sector, *Rittmeister* Georg Höhne and his *I./Panzergrenadier-Regiment 26* counterattacked in their armored personnel carriers and eliminated a deep penetration by the enemy. This counterattack and attacks by the *Stukas* of Hans-Ulrich Rudel's group prevented an attack by Soviet armored forces that had been massing in the area.

"They were the men who always tipped the scales," said one of the men in the division headquarters. "Höhne and Michael, friends for years, were examples to the entire division."

Like Georg Michael, Georg Höhne was killed in combat on 19 February 1945; only one day previously, he had been awarded the Knight's Cross while serving as a *Major* and commander of *Panzergrenadier-Regiment 26*. He had earlier received the German Cross in Gold on 20 January 1944.

On the day of the fighting described above, the *24. Panzer-Division* destroyed a total of 64 enemy tanks and immobilized 12 more. The division's reconnaissance squadron also contributed mightily to the overall success—one of its antitank guns accounted for 8 T-34's alone.

These successes brought the number of armored vehicle "kills" for the *24. Panzer-Division* for a total of 600 within several months of its second deployment to the Eastern Front.

SAPOROSHJE

In mid-December, the Russians began sending more and more forces into their bridgehead across the Dnjepr. A major attack was imminent. It was at this point that the division formed a *Kampfgruppe* under the command of *Oberst* Gustav Adolf von Nostitz-Wallwitz, the commander of *Panzer-Artillerie-Regiment 89*. The *Kampfgruppe* consisted of two troops of tanks, the *II./Panzergrenadier-Regiment 26* under *Rittmeister* Michael, *Panzer-Aufklärungs-Abteilung* 24 and elements of *Panzer-Pionier-Bataillon 40*. In support were the gunners of the *III./Panzer-Artillerie-Regiment 89*.

While *Rittmeister* Michael succeeded in reaching his objective, the tanks became bogged down in extensive minefields. The attack lacked the forces to turn the enemy's flank, but it might have succeeded if the recommendation to commit the entire division had been followed. Michael and his men had to be pulled back. It was a bitter blow to the young officer, because his battalion had suffered significant losses in achieving its objective.

✠

The Red Army counterattacked on 19 December 1943, resulting in a breakthrough. The enemy thus had a clear path to hotly contested "artillery gorge." By midday, the Russians had crossed the gorge and their spearheads were nearing Dnjeprowka.

The armored *Kampfgruppe* of *Oberstleutnant* Müller-Hillebrand attacked again. It was joined by *Oberst* von Nostitz-Wallwitz's *Kampfgruppe*, as it was vital that the Russians be held in check. The latter group was sent south, where it linked up with the *Kampfgruppe* commanded by *Oberst* von Below of *Panzergrenadier-Regiment 21*. Shortly thereafter, the two groups attacked south from Dnjeprowka.

In bitter fighting, the German forces fought their way through the western part of "horseshoe gorge." The *II./Panzergrenadier-Regiment 26* took up position there to meet the expected Russian counterattack. The western arm of the gorge had been denied to the enemy, preventing him from massing forces to the south of it in preparation for another attack.

The enemy attacked the positions held by Michael's battalion. Georg Michael was indefatigable in organizing his defenses. Attacks were halted a few meters from the positions. When the enemy could not break through, he went around, forcing a gap between Michael's men and the Beloserka Defile. The division sent forces to counterattack, but they failed to reestablish contact with the *II./Panzergrenadier-Regiment 26*. It looked like Michael and his men would be forced to fight their way out.

"MICHAEL IS ENCIRCLED!"

On hearing this alarm call, the battered *I./Panzergrenadier-Regiment 26* prepared to counterattack through the Russians. Here is the firsthand account by one of the troop leaders within the *I./Panzergrenadier-Regiment 26* who was involved in the rescue attempt:

> I went up to the division and encountered the liaison officer of the 1st Battalion there. He took me to my troop, which was mounted up in an assembly area. I assumed command from *Oberwachtmeister* Benecke, who had led it up to this point. Other than him, I knew no one. The things I was informed about also were not exactly pleasant. The platoon leaders, noncommissioned officers and the men did not know one another either. Everything had been cobbled together. I attempted to get to know my platoon leaders in a hurry, which was only partially successful in the candlelight of my command vehicle. The squadron commander was *Rittmeister* Thylmann. The 1st Troop was commanded by *Leutnant* Günther; the 2nd by Mathias. All three of us had only assumed command of our troops an hour ago. It was intended for us to attack dismounted at 0100 hours.
>
> The situation was as follows: *Abteilung Michael*—my former troop commander—was almost surrounded. The armored

reconnaissance battalion was to his right, but back some distance. There was considerable separation between the two of them. To the right of the reconnaissance battalion was an infantry regiment. The enemy had been reported to be in the area between the two forces with about 1,000 men. The 2nd [2./Panzergrenadier-Regiment 26] would initially relieve the reconnaissance battalion so that it could move to our right. After that happened, the 2nd and the 3rd Troops would shift further to the left so as to avoid the large open area. When we attacked, we would push our way forward through the cornfield. My troop was the strongest with 60 men and I was to assume the right wing. A troop of assault guns was to provide assistance, if needed.

Everything went well initially. The shift [left] was almost finished, when the Russians attacked the platoon I had held in reserve, yelling their battle cry of "Hurra!" They had allowed both troops to pass within 30 meters of them. The blue beans [soldier slang for bullets] were flying through the air. Communications with the 2nd Troop on the left was broken off. The troop had become completely disorganized and the first one to be killed was my radio operator, with the result that I no longer had communications with the [squadron].

In the light provided by signal flares, I was able to figure out the situation. With a few people quickly gathered together and a "Hurra!" we were able to eliminate most of the Russians. I also had the fortune of bringing order back to the troop. I then attacked with all three platoon on line, with two usually providing cover and one breaking [into the Russian positions] with a battle cry. I was determined to free Michael!

We overran the second Russian position and, as we did so, I saw the 2nd Troop advancing on my left. The Russians fought fiercely, and I took numerous casualties. Nevertheless, at about 0215 hours, I took two antitank guns with a platoon each. The darkness was terrible, and the casualties sustained were no less because of it. The Russians launched a limited immediate counterattack with a "Hurra!" on our right, but we were able to turn it back.

I then identified an antitank gun in front of me and I had a platoon go after it. The platoon leader claimed he was not able to advance, because the firing was too intense. That took a lot of nerve, especially since I was standing up right next to him. I then relieved him of his platoon and advanced on the antitank gun.

Something stirred in front of us, whereupon one squad immediately turned around and pulled back. I had an Italian hand grenade charged in my hand and threw it into the antitank-gun position. Then I dashed forward and suddenly found myself facing a Russian with a fixed bayonet. My machine gun failed to fire; I turned it around and struck the Russian, knocking him down and breaking off the stock of my weapon. The Russian was perhaps 13 or 14 years old and had been the only one who had remained with the antitank gun.

While reorganizing the troop, I identified another antitank gun about 30 paces in front of me. I pointed it out to *Oberwachtmeister* Benecke and intended to have him attack it. But the antitank gun was faster and wanted to take us out. I only saw a spurt of flame and then felt a blow to my face. I fell over. I thought to myself: an antitank round full in the face. I thought about how it was to be dead. While thinking all this over, I came to the conclusion that I should check to see how big the hole in my head was. In the process of doing that, I discovered that my left hand was useless and that two fingers were hanging in front of my face.

This gave me some encouragement. I stood up and saw that I had been lying on Benecke, who had been riddled like a sieve and must have been killed instantly. I then was afraid that I would bleed to death and asked a soldier to dress my arm. He wrapped a dressing around my wrist, which most certainly did not serve any purpose. Before that had happened, I had torn off my index finger, but I did not succeed in doing that to my middle finger, which was still connected to a vein. I started to go back and suddenly noticed that air was coming out of my chest. When I felt there, I was able to put all four fingers of my hand in the hole. After going 30 meters, I ran into a medic, who dressed me properly and requested for me to lie down. He wanted to go for help.

Up front, all of the platoon leaders had become casualties. What was left of the platoon was commanded by an *Unteroffizier*. Two assault guns, which rushed to our aid, were knocked out. A great sadness came over me when I thought about the fact that we had not been able to get Michael out. But I was unable to do anything else . . .

While this individual troop leader was unable to do any more, many more soldiers were able to band together and eventually force a path into the location of Michael's battalion. Once again, fate had smiled on Michael.

✠

The *II./Panzergrenadier-Regiment 26* was then involved in the fighting around Dnjeprowka, which began on 31 December and extended far into January. On the first day of fighting, *Kampfgruppe Nostitz-Wallwitz* knocked out 17 enemy tanks and drove the enemy from the main line of resistance. The fighting raged back and forth, and Georg Michael and his men were always in the forefront. On the night of 16/17 January 1944, enemy assault groups broke into Horseshoe Gorge. *II./Panzergrenadier-Regiment 26* under *Rittmeister* Georg Michael launched an immediate counterattack, supported by three assault guns. The *Rittmeister* was once again the driving force. He and his men halted an infantry attack behind the main line of resistance and drove the Red Army men out again.

Just as they reached the main line of resistance, Georg Michael was shot in the head by an enemy sniper. He immediately collapsed, unconscious. An armored personnel carrier of the *I./Panzergrenadier-Regiment 26* transported him under fire to the frontline hospital. The doctors tried everything to save the life of this unique officer, but their efforts were in vain. *Rittmeister* Georg Michael died on 19 January 1944.

✠

At the time, the division had the following entered into its daily logs concerning this brave officer: "The division has lost one of its best in him. Revered by his comrades, loved by his men, he will live on as an inspiration to us all!"

Georg Michael was buried with full military honors on 23 January 1944. An honor guard fired a final volley over his grave in the military cemetery in Odessa. *Oberleutnant* Schniewind, his last adjutant, delivered the eulogy:

Rittmeister Michael!

We have come here from the Nikopol bridgehead to bid you farewell forever and also to convey the respect and gratitude of the division commander, *Generalmajor Freiherr* von Edelsheim, and the entire division.

The division has lost one of its best, most dashing commanding officers. The [squadron] carries its leader to the grave, a man who was known and loved by everyone and who in turn always had time and concern for the cares and needs of every one of us. He was one of the longest-serving members of the [squadron]—a platoon leader in Holland and France, a troop commander in the first Russian campaign, ever since Stalingrad as commander of his old [squadron].

It is all still difficult for us to comprehend! At exactly the same time one week ago, we attacked. As always, the commanding officer was with us . . . had a kind word for everyone . . . was the soul of the attack . . . only to be taken away fatally wounded, never to return to us.

We are now alone; a gap has been torn that no man can fill. We can only promise you one thing. We vow to continue to fight as you taught us and, if need be, die. In all future fighting we will remember that you are looking down on us and will strive to prove ourselves worthy.

That shall be our solemn promise for the future.

Rittmeister Georg Michael! Your battalion says goodbye to you forever!

✠

At this point, let us turn to the words of the author of the divisional history of the *1. Kavallerie-Division*, which later became the *24. Panzer-*

Division, Ferdinand von Senger und Etterlin. The former *Oberleutnant* and commander of the *3./Panzer-Aufklärungs-Abteilung 24*, who fought shoulder-to-shoulder with Michael on several occasions, wrote the following:

> The young blond from Hamburg was no more. His fine-featured face, too fine for the squat steel helmet, his long, narrow nose, and his often smiling, but mocking lips will never be forgotten.
>
> He stood apart from the majority of the German officer corps, and yet he was a combination of many things that are often encountered only individually. He was a cold-blooded, sometimes brutal fighter. In spite of his pale skin and frail limbs, he had nerves of steel in combat. He stood under fire with an iron calmness, sometimes almost carelessly, as if he thought himself invulnerable, providing an example to his men. Many an old *Wachtmeister* was secretly embarrassed for having showed fear before an action. Michael smiled and advanced slowly, his submachine gun at the ready.
>
> His approach to fighting, which so contrasted with his outward, almost too sophisticated appearance, produced the fascination with his personality. He was not the product of one of the old Prussian military families, which provided so many outstanding leaders in our division, but he possessed all the qualities that they had acquired over the generations.
>
> Neither was he an East Prussian, as most of his men were. But he was an example to them in his outward calm, aggressiveness in the attack and stamina. He was from a Hanseatic town, an area not particularly friendly toward the military, but he was an officer with the self-confidence of an aristocrat . . .
>
> His leadership style was based on intuition and professional skill. We have cited examples of the care with which he issued his orders. He was no impetuous daredevil who saw red when nothing else helped. Instead, he always proceeded according to a well-considered plan, like a good athlete. He never looked any different than his men when in the mud, and he was always at the front! His beaming presence was often the focal point of the division, during quiet times and in combat.

The division perhaps left its stamp on Georg Michael just as much as he was a formative influence on it. His loss was a noticeable extinguishing of one the many flames that provided the division with its inner warmth. Those who survived drew closer together.

On 28 February 1944, Michael was posthumously promoted to *Major* for bravery in the face of the enemy.

A *Panzer IV/F2* of the *24. Panzer-Regiment* in Russia 1942.

A *Stug III Ausf. G* of the *9. Schwadron*. Note the additional bolted-on frontal armor and the *Zimmerit* anti-magnetic paste.

A 5-centimeter mortar, which the soldier's referred to as a "potato tosser."

A larger hole in the ground with a shelter half above it—otherwise known as a company command post.

Oskar Schaub.

CHAPTER 9

Hauptmann Oskar Schaub

WITH *PANZERGRENADIER-REGIMENT 12*
IN THE SOVIET UNION

As morning dawned on 18 November 1941, *Schützen-Regiment 12* of the *4. Panzer-Division* was marching out of its assembly area in Borodino in a depression near Schwaron Creek. The 2nd Battalion, on the right, had been given Jelishewa as its objective; the 1st Battalion on the left was to storm Markowtschina, which was on the far side of the creek. The deep waters of the creek were already frozen over.

"Schaub, cover the left flank of the company!" That was the directive of the company commander of the 4th (Heavy) Company as he returned from the orders conference.

The *Feldwebel* with the goatee nodded and looked around. The men of his machine-gun platoon were gathered behind him. The four heavy machine guns represented considerable firepower. The men were freezing; the temperature that morning registered a frigid -22 (-7.6 Fahrenheit).

Schaub's platoon moved forward into a depression. Off to his right, the rest of the company stomped through the thickly vegetated terrain. The snow, about 10 centimeters high, made it difficult to move. *Feldwebel* Schaub broke through a snow bank once and had to work his way out.

The 3rd and 1st Companies were already making their way to the left and right of the row of houses that constituted Markowtschina. For a few moments, Schaub could make out the vehicles of the 1st Company, which was the battalion's armored company, still riding in its *SPW's.*

All of a sudden, friendly artillery fire commenced when the force approached to within about 200 meters of the village. It was 0615 hours. In response, the men received an occasional 15-centimeter round from the enemy. They impacted into the frozen ground, sending up geysers of snow.

When the 4th Company reached open terrain, the other two companies were already attacking the village. "*Herr Feldwebel,* it looks like they're bogging down in front of the cemetery on the hill!" one of Schaub's noncommissioned officers reported.

"There's the 1st!" one of the men shouted out, and all of them saw the *SPW's* picking up speed for the attack. Muzzle flashes could be seen over the tops of the open superstructures.

Soon, the resistance was broken in the village. The entire village was in the battalion's hands by 0900 hours, and the 4th Company did not even have to be employed. After the men stopped to reorganize, they continued on towards Kubyschewa. The 1st Battalion was in the lead, followed by the 2nd Battalion.

Just outside of Kubyschewa, an enemy antiaircraft gun suddenly popped out from behind a haystack. It fired a few rounds in the direction of the Germans and then disappeared again behind the concealment of the haystack.

The battalion commander, who had made his way forward, ordered his heavy weapons to engage the haystack.

The antiaircraft gun was able to emerge from its hiding place and fire two more times before a round from an infantry gun hit the haystack and set it ablaze. From the village of Kubyschewa, a Soviet 7.62-centimeter gun started to engage the Germans. It was also soon silenced by an infantry gun from the battalion's heavy-weapon's company.

The battalion commander announced to the men would attack after the promised *Stuka* support arrived. The dive-bombers soon approached, easily recognizable in the clear light of the bright November day. Schaub counted 27 machines flying over the company. They dove on the village without engaging their sirens. Schaub watched the impacting bombs through his binoculars. *Oberst Freiherr* von Lüttwitz, the regimental commander, appeared on the scene.

"Looks like we're giving it the full treatment, *Herr Feldwebel?*" one of the platoon runners asked when he saw the commanding officer.

Schaub nodded: "We'll be attacking as soon as it turns dusk."

It was around 1500 hours, when it started to turn dark. The riflemen moved out, with von Lüttwitz in the lead.

The riflemen assaulted the battered village from the south— coming through a depression in which the village was located—and from the west through a large fruit orchard. It seemed as if everything was on fire or glowing. But the Siberians defending there had not been shaken by the aerial attack. It was not possible to eliminate the last pockets of resistance until the tanks came forward.

The next day, the Soviets conducted a counterattack with tanks against the rail station at Dedilowo, which the regiment had taken without a fight. Seven enemy tanks and an armored car were knocked out.

By the evening of 21 November, the lead elements were in Uslawaja. The village was not occupied by the enemy. The Soviets soon started attacking the village, however, and they entered the southeastern portion of the village as it turned dusk. They were able to advance as far as the rail station.

The company commander of the 4th summoned his platoon leaders when he returned from the battalion command post. He briefed his men: "The 1st and 7th Companies have moved out in an immediate counterattack against the Russian forces that have entered the village. Our mission is to eject the enemy infantry out of the fruit orchard south of the rail station. We will be supported by tanks. Schaub, your platoon takes the lead." The company commander then arranged his other two machine-gun platoons to follow behind, echeloned to the right and left.

Four tanks moved up to the machine gunners. *Feldwebel* Schaub waved to platoon leader: "Please don't go so fast, *Herr Leutnant.* We've got a heavy load!"

"Understand, Schaub!" the officer replied. "Stay right behind us!"

Flames shot out of the exhaust stacks on the tanks, and they started to move out slowly. The heavy machine-gun sections followed closely behind.

They had just reached the outskirts of the giant fruit orchard when the first rounds started whipping towards them from the tangle of tree limbs and vegetation. A *Ratsch-Bumm* started taking on the tanks, with the first rounds missing and striking a low outbuilding to the rear.

There were four distinct muzzle flashes to be seen from a building off to the right. The fist section was told to engage at will. The heavy machine gun went into position. With its first burst of fire, one of the muzzle flashes disappeared.

Unteroffizier Klugler called out to *Feldwebel* Schaub: "Group of Russians behind the well off to the left!"

Schaub whipped around. He fired into the Soviet group with his submachine gun. A heavy machine gun joined in, and the enemy force disappeared so fast in the snow it was as if it were not even there.

A house wall collapsed with an ear-deafening din. Flames shot out of the small shed that had been built next to it on the short side of the house. Red Army men ran out of the glut of the fire, their uniforms on fire. They threw themselves down in the snow in an effort to extinguish the flames.

"Klugler's squad, follow me!"

The attackers cut across the terrain and suddenly found themselves in a ditch, up to their chests in the snow. From there, Schaub could see several Red Army men approaching the platoon leader's tank with Molotov cocktails.

"Over there . . . Russians . . . "

As the enemy started to move out to deliver the death blow to the unsuspecting *Leutnant* and his tank, a machine gun started to rattle. Schaub fired from his submachine gun as well, and the Soviets collapsed to the ground in the middle of their movement.

The tank then pivoted on one of its tracks and headed for a sauna. It hit the small building with the front hull, and the edifice soon collapsed. The distraction caused by the tank gave Schaub the opportunity he had been waiting for: "Get up . . . let's go!"

The men gasped for breath as they raced forward with their heavy loads. More and more houses began to catch fire. The Soviets were still defending with the courage of desperation, however. The 4th Company moved forward by leaps and bounds. Off to the flanks, Schaub could see the tanks firing in support, the tracer ammunition streaming towards the enemy like a glowing spear and the main-gun high-explosive rounds exploding with mighty bursts.

From one of the houses, automatic-weapons fire was pouring out at a lively tempo. Schaub and his men approached the building. He fired his submachine gun on the run, emptying his magazine against the house windows. He then let the weapon dangle from its strap while he armed a grenade. He kicked in the front door and tossed the grenade, seeking cover to the side.

As soon as the grenade exploded, he was on his feet again, storming into the house. He took six Red Army men prisoner and entrusted them to the care of two slightly wounded men of his platoon. The other men, inspired by Schaub's example, continued the assault all the way to the rail station, although the Soviets still continued to stubbornly defend, firing from rooftops, attics, basements and outbuildings.

In the meantime, the tanks had another enemy to contend with— four 52-ton KV-series tanks. The were slow moving, top heavy and armed with a 15.2-centimeter infantry gun, but deadly foes, nonetheless, especially since their heavy armor made them almost impervious to German tank guns of the period.

The tank-against-tank engagements started and soon turned into a dramatic struggle. The German tanks, supported by the machine gunners, were able to separate the Soviet escort infantry. Tank hunter/killer teams, armed with shaped charges, snuck up on two of the steel giants and took them out of action. Once that was done, the remaining two started to pull back. The next day, another one was eventually knocked out by one of the tanks supporting the 4th Company. The enemy resistance was broken, however, and the village was soon reported to be in German hands.

On 1 December, Schaub was personally awarded the Iron Cross, First Class, by the newly appointed division commander, *Generalmajor* Eberbach, who had been the long-time commander of the division's *Panzer-Regiment 35.*[1] The young Austrian, with the youthful face and receding blond hairline, had inspired his entire platoon by his actions and contributed significantly to the taking of the stubbornly held village.

✠

Oskar Schaub was born in Krems in Lower Austria on 19 August 1919, the son of the teachers Josef and Johanna Schaub. He attended college preparatory school and was graduated with a diploma in 1937. He entered the Austrian Army as a volunteer for one year of service on 30 September 1937. After undergoing basic training at Lake Neusiedl,

---

1. Editor's Note: See *Knight's Cross Panzers* for the unit history of *Panzer-Regiment 35*, the most highly decorated tank regiment in the German Army in World War II.

he was assigned to *Kraftfahr-Jäger-Bataillon 1*, a motorized infantry battalion. Army life agreed with young "Ossi," as he was called, and he was considered a good comrade by his peers.

As a result of the internal turmoil in the country and the threat of intervention by Germany, Schaub's battalion was deployed to Austria's western frontier at the beginning of 1938. The rest of his regiment remained behind in garrison. At the time, he wrote in his diary: "The danger of a civil war—or of a war against out brothers in Germany—created a depressing and gloomy situation. The government enjoyed little sympathy."

The revolt in Graz and the entry of German forces ratcheted the tension up even further, which did not abate until Austria was annexed—the *Anschluß*—into the *Reich*. For example, on the way to the frontier, the battalion had encountered a cool and reserved reception from the populace. On the way back to its garrison after the *Anschluß*, however, it was greeted enthusiastically.

Schaub's battalion and his parent regiment were earmarked for the formation of *Schützen-Regiment 12*, when the Austrian Army was incorporated into the German Army. On 9 November 1938, the regiment was moved to Meiningen in Thuringia, and Schaub's company became the 4th (Heavy) Company of the regiment.

Unteroffizier Schaub participated in the occupation of Bohemia and Moravia from 11 March to 4 April 1939. In the summer of the same year, the division trained together for the first time as a division at the Jüterbog Training Area. The final exercise of the training period: "Combat Operations of Combined Arms and Coordination of Rifle Elements with Tank Units." On 10 August, the division was moved to the area of Kreuzberg–Oppeln in Silesia, next to Poland. It was there that it prepared for the campaign in Poland.

The campaign there and the subsequent one in the west passed without major incident for Schaub. He was promoted to *Feldwebel* and also designated an officer candidate after he had passed the preparatory course. At the beginning of April 1941, the division was moved to the Eisenstadt area in anticipation of being employed in the Balkans campaign. It was not committed, however. Instead, it was sent to Posen and the Warthe Training Area, starting on 19 April. *Feldwebel* Schaub and his company detrained at Posen West on 29 April.

On the night of 7/8 June, the company departed Posen to head east. On 11 June, it reached an encampment area in the vicinity of Belczac–Suchowola. Amazing rumors started making the rounds. One of them, for instance, had the division moving through the Soviet Union and Turkey to block the Suez Canal.

On the evening of 21 June, Schaub and his platoon moved into the woods west of the Wolka. That same night, they moved farther east to positions along the Bug River, the demarcation line with the Soviet Union. When the 2nd Battalion moved out to cross the Bug around 0315 hours, both of the heavy machine guns of Schaub's platoon fired into the Soviet observation towers on the east bank of the Bug. In the excitement that prevailed that morning, the full moon that was low in the sky was mistaken for an enemy barrage balloon and engaged.

The 2nd Battalion crossed the river and reached Miedna, while the 1st Battalion waited for the engineer bridge to be erected. It was not until the following day around 1100 hours that it was able to cross. *Feldwebel* Schaub and his comrades then set off in the direction of Miedna to join their sister battalion.

Over the next few weeks, Schwab and the men became familiar with the merciless heat of the Soviet summer and the honeycomb clouds of choking dust. During the night of 28/29 June, the riflemen moved through the burning city of Slusk, advancing in the direction of Bobruisk. As it turned dusk on 29 June, the division commander, *Generalmajor* von Langermann und Erlenkamp, received orders to cross the Beresina at Swislotsch and to take Uglata. It was to form a bridgehead on the east bank of the river there. Schaub later wrote about his experiences in that fighting in the regimental history:

> Dusk had started to place its shadows over the road when the 1st Battalion, moving past the column pulled over sharply to the right, headed for Bobruisk.
>
> Order of march: Command staff; 3rd Company; 2nd Company; remainder of the headquarters staff; remainder of the 4th (Heavy) Company; and the 1st (Mechanized) Company. Most of the heavy weapons of our 4th Company were distributed among the rifle companies.
>
> The night turned very cold. Ground fog rose from the broad, wet pasture land. We didn't mind though, since it

formed the shroud of secrecy through which we could sneak through unobserved by any enemy outposts that might appear.

Bobruisk was jam packed with vehicles from the *3. Panzer-Division.* It smelled like a sewer. We turned off the road to the north, left the city and passed the farthest German outposts, which stood there, unmoving, with shelter halves draped over them. We moved forward with security for the column as noiselessly as possible. The old stands of woods lined our route, dark and malevolent. It was difficult to orient ourselves based on the inexact map. The vehicles rolled forward in a tight knot. Just don't lose contact!

An officer from *Panzer-Aufklärungs-Abteilung 7,*[2] who had just returned from a patrol, told us how to get to the Beresina, which would set the direction for us. We continued on through woods, fields and villages. The routes were sandy. The worn-out trails and the abandoned Ford and Moskwa vehicles told us that the enemy had only marched through there a short while ago. Up to that point, we did not have any enemy contact.

The ground fog increased on the morning of 30 June to the point of it being like a laundry room. Things started to stir in the villages. All of a sudden, the steep banks of the Beresina appeared. There was ground fog on the water. We would soon be at our first objective. Our weapons were at the ready.

At the outskirts of Oktjabr, a Russian guard was leaning on an artesian well. He thought we were his fellow countrymen. That mistake cost him his life. We raced through Oktjabr. A Russian column of trains was stopped on the village street. A few bursts of fire, and the soldiers scattered off to the right to the house gardens and to the left into the protective woods.

The race continued on past Uglata. In Sloboda, the reinforced 3rd Company turned off to the right, rolled across the wooden bridge over the Swislotsch and into the locality that was higher above it. The two sentries at the bridge were overpowered; a bridgehead formed. Mission accomplished!

The battalion took the railway bridge as well and established a bridgehead on the eastern side.

---

2. Translator's Note: The division's armored reconnaissance battalion.

The fighting started in the vicinity of the road bridge at Uglata, however. A well-equipped armored train arrived at the Swislotsch rail station. We jumped out of our vehicles and took cover behind the railway embankment. The monstrosity crept ever closer to us.

"If that monster gets across the overpass, then we'll be targets on a range, *Herr Feldwebel!*" Meyer said to me.

Our antitank guns and infantry guns started to fire at that point. White smoke was gushing out of the locomotive initially, then smoke black as a raven. Hit and finished!

The transport train moving behind the armored train also started to burn after the first few rounds hit it. Brown-clad figures started to pour out of the doors of the freight cars. We counted close to 600 that were driven into battle by their commissars. Our defensive fires commenced. A lot of rattling from machine guns. The submachine guns roared, and the rifles cracked. They were joined by mortars, antitank guns and light infantry guns.

The armored train then started firing with 12 very modern antiaircraft guns and just as many quad machine guns. Innumerable individual machine guns protected by armor joined in. We were covered in a hail of steel.

The fighting, which Schaub so vividly describes, continued for some time. All of the heavy weapons of his company were employed. Then the men were threatened with a shortage of ammunition. Like all of the other platoon leaders, he had to force his men to single shot mode.

It was 1000 hours. The fighting had already been going on for six hours, when a second armored train arrived at the Swislotsch rail station. It was also set ablaze. The Red Air Force attacked with bombers and fighter-bombers. At 1300 hours, a third armored train came chugging forward. It was firing with everything it had. At the same time, ground elements of the Red Army also moved out to attack.

Schaub's company commander directed him to fire at the enemy flanking forces. The heavy machine guns rattled away with short bursts among the ranks of the charging Soviets, who nevertheless seemed to be getting ever closer.

Suddenly, nine *Stukas* appeared on the horizon. They dove on the armored train and released their bombs. The train was torn apart in cascades of explosions that sent clouds of debris, smoke and dirt into the air. There was nothing more to be heard from that threat.

As the sound of the explosions receded, Schaub could hear the sounds of tank tracks. Whipping around quickly, he saw four German tanks approaching, which also started opening fire.

The acting company commander ordered the men to follow the tanks.

They jumped up, grouped up behind the tanks and entered the nearby woods. By 1500 hours, both of the bridgeheads were firmly under the battalion's control. *Major* Ernst-Wilhelm Hoffmann's men had proven themselves once again.[3] The advance continued, seemingly without end. The Dnjepr was crossed at Stary Bychow. The Stalin Line was forced. Schaub continued to excel, especially in the fighting around Bachmatsch and Baturin.

Despite the bitterness of the fighting, there was an occasional amusing interlude. One day, in the fighting northeast of Kiev in the vicinity of Schelkowiza, the men were being harassed by enemy tanks when one of them saw a German tank positioned along the wall of an outbuilding in a collective farm.

"Hey . . . fire at them . . . asshole!" one of the men yelled out.

The commander's cupola opened up, and the tank battalion commander popped out. "Who's an asshole!" he called out. "Try firing with a wooden cannon sometime, if you can!"[4]

The *4. Panzer-Division* remained in its positions there until 26 September, helping maintain the ring of encirclement around the Soviet forces surrounded in the Kiev Pocket. The division then advanced to the northeast, moving through Seewsk, Kromy and Orel in the direction of Mzensk. From there, it proceeded towards Tschern

3. Author's Note: Hoffmann was a recipient of the Knight's Cross to the Iron Cross on 4 September 1940 as the commander of the *1./Schützen-Regiment 12*. As the regimental commander, he received the Oak Leaves to the Knight's Cross to the Iron Cross on 9 June 1944, the 494th member of the German Armed Forces to be so honored at the time.

4. Author's Note: The command-and-control tanks for the battalion and regimental commanders had their main guns removed to make room for more radio equipment in the vehicles. The main guns were replaced with a wooden dummy "gun," which was intended to deceive the enemy as to the true purpose of the vehicle. These vehicles were designated *Panzerbefehlswagen III Ausf. H.*

and Wenew. On 21 October, *Feldwebel* Schaub received the Iron Cross, Second Class.

On 2 December, the riflemen participated in the assault on Tula outside the gates of Moscow. The riflemen mounted up on the rear decks of the tanks. The main road running from Tula to Moscow was reached in a biting east wind with temperatures hovering around -28 (-18.4 Fahrenheit). During the night of 4/5 December, the temperature sank to -35 (-31 Fahrenheit). The next night, with the wind chill, the temperature went even lower—down to -50 (-58 Fahrenheit) in unprotected areas.

The men were greeted by Stalin organs and mortar fires on 12 December. The German position became untenable. Schaub wrote in his diary: "General retreat! And how!"

The division, some of its elements horse-drawn, had to withdraw from the area northeast of Wenew back as far as Orel. Schaub fought in the rail elements of *Schützen-Regiment 12* as part of the rearguard.

Schaub and the other men spent Christmas Eve in Orel. The regiment was alerted on Christmas Day and sent to defensive positions northeast of Orel.

The division then pulled back to the Oka River, moving by way of Bjelew and Bolchow. Schaub's platoon, which was authorized four heavy machine guns, had only one operational on 30 December. New Year's Eve passed quietly, and the men wished each other wishes for the New Year at midnight, mixed with their usual gallows' humor: *"Hals- und Bauchschuß."*[5]

In the vicinity of Karagaschinska, the Russians succeeded in penetrating the lines in the early part of January and advancing as far as the command post of the 1st Battalion in the thick snow squalls. Schaub was attached in support of the 3rd Company and joined its company commander and five men in conducting an immediate counterattack in an effort to eliminate the Soviet elements. The men assaulted the enemy, armed only with a light machine gun, four rifles, two pistols and a flare gun. The Soviets, for their part, were still in

---

5. Translator's Note: *Hals- und Beinbruch* is what is usually said before theatrical productions in German-speaking countries and is the equivalent of "Break a leg!" In German, it goes a step further, by telling the recipient to break his neck as well as a leg. The soldier version given here takes it another step further: "Break your neck and get shot in the stomach!"

a state of flux in the snowstorm and the normal disorientation that followed a penetration through the enemy lines.

"Let's go!" the *Hauptmann* called out as the Soviets suddenly appeared in front of them. The Germans shouted their battle cry, and Schaub fired his flare gun as they ran forward. The rushing, glowing round knocked several of the Soviets over. Schaub's machine gun fired from the hip. The *Hauptmann* yelled out orders to units that did not exist in an effort to deceive the enemy as to their true size.

The Soviets started to run and soon disappeared. As a result, seven men were able to restore the former main line of resistance. The company commander had four men remaining in place, while he, Schaub and another man continued to move forward. Ossi Schaub took the light machine gun with him. The three men continued forward, noiselessly, through the freshly fallen snow and the storm. They moved up a *balka,* and saw the turned-up dirt for an earthen bunker and dugout that was still being constructed. Some 30 meters away, the area was crawling with Soviets—about 50 of them—with an officer issuing orders to them.

"Give them some lead, Schaub!" the *Hauptmann* ordered the senior noncommissioned officer. Schaub went into positions, charged the weapon and depressed the trigger: Click! Misfire! Despite the -48 degree temperature (-54.4 Fahrenheit), sweat started to bead on his forehead. He pulled out the jammed round and recharged the weapon. Once again, the only thing to be heard when he depressed the trigger was the slamming of the bolt. He went through the procedure again and took up aim for a third time. Another misfire. Fortunately for the men, the Soviets had not heard anything in their thick winter uniforms.

"We'll fire at them with our small arms. Take them under fire with your flare gun, Schaub!" the officer commanded.

They opened fire simultaneously. Despite the lack of a machine gun, the Soviets were so surprised by the sudden fires and the uncommon use of the flare gun that they immediately fled the area.

✠

In the weeks that followed, Schaub was frequently chosen to lead patrols across the winter landscape, since he was an avid and capable skier. During those patrols, the men often advanced far into the Soviet lines.

On 26 February 1942, Schaub wrote in his diary: "Haven't found a louse for the first time in a long time. Took a bath for the first time in three-quarters of a year. Simply great! And in Russia, to boot!"

On 1 March, Schaub received his commission and was promoted to *Leutnant*. His regimental commander, *Oberst* Lüttwitz, congratulated him at the small celebration on the occasion, but also told him the following: "Schaub, no more beard in the future . . . understood?" That was the next thing the newly coined *Leutnant* did.

On 5 March, the Soviets entered Slobodka with tanks. The close-in fighting for the city lasted until 8 March. While defending against an attack on 6 March, one machine gun alone fired more than 5,100 rounds, the equivalent of 17 boxes of ammunition.

In the end, four German rocket launchers succeeded in driving the Soviets back for a while, but they were soon crawling back in their white snow outfits.

Some 140 Red Army men succeeded in entering the southwest portion of the main line of resistance. The inexperienced replacements that had been committed there were pushed back in the afternoon. The village changed hands several times. Soviet mortars and Stalin organs pounded the German positions. Those were days of fighting that no one who was there would ever forget as long as they lived.

On 13 March, *Oberst* Lüttwitz was reassigned from the regiment, after having received the Knight's Cross to the Iron Cross on 14 January of the same year. The new commander was *Oberst* Spitta. The commander of the 1st Battalion also received a transfer, and the acting commander of the 2nd Battalion, *Hauptmann* Ecker, was wounded.

On 6 April, the regiment was pulled out of the line and sent to Schtschigri, south of Karatschew, to undergo a battlefield reconstitution. For a short while, Schaub was designated as the acting commander of the 4th Company. At the end of May, the regiment was transported on three trains to Dumtschino, marching from there to Mzensk. The *4. Panzer-Division* was allocated to the command of the *XXXV. Armee-Korps. Schützen-Regiment 12* relieved elements of the *26. Infanterie-Division (mot.)*, which were fighting in that sector. Facing the regiment across the Susha River was the Soviet 283rd Rifle Division.

On 10 July, the regiment was redesignated as *Panzergrenadier-Regiment 12*, along with all of the other rifle regiments of the German Army. Around that time, Schaub was transferred to the 1st Company as a platoon leader, where he would remain for a long time and eventually become its commander.

While the division was involved in positional warfare in the large bridgehead around Mzensk, the Germans were launching their summer offensive in southern Russia, which had as its objective the capture of Soviet oil resources. Its end result, however, would be the debacle of Stalingrad.

The Soviets launched an offensive in the division's sector on 29 August. More than 10,000 artillery shells were fired into the German positions, coupled with a one-hour pounding by the Red Air Force. Following the preparation, the Soviets moved out. They hit the sector of the *II./Panzergrenadier-Regiment 12*, where their attack bogged down after capturing a sector of the main line of resistance measuring some 200 by 200 meters.

The area was mopped up around noon after two immediate German counterattacks had been launched. A Soviet attack against the 1st Battalion's sector remained without success.

✠

On 1 October 1942, Schaub was promoted to *Oberleutnant* and installed as the commander of the 1st Company, which was the *SPW* company of the battalion.

Winter set in. When the Soviet counteroffensive started around Stalingrad on 19 November 1942, everything remained quiet around Mzensk. The only causes of casualties were from the frequent reconnaissance and combat patrols. Schaub wrote in his diary: "The men in the trenches experience the same things every day. The monotony hides the danger of lethargy. It is the main mission of the leadership to shake up the men and keep them busy through mental challenges."

For instance, a competition was organized. A song for *Panzergrenadiere* was the object of one such contest. An *Obergefreiter* from the 4th Company won first prize. His song was soon known among all of the *Panzergrenadier* regiments of the German Armed Forces.

On 23 January 1943, the regiment started to be relieved by elements of *Grenadier-Regiment 80* of the *34. Infanterie-Division*. The *4. Panzer-Division* was being moved to a new area of operations around Woronesch and Kursk, where the Soviets had launched an offensive on 14 January. By the end of January, the *2. Armee* had been badly battered. The neighboring Hungarian 2nd Army was practically wiped out. In the sector of the Italian 8th Army, only one corps was still combat effective.

On 1 February, *Panzergrenadier-Regiment 12* detrained at Schtschigry. That same day, the 1st Battalion was committed in an attack on Issakowo. *Oberleutnant* Schaub led his company to the village outskirts. The sharp wind from the northeast blew snow and ice into the faces of the Germans. It was -31 (-23.8 Fahrenheit). Schaub directed his organic and attached heavy weapons to support the attack through flanking fires.

The men dismounted for the attack into the village. Soon they were joined by the rest of the battalion. Unfortunately, the attack could not carry through; it bogged down, and the men set up for the defense along the western portion of the locality.

Eventually, the regiment had to pull back to Schtschigry, when the Soviets resumed their attack and threatened to bypass the Germans. Despite the withdrawals, the division was able to hold open significant sectors of the front to allow other German formations to pass through to the west. The division then pulled back in the direction of Kursk, with the 1st Battalion serving as a rearguard in the area around Wjasowoje. The *4. Panzer-Division* was singled out for praise in the Armed Forces Daily report for its efforts in the defensive struggle.

It then appeared that the division, along with the *8. Infanterie-Division*, would be encircled in Kursk, however. To that end, the 1st Battalion received a special mission on 8 February. It was reorganized as *Kampfgruppe Stäuber*, receiving the regiment's 9th (Infantry Gun) Company, an antitank company, a battery of self-propelled artillery and a battery of assault guns in support. It was directed to move to Obojan, some 65 kilometers from Kursk. It was there that the *Kampfgruppe* was to establish a blocking position and passage point for the withdrawing formations of the *VII. Armee-Korps*.

At the time, Schaub almost came before a court-martial. At the Konotop rail station, he had "procured" a brand-new *Muli*, a cargo truck with a fully tracked rear drive. The vehicle was "camouflaged" with papers and a license plate for a vehicle that had been lost in the company, but the cat was soon out of the bag, and there was talk of charges against the officer. Because of his stellar service record, however, the charges were never brought.

On the evening of 25 February, Schaub was summoned to the command post of the *Kampfgruppe* commander. His battalion command reinforced his company with a section of light infantry guns, a platoon of engineers and a section of artillery. He wanted Schaub's *Kampfgruppe* to advance that night and occupy Lipowaja Dolina at first light.

At 0100 hours, Schaub gave his men the order to move out. The column set out slowly from the snowed-over streets of Ssassulje. His men then crossed a section of woods, which they had assaulted and crossed once before—on 21 September 1941.

After covering 33 kilometers, the small *Kampfgruppe* reached Lipowaja Dolina. At first light, it moved forward, took the village, and was ordered to continue its move east. After another 45 kilometers, Grun was reached. The division then followed. It was soon to be a time when the name of *Oberleutnant* Schaub would become well known within the division and beyond.

On the morning of 1 March 1943, the 1st Battalion launched an attack with a battery of assault guns in support. Schaub's company remained behind as the battalion reserve.

When the Germans reached the vicinity of Mesheritschi, they started to receive strong defensive fires from antitank guns, infantry guns and a number of machine guns. The attack bogged down on the steep approach route to the locality. The effort to advance along the road failed several times. It appeared that the men would not be able to take the village and enjoy warm quarters for the evening.

The 1st Company was called forward.

"Everyone follow me! Step on it!" *Oberleutnant* Schaub ordered as the *SPW's* passed the bogged-down companies of the battalion. The company picked up speed. Antitank guns started to take the vehicles under fire. Rounds came whizzing just over the top of the commander's vehicle. He headed his vehicle towards a still standing building; the rest followed.

A couple of brilliant tongues of flames snaked there way towards Schaub's vehicle. Machine-gun rounds hit the armor and ricocheted skyward. The cannon group of the company fired rounds into the main pocket of resistance. Mortars plopped their shells towards the enemy; the sound of automatic-cannon fire could also be heard. The battalion's attached artillery fired in support.

An enemy antitank gun suddenly appeared around the corner of a building and started to take aim at Schaub's vehicle. It was only about 80 meters away. Schaub reached for his submachine gun and emptied a magazine. His aim was good; the crew was eliminated.

The heavy weapons fired concentrically on the Soviets. All of a sudden, it was quiet.

The battalion commander knew the time had come for the remaining companies to resume their movement: "2nd and 3rd Companies: Follow!"

The companies got on their feet again and mopped up any pocket of resistance that the 1st Company had not already crushed. The battalion moved to the outskirts of town and consolidated for the night. That night, whatever Soviet forces remained in the village proper evacuated their positions. The 2nd Battalion took the lead for the advance the following day. The 1st Battalion remained in the village until it was relieved by elements of *Infanterie-Regiment "List,"* an elite formation. It moved out during the afternoon, heading towards Grun in a march that continued on into the night and through a heavy snowstorm.

The 1st Battalion then rolled east across the bridge over the Dessna there. Early on the morning of 8 March, Schaub and his company reconnoitered in the direction of Iwot. It was determined that strong enemy forces were there. An attack was ordered on the locality for 10 March, after the regiment had reorganized all of its forces. The attack was to be conducted by three separate *Kampfgruppen.*

Schaub's company was part of the second attack group. It was directed to move out of Sswirsh along the Pogrebki–Iwot road. The attack started at 0700 hours. After a five-minute artillery preparation, *Oberleutnant* Schaub and his *SPW's* approached Iwot. They entered the northern and northwestern portions of the locality, where they saw the enemy's antitank guns—but from the rear. The enemy had expected the attack from the opposite direction. In that regard, he was partially right, since one of the three *Kampfgruppen* was also attacking from that direction.

Schaub ordered his men to pick up the tempo and charge the antitank-gun position. The weaponry on the *SPW's* opened fire as the vehicles picked up speed. The rounds slammed into the enemy's positions. As the company started to roll up the enemy positions from the rear, Schaub ordered the company to complete its move through the village and on to the bridge.

Schaub's *SPW* ran over a machine-gun position. The *SPW's* of the company fired with everything they had. They raced through and around the surprised enemy and took the bridge. The riflemen from the other companies then proceeded to mop up, house-by-house. *Flak* fired into the pockets of resistance. Partisans also took part in the fighting. The acting commander of the regiment's infantry gun company was gunned down by a 10-year-old Soviet boy with a submachine gun.

When the news arrived that the two other *Kampfgruppen* were having problems in advancing on Antonowka, *Oberleutnant* Schaub and his men were summoned in that direction. He was given a Hungarian tank company in support.

Schaub had two of his platoons dismount and attack from the west. He moved around Antonowka with his heavy weapons and entered the village from the north. His heavy weapons opened up and let loose with a thunderous roar. A heavy machine gun that fired on Schaub's vehicle was silenced by a direct hit.

The Soviets engaged the armored vehicles with antitank rifles. One round struck the side of Schaub's vehicle. There was a murderous crash, but the vehicle remained undamaged. Five minutes later, the fighting for the village was over. Schaub's men had taken two villages. Schaub had his men set up defensive positions; he ordered patrols sent out.

When the chief of staff of *Heeresgruppe Mitte* visited the division command post on 10 March, he was briefed on the extraordinary success by Schaub and his company on the previous day.

It was directed that the attack be continued on 12 March. There was brilliant sunshine as the *SPW* company rolled out in the direction of Lunew and Gudiowtschino. A Soviet outpost was overrun, but the walls of snow in the village prevented further progress by the company.

Schaub ordered his tracked vehicles to bypass the village to the east. He had the wheeled elements remain behind in the small locality.

The *SPW's* moved out. They caught up with fleeing Red Army men on horseback and sleds in the vicinity of Salesje. There was a short skirmish, before the enemy forces surrendered. The Soviets had sustained a number of casualties, and Schaub directed they be treated immediately. He later wrote: "[The fact] that the Russians did not leave their wounded to their fate—instead, evacuated them all—spoke well for the excellent morale of the forces opposing us."

Towards noon, the *SPW's* of the 1st Company attacked the southeastern outskirts of Wowna. Moving behind the smoke generated by a few barns that had been set of fire, the *SPW's* approached close to the village. When the enemy positions were identified—positions that had held up the attack of the 2nd Battalion earlier—the weapons mounted on the *SPW's* opened fire. Schaub had his vehicle swing out to the east and then attack the village from that direction.

The Soviets lost their nerve. Using sleds, they abandoned their positions in droves. A complete cavalry regiment galloped wildly away to the east and south-southeast, where they ran into the leveled barrels of the 1st Company. The fanatic Cossacks did not entertain the thought of surrender. Elements of the regiment went into position and opened fire.

The *SPW's* replied in kind. Horses collapsed; riders were thrown from their saddles. It was a horrific scene. The *SPW's* then advanced on the Cossacks. One of the vehicles remained behind; its driver had been wounded.

All of a sudden, there was a thunderous crash. Schaub, who had made it through the terrible victory over the riders, had seen a brilliant flash of light just momentarily before. Everything was followed by terrific pain, before he fell to the floor of his *SPW,* unconscious.

Schaub's *SPW* had been hit by a mortar shell. There were four wounded in all. He had been hit the worst, however. A piece of shrapnel had lodged itself in his spine; he was completely paralyzed from the hips down. This severe wound signaled the end of combat operations for the young officer. He was sent to a military hospital in Warsaw and then on to Vienna, where a noted surgeon, *Oberstabsarzt Prof. Dr.* Schönbauer, operated on him.

On 22 April 1943, *Oberleutnant* Schaub was awarded the Knight's Cross to the Iron Cross for his decisive contribution to the success of the battalion's and regiment's operations. He was presented the Wound Badge in Gold by Schönbauer on 20 May.[6]

With the same energy he had devoted to his military career, Schaub, who had also been promoted to *Hauptmann,* tried to learn a new occupation, since the operations had been unable to restore him the use of his legs. He was confined to a wheelchair. In November 1943, he started studying law at the university in Vienna, still officially in the military. Due to complications from his wounds, he returned to the hospital in Ischl numerous times in the spring of 1945. With the approach of the Americans, he was released from his military service obligations.

After the war, Schaub was prohibited from studying at the university because of his wartime status as an officer and Knight's Cross recipient. As a result, he attended a trade school for woodworking from 1946 to 1947. He also worked as a journalist and wrote military articles of a professional nature for German and Austrian periodicals. He also wrote the history of his regiment, *Panzergrenadier-Regiment 12,* which he completed in 1957.

In 1956, he was able to study at the university in Vienna again, where he studied journalism. He died on 19 May 1958 and was buried in Vienna at the Grinzing Cemetery.

✠

For 15 years, Oskar Schaub had borne the hard fate of a severely disabled war veteran. No one ever heard him complain. He was an exemplary father and husband to his daughter and wife.

Many of his former comrades made the journey to his burial service. They had come from all parts of Germany and Austria. His personal friend, the last commander of *Panzergrenadier-Regiment 12, Major* Heinz von Heyden, gave the eulogy:

---

6. Translator's Note: Normally, the Wound Badge in Gold was presented only after sustaining five separate wounds in combat. In the case of severe wounds, such as the loss of eyesight, limbs or the use of limbs, the highest level of the badge was automatically awarded.

May the youth of today recognize through the example of this man that those of their fathers' generation, who wore the field-gray service dress [of the German Army], have nothing to be ashamed of.

A rocket-firing version of the Opel *Maultier* "Mule." The standard (unarmored) version was an extremely useful supply vehicle with good cross-country performance.

Remy Schrijnen

CHAPTER 10

SS-Unterscharführer Remy Schrijnen

FACING MASSED ENEMY ARMOR ON HIS OWN

With the outbreak of armed conflict between the Soviet Union and Germany on 22 June 1941, a young Flemish miner by the name of Remy Schrijnen volunteered for duty with the *Waffen-SS*, the field branch of Himmler's *SS* organization. He was initially not accepted for duty because he did not meet the size requirements.

As a youth in Kümtich, a village near the Belgian city of Löwen, Schrijnen had close contact with Germans. His teacher at school, who had been a soldier on occupation duty in Germany, received a German couple every year on visits. The Germans brought along their children, with whom young Remy often spent time.

As a result, the youth developed a fondness for Germany. When the call was issued to the Flemish to fight against the Soviet Union in order to build a new Europe in which the rights of the Flemish homelands in Belgium and Flanders would be guaranteed, the promise did not fall on deaf ears and many volunteered.

The Flemish fought alongside the Germans in the Soviet Union as part of the *Legion Flandern* in 1941.[1] It participated in the assault on Tichwin. The "legion" was one thousand men strong at that point and was under the command of *SS-Sturmbannführer* Lippert.[2] In the

---

1. Translator's Note: Actually, the formation was known as *SS-Freiwilligen-Standarte Nordwest* at the time, but it and its subsequent incarnations, eventually becoming a nominal division by the end of the war, are quite confusing, even to those well versed in the subject. For simplicity's sake, the Flemish volunteers will generally be referred to as the *Legion Flandern*. For the purists, here's the succession of re-designations and reorganizations: *SS-Freiwilligen-Standarte Nordwest* (*SS* Volunteer Battalion *Nordwest*); *SS-Freiwilligen-Verband Flandern* (*SS* Volunteer Formation *Flandern*); *SS-Bataillon Flandern* (*SS* Battalion *Flandern*); *SS-Freiwilligen-Legion Flandern* (*SS* Volunteer Legion *Flandern*); *SS-Freiwilligen-Sturm-Brigade Langemarck* (*SS* Volunteer Assault Brigade *Langemarck*); *6. SS-Freiwilligen-Sturm-Brigade Langemarck* (6th *SS* Volunteer Assault Brigade *Langemarck*); *27. SS-Freiwilligen-Grenadier-Division Langemarck* (27th *SS* Volunteer Grenadier Division *Langemarck*).

2. Translator's Note: The major *SS* ranks are presented in a table at the back of the book for those not familiar with them.

fighting in January 1942, the Flemish force particularly distinguished itself. The German Armed Forces Daily report announced:

> In the course of the hard fighting in the northern sector, the *Legion "Flandern,"* which has been committed in the hot spot of the fighting, has inflicted extremely heavy and bloody losses in defending against the attacks of the Russians.

The fighting continued for several months and the "legion" was again mentioned in the daily report on 4 March 1942:

> In the course of a local offensive operation, the enemy was ejected from his positions. In the course of intense close combat, the volunteers of *Legion Flandern* took 25 enemy bunkers.

SS-Sturmbannführer Lippert was badly wounded in the course of the fighting in the Wolchow Pocket. That began a quick succession of changes in command for the "legion": Lippert was first succeeded in command by *SS-Sturmbannführer* Paul von Lettow-Vorbeck,[3] who was killed in an accident shortly thereafter. *SS-Sturmbannführer* Vitzthum then assumed command. He was succeeded by *SS-Sturmbannführer* Schellong on 11 July 1942, following the Flemish celebration of the "Battle of the Golden Spurs" of 1302.[4] Schellong ended the rapid successions of command and would lead the formation in its various incarnations until the end of the war.

---

3. Translator's Note: The nephew of the famous colonial fighting in Africa in World War I.

4. Translator's Note: According to Wikipedia, The Battle of the Golden Spurs (Dutch: *Guldensporenslag,* French: *Bataille des éperons d'or,* or *Battle of Courtrai*) was fought on July 11, 1302, near Kortrijk in Flanders. The date of the battle is the official celebration day of the Flemish community in Belgium. The large numbers of golden spurs that were collected from the French knights gave the battle its name; at least a thousand noble cavaliers were killed, some contemporary accounts placing the total casualties at over ten thousand dead and wounded. The French spurs were hung in the Church of Our Lady in Kortrijk to commemorate the victory. The outcome of the battle—the annihilation of a large cavalry force, thought invincible, by a relatively modest but well-armed and tactically intelligent infantry—was a shock to the military leaders of Europe. It contributed to the end of the perceived supremacy of cavalry and led to a deep rethinking of military strategies.

During the Flemish celebration, the commander in chief of the *18. Armee, Generaloberst* Lindemann, presented the Iron Cross, First Class, to Julius Geuerts, the first Flemish soldier to be so honored.

In the summer of 1942, Schrijnen finally was allowed to join the *Waffen-SS.* He underwent basic training in Graz (Austria), before being sent to the Soviet Union. He was assigned to the 5th Company, which was an antitank-gun company. The Flemish soldiers were outfitted with guns of all calibers and from differing countries of origin.

Schrijnen, a small-framed man with dark eyes and a shock of dark hair, was employed as a foot messenger for his unit and had to make his way from his company to the battalion headquarters several times each day. He frequently had to make his way through enemy fires and sniping attacks, since messengers were a favorite target for enemy snipers.

In the same sector of the front—the area around Krassnoje Sselo and Duderhof initially, then Puschkin, Zarskoje and Sselo—the Flemish men fought side-by-side with volunteers from Latvia and Spain. The "legion" was then moved to the great bend of the Narwa River at Krasny Bor. The Soviets were attempting to attack across the frozen river there, thus rolling up the positions of the Spanish "Blue Division." After a tremendous preparatory barrage on 12 January 1943, the Soviets opened the second Ladoga battle and took the Spanish "Bastion" outpost. It became the mission of the *Legion Flandern* to retake it.

✠

SS-Obersturmführer Dedier summoned Schrijnen.

SS-Sturmmann Schrijnen waited for the next salvo of artillery to land before moving out. After the mortar shells impacted and the high-explosive rounds sent their shrapnel in all directions, he took off. Soviet artillery screeched overhead.

"*Obersturmführer?*"[5]

"Report to the 5th. Tell them to close up behind the 3rd on the road and eliminate the enemy positions identified there."

Schrijnen carried out his mission and raced back to the headquarters. The antitank guns of the 5th Company rolled forward

---

5. Translator's Note: In contrast to the Army, *Waffen-SS* personnel did not address their superiors with the prefix of *Herr.*

and joined the 3rd Company, which was decisively engaged. Just at that point, the Soviet tanks also started attacking.

The Flemish gunners serviced their French-made 7.5-centimeter guns, which had been mounted on a German 5-centimeter *Pak 38* carriage.[6] With the fighting reaching its crest, Schrijnen was sent back to his company to help. He hauled ammunition for the guns. He saw a long lance of flame shoot out of the end of a 7.62-centimeter main gun of a T-34. Off to the right, where one of the two captured Soviet 5-centimeter guns was in position, there was a thunderous crack. Cries could be heard penetrating through the sounds of battle over to Schrijnen. A piece of shrapnel whizzed past his ear and sparked against the gun shield of a cannon.

SS-Obersturmführer Dedier appeared; he was bleeding from a shrapnel wound.

"The 3rd is being pushed back, *Obersturmführer!*"

"German tanks!" Schrijnen then announced, as he saw armor bursting out of the woods off to the left. Two 8.8-centimeter *Flak* followed and soon went into position.

The tanks took up the fighting with their enemy counterparts. Round followed round in an indistinguishable roar. The 8.8-centimeter *Flak* were also soon involved in the fray, firing—and hitting—targets at up to 2 kilometers away. Several T-34's and KV-II's were soon burning out in the open.

Schrijnen resumed his messenger duties: "The 1st and the 2nd have moved past us on the right, *Obersturmführer.*"

"Good, let's go!" After a short pause, the officer exhorted the men to move out.

The tanks took the lead. The attack started to make good progress and made it past the burning hulks of the Soviet tanks. Off to the right, the men could see their comrades reoccupy the former main line of resistance of the Spanish Blue Division. Then they ran into the enemy again.

Machine-gun fire raced towards Schrijnen. He threw himself to the ground, crawled to a ditch and then continued to crawl on through the

---

6. Editor's Note: This *PAK 97/38* gun was an expedient design intended to help combat the Soviet T-34 and KV tanks until the excellent *PAK 40* came into widespread service. Due to its relatively low muzzle velocity and instability when fired, the *97/38* was not very effective or popular with those troops using it.

wet snow and the muck. When the men of the 3rd Company jumped up and started to charge, Schrijnen joined them. They entered the enemy trench line. Schrijnen came face-to-face with a Soviet as tall as a tree. He instinctively aimed his submachine gun and let loose with a long burst, laying low the enemy soldier who had charged him from the left.

Then he saw another attack, springing towards him. Actually, the only thing he could focus on was the triangularly shaped bayonet that was jutting towards him. He threw himself to the side. He was quick, but not quick enough. He felt a stabbing pain on his right cheek. Nonetheless, he pointed his submachine gun upwards and fired from the trench floor. Another enemy soldier was eliminated. With a sigh of relief, he saw that the next men approaching him were comrades. The enemy position had been rolled up.

With the stab wound to his cheek, Remy Schrijnen had suffered his first battlefield wound.

That night, the Soviets launched immediate counterattacks to try to regain their lost positions. The 5th Company had moved forward into the retaken positions. The cannon fired high explosive, but the Soviets were able to achieve a penetration into the Flemish lines nonetheless.

Once again, the Flems were involved in hand-to-hand combat. Schrijnen was right in the midst of the melee as well. Despite his earlier wound, he only had a field dressing applied. He stayed with his comrades as he felt better being among his peers; the "Legion" had become his second home in that faraway country.

For a week, all of the enemy efforts were repulsed. Many of Schrijnen's comrades fell or were badly wounded. Despite the intensity of the fighting, he remained spared after the first wounding.

The gaps in the ranks became ever greater. Of the 500 men who had headed east originally, only 45 remained in the front lines. A light infantry battalion from the *5. Gebirgs-Division* was directed to relieve the Flems, and two trucks picked up the remaining men to evacuate them from the front lines. *Legion Flandern* had been effectively wiped out. The remnants of the formations—including convalescing men arriving back to the field—assembled at the Debica Training Area. On 1 July, the "Legion" was sent on to the Milowitz Training Area near Prague. The formation underwent a reconstitution and was redesignated as the *Sturm-Brigade "Langemarck."* Remy Schrijnen was assigned as a gunner on one of the newly issued 7.5-centimeter antitank guns with the long barrels.[7] He was reassigned to the newly formed 6th Company.

The reconstitution lasted until December 1943. The brigade had an end-strength of 2,000 men by the time it was done, some 300 more than authorized. On Christmas morning, Schrijnen and the others discovered that they would be departing for the Eastern Front the next day.

The brigade was attached to *SS-Panzergrenadier-Division "Das Reich,"* which was involved in heavy defensive fighting east of Shitomir. One of the Flemish companies was already being engaged on New Year's Eve at Dawidowka. It was able to hack out a transport column of the division that had been encircled.

A short while later, the remaining companies were employed against the lead elements of Marshal Vatutin's 1st Ukrainian Front along the edge of the woods 30 kilometers southwest of Shitomir, some 5 kilometers west of the highway.

✠

"Sounds like tanks, Remy!" the gun commander said to his gunner as the rumble of a lot of engines increased.

"T-34's, Jan!" Schrijnen stated, confirming that he also thought it sounded like tank engines. But as he searched through the gun optics, he could not make out any tanks to the front, along the wood line or in the woods proper.

It turned noon. Schrijnen took his time eating the cold rations.

An hour later, he spied the first enemy tank as it slowly edged its way out of a depression.

"There they are, *Hauptsturmführer!*"

Knorr, who had just arrived at the gun position, raised his binoculars and looked at the enemy tanks that had started to advance on a broad front from the woods and out of the depression.

The officer quickly issued orders: "Alert everyone . . . get ready to engage!"

Schrijnen started to count and stopped when he reached 25, since the lead vehicle was already about 1,800 meters out.

---

7. Editor's Note: This would be the highly effective 7.5-centimeter *PAK 40*, a weapon capable of defeating all Soviet tanks at most combat ranges.

"Well, Remy, I guess we'll find out how well the gun shoots!" It was the first time they had seen action with the new weapons.

Schrijnen took up a sight picture on the lead tank. He let it approach to within 200 meters. When the tank stopped momentarily on a slight rise, a lance of flame came out of its barrel. Schrijnen thought he could almost see the round headed in his direction. It whizzed passed him and the gun—high and to the left. He made a final adjustment to his sight picture and fired. The round raced towards the enemy.

The round smacked into the area between the turret and the hull—a perfect shot. The turret was ripped off of its race and seemed to fly through the air. "Target!" someone yelled out. There was little time to celebrate, however. By then, the 25 enemy tanks had all started firing furiously.

The next round was rammed home, and Schrijnen fired a fraction of a second later. The second round impacted into the ground next to an advancing T-34. The enemy tank had moved at just the right time to miss the fate of his comrade. All hell started to break loose. A main-gun round slammed into the ground next to the antitank gun. Shrapnel tore through the air. A piece of hot steel bounced off his helmet. Schrijnen shuddered involuntarily.

There was another thunderous roar. Hot shreds of metal pelted the gun shield. He felt a blow to his shoulder, but he was still able to move his arm. He took aim and fired. One of his comrades collapsed behind him, mortally wounded.

The enemy tanks came ever closer. They were firing in a devilish rhythm. Several of the nearby haystacks went up in flames. When Schrijnen looked back, he could see thick clouds of smoke rise skyward. Many of the men who had taken up positions there never emerged from the smoking hell.

"Off to the right . . . 600 . . . just a thumb to the right of the vegetation!" the gun commander called out.

Schrijnen observed the area. He saw the hull of a T-34 emerge from a defile.

"Identified!"

He aimed feverishly. Half of the tank was already in his sights. The gun reported and the impact was almost instantaneous, due to the distance. An explosion rocked the area surrounding the stricken tank. The commander's hatch flew open, and flames shot out. A hand emerged, only to fall back in again, never to leave the blast furnace that the interior of the fighting compartment had become.

Three, then four enemy tanks started to engage Schrijnen's gun. Rounds tore open the earth. The second man of his crew was hit, badly wounded. Schrijnen himself received shrapnel to his rear end.

Soviet infantry appeared behind the tanks. They assaulted around the burning tank hulks and headed for Schrijnen's gun. He grabbed his submachine gun, firing a complete magazine in a single burst. Although he hit most of the closest attackers, one of the Soviets managed to strike him in the throat with his bayonet. Schrijnen could taste his own blood in his throat.

The Soviet who had hit Schrijnen was shot by one of the gunner's comrades. The remaining Soviet infantry turned to flee, but they were soon replaced by more enemy tanks. Schrijnen pressed a dressing to his wound. His gun commander finished applying the dressing, and the plucky Flemish soldier was back behind his sights again. The T-34 headed for the gun was able to get off two rounds—both of which were high—before Schrijnen could take up a good sight picture. Then the tank turned slightly, inadvertently exposing its flank. Schrijnen fired and the round was a direct hit. Within a few minutes, the entire vehicle was engulfed in hot, oily flames, punctuated by occasional explosions from ignited main-gun ammunition.

When it was all over, there were 19 enemy tanks smoldering in front of the Flemish positions. The other guns of the company had contributed to the defensive success as well.

Schrijnen was evacuated to the main dressing station. He was supposed to be sent to a field hospital, but he requested not to be sent. He didn't think the three wounds he had sustained were so serious. He stayed with his unit and received the Iron Cross, Second Class, on 2 January 1944. He also received the Wound Badge in Silver.

On 6 January, Schrijnen was involved in the fighting around the Olschansk rail station, which was eventually lost in the face of a ten-fold Soviet superiority. The brigade was able to hold out at Steskowzy and Sewerinewka until the middle of February. Schrijnen recovered from his wounds and steadily manned his 7.5-centimeter gun.

The brigade reached Jampol by 28 February. Flemish reinforcements arrived there, being brought forward from Breslau. To the north and northeast of Jampol, the Flemish formation occupied positions along a hilly 21-kilometer stretch of land. The deep snow and broken terrain offered the enemy good opportunities to approach the defensive positions unobserved. Once again, Schrijnen and his gun were in a forward position.

The small Flem, with his alert eyes and constant good spirit, had become something of a mascot for the rest of the company. The men all seemed to agree: wherever Schrijnen was, nothing could probably go wrong.

On 29 February, Soviet snipers took the gun positions under fire. Patrols reported enemy mortars going into position. It seemed an attack was imminent. The Soviets did not disappoint. On 2 March, they launched a massed attack. Schrijnen took the escorting tanks under fire. Once again, the antitank gun, along with some support from assault guns of *SS-Panzergrenadier-Division "Das Reich,"* stopped the enemy cold.

The Flemish soldiers were in the thick of the fighting. The enemy attempted to envelop them to both the right and the left. Schrijnen saw the enemy bypassing the Flemish gun positions, out of range. A number of Soviet antitank guns followed in their tracks. A messenger informed the brigade commander, *SS-Obersturmbannführer* Schellong, that the withdrawal route had been blocked by the Soviets. That was on the morning of 3 March. He directed his antitank guns forward, with the rest of his brigade following. The Flemish antitank-gun company soon encountered approximately 40 enemy antitank guns that had set up along the road to block the withdrawal. A bitter struggle ensued.

The antitank guns barked. Soon, two of the Flemish guns were silenced by direct hits. The only gun left firing was that of Schrijnen.

It truly became time for him to shine. The small *SS-Rottenführer* demonstrated both technical and tactical proficiency and incredible bravery. He trained on the muzzle flashes of the enemy; soon, one enemy gun was blown to bits. Another gun received a direct hit as it attempted to engage the German 7.5-centimeter gun.

He rapidly changed positions, so as to avoid becoming a target himself. A Stalin organ fired an entire salvo of rockets against Schrijnen's perceived position, only for the deadly missiles to churn up empty ground. But there were so many Soviets and only one Flemish gun. Despite constantly changing position, the men of the gun crew started to become casualties. Eventually, there was only one man left to slam home rounds in the gun for Schrijnen to fire.

Eventually, his helper was wounded and no longer able to assist. Schrijnen found himself facing 30 enemy guns—all by himself. He had to get ammunition, load it, aim the weapon and fire. Despite the impossibility of the task, he accomplished it. Rounds impacted, ever closer, to his left and right. He had to increasingly take cover against the massed fires and walls of steels that were being directed against his position. Miraculously, he emerged each time, unscathed. He continued to fire. And it seemed that every round was a direct hit. While the enemy rounds sought his death, he continued to fire as if on a gunnery range.

And then the miracle happened . . . the Soviets pulled back and the road was open. One of the final rounds fired against Schrijnen landed a bare 5 meters from the plucky gunner. He heard the thunderous roar. Then he felt the sharp bite of shrapnel—three times—in his upper thigh.

Schrijnen was evacuated by his comrades and loaded on a truck, one of almost all the soldiers that were able to make it out of the threatened encirclement. This time, his wounds required evacuation. He went to the military hospital at Troppau. He was immediately awarded the Iron Cross, First Class, for his incredible performance. By the end of June, he was on his way back to his company.

By then, the brigade was at the Knowitz Training Area, where it was being reconstituted. *SS-Obersturmbannführer* Schellong had also been wounded; *SS-Hauptsturmführer* Rehmann assumed acting command of the brigade in his absence. On 19 July, the brigade was alerted and loaded by rail in Beneschau and sent to Toila. On 25 July, it occupied positions in the woods west of Marwa. By noon of that same day, the Soviets were already pressing against those positions. The nominal brigade—it had not finished its reconstitution and had only four operational companies, which were referred to as *Kampfgruppe Rehmann*—suffered heavy losses. During the morning of 26 July, the command post of the *Kampfgruppe* was hit by an artillery round. Rehmann was wounded; three officers, who were there for an orders conference, were killed. As a result, the *Kampfgruppe* had lost almost all of its leadership on the second day of its employment. *SS-*

Untersturmführer D'Haese assumed acting command and performed splendidly, despite his junior rank.

The next day saw the Flemish soldiers undergoing a punishing barrage fire. From his gun position, Schrijnen could see the first enemy tanks approach. The gun commander wanted to engage the tanks when they came into range. Schrijnen had to remind the new man that they were supposed to be in an ambush position.

"Shit, they're going to overrun us!" one of the newer replacements cried out under the stress of seeing the steel behemoths approach ever closer.

Schrijnen waited until the lead tank had closed to within 250 meters. He fired at a range where he could not miss. He had not been given the order to fire, but he knew he could wait no longer.

The round slammed home and penetrated the turret. The tank went up in flames almost instantly.

For the next 15 minutes, Schrijnen and his crew did nothing but fire. The heavy and accurate gunfire from the single gun seemed to so shock and surprise the Soviets that they acted paralyzed. Four T-34's were knocked out before there was any aimed fire against the antitank gun at all. Schrijnen kept up his fires. Soon, two more enemy tanks were eliminated. The enemy hesitated and stopped his attack.

The men then received the order to pull back. The new position ran from the road to the Blue Mountains. The names the hills had been christened—Grenadier Hill, Love Hill and Children's Hill— would remain forever etched in the memory of Remy Schrijnen.

The Soviets soon recovered from the shock and continued their attack, directing it against these new defensive positions. Once again, the Flemish gunner had positioned his piece well. He waited for the enemy. The Soviets soon came into view, attacking in waves. He opened fire with high-explosive rounds, tearing huge gaps in the brown-clad ranks.

The enemy infantry started to return fire, supported by mortars. Shreds of steels ricocheted off the gun shield whenever it was hit. Schrijnen was slightly wounded. Once again, he started to lose his fellow crewmembers. The Flemish and German grenadiers started pulling back on both sides. They were unable to hold out against the Soviet's vast superiority in numbers.

Schrijnen also intended to start pulling back when he saw 30 enemy tanks approach from behind the enemy infantry. A messenger came racing up, gasping: "Schrijnen, pull back!"

But the wiry Flem knew what would happen if he did that. He stayed and fought. He initially engaged the five heavy Josef Stalin[8] tanks; they were the biggest threat.

A main-gun round shattered his gun shield. Schrijnen did not lose his composure. He continued aiming and then fired. The round struck a mortal blow to the offending Josef Stalin. Despite the oily flames from the stricken comrade, the other tanks continued advancing, getting ever closer to the solitary gun. He knocked out two T-34's; then his spent shell-casing ejector started to malfunction. He had to manually extract each of the hot casings by pushing them out through the gun barrel from the front with an extracting rod.

Needless to say, every time he appeared in front of his gun, he was subjected to all sorts of fire from machine guns and snipers. The rounds hissed overhead and slammed into the ground around him.

A wounded artillery forward observer ordered fires placed on the German positions that had already been abandoned. The artillery helped take some pressure off of Schrijnen, who could reload his gun without as much interference.

An inner voice told him to run away. But his sense of duty was stronger. He knew the tanks would grind his comrades into the ground if he didn't give them the opportunity to get away. And so he stayed and fought. In a fight of one against all, Schrijnen ultimately emerged the victor. He knocked out a second Josef Stalin. Then another two T-34's that had approached to within 400 meters. The enemy hesitated at that point, giving Schrijnen some breathing room.

The enemy then called in artillery on his position. The T-34's fired as fast as they could, while the remaining heavy tanks continued to approach. The brave Flem was able to hear the rattle of tracks and roar of engines in the short intervals between firing.

He was alone, but he still had ammunition. That meant: fire . . . fire . . . fire!

---

8. Editors Note: Basically, the Stalin was a new hull and turret on a KV chassis. Front hull armor was over 100 millimeters thick and the tank mounted a massive 12.2-centimeter main gun.

There were seven tanks on fire in front of his position. Three or four others were hit in the turrets or suffered some other battle damage that either required them to turn away or immobilized them.

All the while, Schrijnen had to run in front of his gun after each round was fired. He was followed by bursts of machine-gun fire, and the tanks approached ever closer.

A Josef Stalin rumbled forward. Schrijnen fired but missed when the steel giant turned unexpectedly. The enemy tank fired and the 12.2-centimeter round seemed to clip the top of what remained of the gun shield. The tank engine started to roar. Schrijnen raced around to the front of his gun, pushed the round out, loaded another and took up his position at the gunner's station. The enemy tank was only 30 meters from him. With his life in the balance, Schrijnen fired, but the main gun of the enemy tank also fired at the same moment. Both rounds hit. The tank was knocked out. But Schrijnen's gun was destroyed as well, and he was tossed away from the gun by the resulting explosion. He was unable to move, bleeding profusely from numerous wounds.

The Soviets did not follow up even though all effective resistance had been eliminated at that point. They hesitated and then turned back, affording the Germans the opportunity to reoccupy their positions in the subsequent immediate counterattack. When the Germans reached the area of Schrijnen's destroyed gun, they counted 12 knocked-out enemy tanks. They also found Schrijnen, miraculously alive. He was evacuated to a field hospital.

On 29 July, Schrijnen was recommended for the Knight's Cross to the Iron Cross, which was eventually awarded to him on 21 September. He was the only soldier of the entire Flemish formation to be so honored. Of course, he also received the Wound Badge in Gold due to his innumerable wounds.

The Flemish formation was effectively wiped out once again. It was withdrawn from the front and underwent a battlefield reconstitution. It was given nominal divisional status and redesignated as the *27. SS-Freiwilligen-Grenadier-Division Langemarck.*[9] Because of bravery in the face of the enemy, he was promoted to *SS-Unterscharführer.* At the end of January 1945, the division was moved to Outer Pomerania. The division participated in the final fighting around Berlin. In the final

9. Editor's Note: This so-called division never exceeded brigade strength.

weeks of the war, *SS-Unterscharführer* Schrijnen was credited with an additional 22 enemy tanks, in addition to innumerable enemy antitank guns.

After the war, Schrijnen was imprisoned in his native Belgium until 1950. Many Flemish soldiers who fought for the Germans were sentenced to death, even though they never fought against their country. In 1953, Schrijnen was again imprisoned, that time for demanding a general amnesty for all of his comrades. He remained behind bars until 1955. When he attended a meeting of the Knight's Cross association in Germany in 1962, he was again threatened with imprisonment if he returned to Belgium. He thus remained in Germany, remaining there until his death on 27 July 2006.

A column of JS 2 (IS 2) "Josef Stalin" tanks in the rubble of Berlin. The JS 2 was heavily armored: 160 millimeters (6.3 inches) on the front of the turret and 110 millimeters (4.3 inches) on the full front. The main armament was the formidable 12.2-cm D-25T gun that fired a massive 50 kg (110 lb) round.

The 7.5-cm *PAK 97/38*. a French 7.5-centimeter field gun mounted on a *PAK 38* chassis. The large, perforated muzzle-brake was intended to reduce recoil. At a range of 500 meters, this weapon could, under favorable conditions, knock out a T-34.

The deadly 7.5-centimeter *PAK 40*, Germany's standard antitank gun from late 1941 until the end of the war. Firing a standard armor-piercing round, armor penetration was 116 millimeters (4.6 inches) at 1,000 meters. This was more than enough to destroy a T-34 at that range.

Friedrich-Carl von Steinkeller

CHAPTER 11

Generalmajor Friedrich-Carl von Steinkeller

STRONGPOINT SSLAWJANSK

The *7. Panzer-Division* was alerted on 9 May 1940 and sent in the direction of the Meuse River. Its advance guard, consisting of *Kradschützen-Bataillon 7, Hauptmann* Hüttemann's tank company from *Panzer-Regiment 25* and *Hauptmann* Oll's battery from *Artillerie-Regiment 78 (mot.)*, was led by *Major* von Steinkeller, the commander of the motorcycle battalion.

The march to the forward staging areas for the initiation of the campaign in the West was made especially difficult by the fact that other divisions had moved forward ahead of schedule to the Belgian frontier and were blocking the approach routes for von Steinkeller's force. Despite those difficulties, *Kampfgruppe Steinkeller* was able to move into Belgium across the Ourq at 0532 hours on 10 May.

Von Steinkeller's men moved rapidly across that portion of Belgium and into the northern tip of Luxemburg. Once they crossed the Luxemburg-Belgian border, they encountered Belgian outposts, which pulled back after a short firefight.

The advance continued through a belt of woods. The men were especially alert since this was where a concerted defensive effort could be expected. But the advance guard did not encounter any more enemy resistance until it reached Chabrehez. The village was stubbornly defended by light infantry from the Ardennes region.

The motorcycle infantry had to dismount. The Belgian forces put up a good fight, and it was not until artillery and tank were employed that the enemy was ejected from the village around 2200 hours. It turned out to be one of the hardest engagements the battalion was to fight in the campaign in the West.

That day, the commander of the 2nd Company, *Hauptmann* Kleinschmidt, was wounded. Von Steinkeller placed *Oberleutnant* von

Petersdorf in charge. For the actions of the day, *Unteroffizier* Fischer would later receive the Iron Cross, First Class, the first man of the battalion to be so honored.

The motorcycle infantry battalion secured the terrain it had won and billeted in the village that night. Curiously enough, a small shop opened after the fighting had ceased, and the German soldiers were able to buy cigarettes and chocolate, just as if they had been back home at their garrison.

The morning of 11 May dawned. Thick ground fog covered the terrain, when the radio operator reported to von Steinkeller: "Radio message from division, *Herr Major*!"

Von Steinkeller read the characteristic formulation from *Generalmajor* Rommel, the division commander: "*K7*[1] crosses and exploits the Ourthe!"

Exploit—exploit! That was Rommel's motto, a philosophy that brought him quick success later on when he was in Africa.

Von Steinkeller rapidly led his forces to the river. Just before the ground fog lifted, the lead elements were on the high east bank of the river. The *Kampfgruppe* commander ordered a crossing bridge be built for the motorcycles.

It took 20 minutes for the provisional bridge to be erected. They had practiced this type of hasty crossing so many times along the Mosel that it had become second nature by that point.

The commander ordered a patrol across, with instructions to advance west, reporting any enemy contact. The patrol immediately went across the river. While the main body was still pushing its motorcycles across, the patrol had already advanced 3 kilometers to the west, where it encountered French reconnaissance forces, which were turned back.

In the meantime, the armor and the artillery had found a ford and not a single hour had passed since the river had been reached before the entire advance guard was across it. Because of his bold, decisive action, he was winning the race against the enemy.

The report from the patrol told von Steinkeller that the enemy's main body would be no more than 8 kilometers west of the river. If the French had succeeded in beating the Germans to the river, then a crossing would not have been possible. It was also apparent to von

---

1. Translator's Note: *Kradschützen-Bataillon 7*.

Steinkeller that he would initially have to face the enemy force with just his advance guard. As an ex-cavalry officer, that could mean only one thing: strike the first blow in a powerful and rapid manner.

Correspondingly, he had the armor and the artillery fall in behind the lead company. Any vehicle that was not immediately needed was placed towards the rear of the column. He ordered his reorganized force to move out.

Five kilometers west of the river, the lead German elements encountered French motorcycle forces. The lead elements immediately attacked the French lines, firing with everything they had and drove the enemy forces back.

The lead elements continued pressing hard and reported that strong French armor and infantry forces were in the village of Waha, a bit farther west. Von Steinkeller ordered his artillery forward to take up open field positions. He ordered Hüttemann's tanks to swing right to envelop the village and attack it. The tanks rattled off as fast as they could to the right, joining the firing on the enemy that had just been opened by the artillery.

By the time the motorcycle infantry reached the village, it had been abandoned—a surprise! Von Steinkeller ordered Oll's gunners to shift their fires to the patch of woods west of the village. The woods were packed full of vehicles, tanks and guns that were fleeing wildly to the west. All of a sudden, French tanks appeared outside of the village. The artillerymen engaged the armor over open sights. One tank was immobilized when its tracks were hit; a few moments later, it was the victim of a direct hit. The two remaining tanks turned away, emitting smoke. The battlefield was firmly in the hands of the Germans.

✠

The advance guard was relieved on 12 May, with the motorcycle infantry being attached to the division's tank regiment for combat operations. *Panzer-Regiment 25*, commanded by *Oberst* Rothenburg, fought with French mechanized forces the entire day.

The enemy lines were penetrated at Haversin; around midday, the high ground west of Leignon was reached. Towards 1700 hours, the German forces were in the area around Fréche–Try, northeast of Dinant, along the eastern edge of thick vegetation that stretched along the east side of the Meuse River.

All of a sudden, Rommel appeared at von Steinkeller's location: "At first light, cross the Meuse with your battalion east of the *Ferme La Grange* and establish a bridgehead on the west bank. The crossing will be supported by artillery and Hüttemann's tank company."

The battalion dismounted and all of the vehicles were staged to the rear. The heavy weapons, infantry guns and antitank guns were manhandled forward. The motorcycle infantry dragged the rafts forward. Snaking forward to the west, using a compass to negotiate the woods, the long single column made its way to the river, with von Steinkeller in the lead. Like a ghostly procession tapping its way forward, the battalion needed four hours to cover five kilometers. But the procession remained unseen and unheard by the enemy and, around 2200 hours, the men reached the road that ran along the east bank of the river.

Major von Steinkeller was with his 1st Company, led by *Hauptmann* Heilbronn. The company was to be the first across the river. The rubber rafts were inflated and staged.

Noises could be heard the entire night on the other side of the river. Half-loud orders could be distinguished; an occasional flashlight lit up on the enemy side. During the night, the French battalion that had been in place there was relieved. But that was something the German attackers could not have known at the time.

When it turned first light, the German artillery opened fire. It was joined by the infantry guns of the battalion and Hüttemann's tanks that came racing towards the river. At that moment, Heilbronn gave the signal to move out. The 1st Company raced across the road and into the water with the rafts. The motorcycle infantry paddled furiously to get across the Meuse. They were halfway across before the enemy identified them.

By then, Rommel was also on the scene. He watched as von Steinkeller crossed the river with *Oberleutnant* von Peterdorf's 2nd Company in the second attack wave. By then, the enemy had recovered from his surprise. Machine-gun fire ripped towards the rafts. The enemy artillery registered its fires on the crossing point. A few of the vessels sank when the rubber was punctured.

Hauptmann Heilbronn was wounded; von Steinkeller temporarily assumed command of the company. He ordered the men to prepare to attack the high ground. While the artillery and tanks identified targets on the slopes of the Meuse and eliminated some of them, von Steinkeller and his two companies assaulted up the slope. After a short fight, the high ground was taken. The western edge of the woods across from the *Ferme la Grange* was occupied.

In the course of the attack, both the adjutant, *Oberleutnant* Pflug, and the liaison officer, *Leutnant* Malsch, were killed. Patrols soon determined that the enemy had pulled back from the woods and reestablished himself in a village to the west of *Ferme la Grange*.

At that point, the battalion had only one 3.7-centimeter antitank gun with it. The battalion's infantry guns could not yet get across the river and there was no communications with them. The enemy was placing heavy fire on the crossing point, preventing reinforcements from coming forward.

It took eight hours for *Leutnant* Häusler to get back across the Meuse and inform Rommel of the situation on the far side. Friendly artillery was finally called in on the enemy gun positions. Once those were eliminated, other elements of the division could finally be brought across.

While all that was occurring, the two motorcycle infantry companies were desperately holding their ground, well aware that any one of the enemy's immediate counterattacks could force them out of their precarious positions and back off the high ground. The enemy was concentrating his artillery fires on the motorcycle infantry.

During the afternoon, enemy tanks entered the woods. They were engaged by hunter/killer teams and driven out. It was during that fighting in the thick vegetation that *Leutnant* Neubrandt[2] especially distinguished himself, later becoming one of the first members of the division to be honored with the Knight's Cross to the Iron Cross.

Towards evening, von Steinkeller was wounded in the foot by a tank main gun round and had to temporarily relinquish command of the battalion to *Hauptmann* von Hagen, the commander of the heavy company. By then, however, the situation was essentially stabilized, and the division was able to relieve the beleaguered force and continue its advance into France.

✠

---

2. Translator's Note: The young officer was a platoon leader in *Aufklärungs-Abteilung 37* of the *7. Panzer-Division*. He was killed in action in the Soviet Union on November 1941 in the area around Viazma. He was a company commander at the time.

Friedrich-Carl von Steinkeller was born on 28 March 1896 in Deutsch-Krone in West Prussia. His father, *Oberst* Ewald von Steinkeller, was killed along the Somme in September 1916 while in command of a regiment. Von Steinkeller spent his youth in West Prussia and Thuringia. In August 1914, he received his college preparatory diploma from the *Königliches Gymnasium* in Graudenz. A few days later, he entered *Ulanen-Regiment 3* at Fürstenwald (Spree) as an officer candidate.

He participated in the fighting in the Great War in Poland, East Prussia, Kurland, Romania and France, initially as a platoon leader, then as a troop commander in *Reserve-Ulanen-Regiment 3*, which was later reorganized and redesignated as *Reserve-Ulanen-Schützen-Regiment 9*.

In March 1915, *Fähnrich* von Steinkeller was awarded the Iron Cross, Second Class, for his leadership of several successful patrols. As a *Leutnant* and platoon leader, he received the Iron Cross, First Class, in July 1916 for his actions during the battle of Eckau/Kekkau. After being badly wounded, he served for a year as the assistant operations officer for the *216. Infanterie-Division,* which was conducting operations in Romania. In November 1919, *Oberleutnant* von Steinkeller was released from active service.

He took up agriculture for a living in Pomerania, also living in Mark and Mecklenburg. In 1921, he participated in the fighting in Upper Silesia as part of *Freikorps Richthofen.*[3] Following that, he was the director of an agricultural bank in Thuringia from December 1925 to the end of 1933.

On 1 July 1934, von Steinkeller re-entered the military as a *Rittmeister* in *Reiter-Regiment 16* in Erfurt. He soon became involved with the fledgling motorcycle infantry forces, serving as a company commander in *Kradschützen-Bataillon 2* in Eisenach and Kissingen until October 1938. On 1 October of the same year, he was promoted to *Major.*

When the *XV. Armee-Korps (mot.)* was established, von Steinkeller was transferred to its administrative staff as the personnel officer for the corps' noncommissioned officer corps and enlisted personnel. *Generalleutnant* Hoth, the commanding general, was an example the young field-grade officer later sought to emulate.

---

3. Translator's Note: Lothar von Richthofen, the commander of the free corps, was the younger brother of the famous Great War ace, Manfred von Richthofen.

During the campaign in Poland, von Steinkeller was still assigned staff duties at the corps. On 17 October of the same year, he was assigned as the commander of *Kradschützen-Bataillon 7*. At the time, the division commander was *Generalleutnant* Stumme. On 1 February 1940, *Generalmajor* Rommel assumed command of the division. During the campaign in the West, Rommel started to gain notice as a large formation commander. The enemy referred to his force as the "Ghost Division."

At the start of the campaign in the East, von Steinkeller had convalesced from the wounds sustained in France and had resumed command of his motorcycle infantry battalion. The offensive started at 0305 hours on 22 June 1941. The division's advance guard was *Kampfgruppe Rothenburg*, the commander of *Panzer-Regiment 25*, consisting of Rothenburg's 1st Battalion and *Kradschützen-Bataillon 7*. By 1245 hours, the men had already reached Olita. After a short skirmish in the city, it was possible to take the northern bridge over the Njemen intact as a result of the aggressive actions of the *Kampfgruppe*. When the *Kampfgruppe* then proceeded to advance farther to the east from the bridge site, it started to receive heavy fire from enemy forces along the ridgeline, some of them dug in.

The German armor took considerable losses. Despite that, the *Kampfgruppe* succeeded in establishing a bridgehead. For the rest of the day, the men had to defend against Soviet attacks, which were all driven back. It was thanks to the death-defying actions of the tankers, who knocked out 82 enemy armored vehicles that day, as well as the motorcycle infantry, who pushed back attack after attack with great stubbornness, that the bridgehead was held and, in fact, expanded during the night.

On the evening of 23 June, von Steinkeller received orders, along with the tanks, to attack the city of Wilna from the south the following morning at first light. As a result of the loss of radio contact with the division during the night, von Steinkeller did not discover that the tanks had been pulled back to the area southeast and east of the city.

Just before 0300 hours, as it started to turn light, von Steinkeller's men were in their designated positions to the south of Wilna. Of course, there was not a tank to be seen. Regardless, von Steinkeller ordered the attack to be launched, supported by the battery of artillery that had been attached to him. The motorcycle infantry rode out at high speed, with the southern edge of the airstrip at Wilna soon coming into sight. A few Soviet machine-gun positions opened fire.

"Dismount!"

The attacking company rapidly dismounted its motorcycles, with the vehicles soon being placed under cover. A short, sharp fight ensued, with the enemy soon withdrawing his positions at the airfield, where the German force captured 25 operational aircraft.

The main body of the battalion continued attacking east of the airfield and headed directly for the city. It overran Soviet outposts. Any resistance in the city was reduced by *Oberleutnant* Grünert's 1st Company. Around 0500 hours, the train station and the important bridges over the Wilejka were in the hands of the motorcycle infantry.

A short while later, the Lithuanian flag was raised over the city, with all of the church bells in the city ringing. The local populace flooded the churches to celebrate the end of Soviet domination.

For the fighting around Olita and Wilna, von Steinkeller received a certificate of appreciation from the commander in chief of the Army, *Generaloberst* von Brauchitsch. In the Armed Forces Daily report of 8 July 1941, it was announced:

> *Oberst* Rothenburg, the commander of a tank regiment, and *Major* von Steinkeller, the commander of a motorcycle infantry battalion, especially distinguished themselves through their bravery.

On 22 July, von Steinkeller conducted reconnaissance in his staff car prior to an attack on the city of Jarzewo. As his vehicle moved down the road, it was suddenly tossed to the side by a mighty blow. Flames rose skyward. The vehicle had run over a mine; a few seconds later, it was engulfed in flames. Von Steinkeller was pulled from the stricken staff car, but he suffered bad burns and internal injuries. He was immediately evacuated to the main clearing station and then a field hospital, finally being sent to Germany and the military hospital in his garrison city of Jena. On 1 September 1941, while still a patient, he was promoted to *Oberstleutnant*.

On 25 December, von Steinkeller was back at the front, even though he had hardly recovered from his wounds. He resumed command of his motorcycle infantry battalion, which was used over the next few months as the rearguard for the division in its withdrawal to the Königsberg Line. The battalion fought for every village—usually in deep snow and sometimes at temperatures of -25 (-13 Fahrenheit). With his *Kampfgruppe,* von Steinkeller prevented the Soviets from breaking through in the area east of Bjeloj. Later, north of Duchowtschina, it was his battalion again that mastered a dangerous situation that had threatened the entire division.

For his superior performance and achievements in the fighting associated with the withdrawal, von Steinkeller was awarded the German Cross in Gold on 25 May 1942.

In the middle of April 1942, he was selected to lead the advance party of the division that was returning to France for the formation's reconstitution. The rest of the division followed in May. Originally, the division was billeted in the area around Niort. In August, it was moved to the vicinity of Angers–Cholet.

That summer, the division was brought back up to full strength in both personnel and equipment. During the 10 months it had been employed in the Soviet Union, it had suffered heavy casualties: 114 officers and 1,941 noncommissioned officers and enlisted personnel had been killed. An addition, 5,700 men had been wounded; 300 were reported as missing.

The division commander at the time, *Generalleutnant Freiherr* von Funck, oversaw the intensive training program that resulted in the old "Rommel division" being ready for commitment again at the end of the year. During the reconstitution, von Steinkeller was given command of one of the division's rifle regiments, which was redesignated as *Panzergrenadier-Regiment 7* during the same time frame. On 8 November, the division was alerted; the Americans had landed in northwest Africa.

The division was sent to the southern part of France, which had heretofore not been occupied by the Germans. It was given security missions along the Mediterranean coastline from the Spanish border to the area around Narbonne. The occupation took place without incident. Von Steinkeller's regiment was billeted in the Narbonne area until 24 November, when it moved with the division to Aix-en-

Provence, north of Marseilles. On 26 November, the division, along with other German forces, received orders to take the French naval port of Toulon by surprise and capture its high-seas fleet.

Von Steinkeller was put in charge of one of the *Kampfgruppen* formed for the raid. Without encountering any resistance, his men were able to occupy the French forts and the fortifications on the island of St. Mandrier, which is located in the harbor.

At the end of December, the division was sent back to the Soviet Union. It assembled in the area around Forschtadt in the early part of January 1943. On 6 January, the main body of the division was committed in an attack against advancing Soviet forces east of the Kalitwa River and in the direction of Millerowo. At the same time, von Steinkeller's reinforced *Panzergrenadier-Regiment 7* was able to take Kononoff and Wyssokij-Talowyj (30 to 35 kilometers north of Forschtadt) in aggressively conducted operations. It advanced as far as the area around Petrowskij. The regiment was then forced to transition to the defense by a numerically vastly superior enemy.

On 8 January, *Hauptmann* Grünert's *I./Panzergrenadier-Regiment 7* was left in place to defend, while von Steinkeller was given the mission of screening the northern flank of the division in the area east of the Kalitwa as far as the Bystraja. With *Kampfgruppe Steinkeller* was the *II./Panzergrenadier-Regiment 7* (*Hauptmann* Walsberg), a battalion from *Panzer-Regiment 25* (*Hauptmann* von Gember), a battery from the divisional artillery and some other forces. The division committed its main body against the enemy advancing north of the Don in the direction of Tazinskaja.

Both *Kampfgruppe Grünert* and *Kampfgruppe Steinkeller* were subjected to unceasing attacks of ever-greater intensity and supported by armor. In Grünert's sector, all of *Leutnant* Gothe's platoon was lost. The Soviets constantly fired artillery on the German positions, especially in *Hauptmann* Walsberg's sector. In the course of the intense fighting, some 30 T-34's were knocked out.

During the night of 10/11 January, Soviet tanks were able to penetrate a sector of the front that had not been occupied due to a lack of forces. They attacked the regimental headquarters at Nowotscherkasskij. The fighting raged around the command post the entire night, with *Oberleutnant* Bunge, the adjutant, distinguishing himself through his bravery and decisive actions. As it turned first light, the meager German forces were no longer able to conceal their hopelessly numerically inferior strength and had to pull back to a prepared blocking position. The enemy had succeeded in separating the command-and-control apparatus from the forces in the field. German tanks and mechanized infantry elements were encircled.

In that desperate situation, von Steinkeller broke through the enemy lines in a single *SPW*. Chased and fired at by T-34's, his *SPW* was able to conceal itself in a deeply broken up defile and eventually reach the encircled forces.

He immediately reorganized the defenses, turned to face the Soviet forces that had been preparing to launch another attack with armor and launched his own preemptive attack against the Soviet tanks staging at Nowotscherkasskij. The totally surprised enemy forces were eliminated as it started to turn dark. The *Kampfgruppe* was able to escape the Soviet encirclement through the glare of burning enemy tanks.

In the days that followed, von Steinkeller continued his determined defense in the area between the two rivers. Later on, also employed west of Kamensk along the Don, he was also able to turn back Soviet attacks across the frozen waters.

On 22 January, he was ordered 40 kilometers north of Kamensk with his *Kampfgruppe*. The Soviets had advanced west into the sector of an infantry division there, attacking across a bridge made of ice over the Ssewernij-Donez. The regimental commander had received the mission of clearing the west and south banks of the river between Dawido-Nikolskij and Marakoff of the enemy.

Generalleutnant von Manteuffel, one of the commanders of the division, later wrote:

> In a bold and decisive move, the *Kampfgruppe* succeeded in wresting Iljewka and Krushilowka from the enemy by the evening of that day. On 23 January, the *Kampfgruppe* also took back Marakoff, thus accomplishing its assigned mission.

Since the effort to extricate the *7. Panzer-Division* from its former area of operations around Kamensk and reassemble in the area west of Krushilowka was delayed, von Steinkeller was given orders to cover the area along the southern bank of the Donez between Dolgoje and Krimskaja.

The Soviet forces attacking north of the Donez to the west then directed their efforts towards Sslawjansk. They were determined to take the bridge south of the city, which led across the Kasennyi-Torez. It was imperative for the German forces to get there first, if they did not want the Soviet armored forces under Popoff to eliminate this important bulwark of the Donez front.

Consequently, von Steinkeller was ordered to the city on 31 January. Initially, he only had his 1st Battalion to accomplish the mission of holding the city and the bridge under all circumstances. Sslawjansk was declared a *fester Platz.*[4]

After a forced march at night over iced-over roads that were difficult to negotiate, the lead elements of the *Kampfgruppe* encountered enemy forces at first light on the morning of 1 February. The enemy had reached the city just to the east of Sslawjansk and the river, Ssemenowka-Mostowaja. The Soviets were in the process of moving on the important bridge.

In that critical situation, von Steinkeller committed his forces as they arrived on the battlefield. *Hauptmann* Grünert, a seasoned and highly capable commander, held up the advancing Soviets with his 1st Battalion. Rallied by the inspirational example of their commander, the *Panzergrenadiere* took Ssemenowka-Mostowaja from the enemy, even though it was stubbornly defended. They then went on to take a factory located on dominant terrain. By doing so, they covered the northeastern approaches to Sslawjansk.

While the fighting was going on, von Steinkeller and his regimental staff entered the city of Sslawjansk proper. The city still appeared to be asleep, apparently unaware of the dramatic turn of events to the east. Von Steinkeller assumed command of the entire area defenses and impressed a security battalion, which was in positions north of the city, into his command. He also commandeered a unit of replacements that had been making its way to the front. With those forces—the replacements having had no or very little combat experience—he hastily established a defensive front.

4. Translator's Note: "Fortified area." This is somewhat analogous to the U.S. Army's concept of a "strongpoint," which is designed to be any area to be denied to the enemy under all circumstances.

In the meantime, the division had sent some reinforcements to von Steinkeller's meager forces: a battalion of artillery under *Hauptmann* von Kahlden, elements of *Panzer-Pionier-Bataillon 58*, four light tanks under the command of *Oberleutnant* Baranek and a single 7.5-centimeter antitank gun.

In the days that followed, the enemy continuously brought up reinforcements. Von Steinkeller's force—barely a regiment in size—eventually found itself facing three newly committed Soviet divisions. Despite that, the enemy was constantly turned back, even though the *Kampfgruppe* had to cover more than 20 kilometers of frontage.

The conditions in Sslawjansk grew more critical by the hour, but von Steinkeller's ability to rapidly assess the situation enabled him to continuously read the Soviet command's intent in investing the city and thereby thwart their plans. By 4 February, even the narrow corridor to the south had been cut when the enemy occupied Kramatorskaja with his II Guards Corps. The *Kampfgruppe* was completely encircled.

During the night of 5/6 February, the Soviets succeeded in making a deep penetration into the broken up industrial area of the city. It seemed as though the end was in sight for the beleaguered force. But von Steinkeller again proved to be a tough nut to crack. Using every last one of his men—including headquarters drivers and clerks—he personally conducted an immediate counterattack that succeeded in stopping the Soviets.

The men had to face the enemy around the clock. Whenever one attack was thwarted, it seemed another attack flared up at some other point on the line. It was thanks to the exemplary combat élan of the men that the Soviets were never able to strike the decisive blow. The engineers and the tanks were employed as the reserves, and they made their mark at the hot spots of the fighting, always distinguishing themselves. For von Steinkeller, the defense of *fester Platz Sslawjansk* was the most difficult challenge of his entire military career.

On 17 February, the division was finally in a position to relieve von Steinkeller and his men. For his magnificent performance, he was later awarded the Knight's Cross to the Iron Cross and was promoted to *Oberst* ahead of his peers. The division published an order-of-the-day concerning the stalwart defense of the city:

With great pride, the division looks back on the hard but successful fighting of *Kampfgruppe Steinkeller* from 2 to 17 February, in which it was possible to hold this important bulwark of the Donez Front against superior numbers of the enemy, thanks to the unshakeable attitude of its commander. As a result, it contributed to a decisive change in the course of the winter fighting. *Kampfgruppe Steinkeller* turned back the Russian onslaught over and over again in especially difficult fighting, in days and nights full of extreme stress, in tough defense and in stubbornly conducted immediate counterattacks. All of them, from the determined commander down to the last individual soldier, who held out in exemplary fashion, have held high the honor of the German soldier . . . *Kampfgruppe Steinkeller* has earned my special recognition and thanks for this tremendous achievement, which continues to have far-reaching effect.

✠

In the period from 1 March to 6 April 1943, *Kampfgruppe Steinkeller*, consisting of *Panzergrenadier-Regiment 7*, the *I./Panzergrenadier-Regiment 6* (*Hauptmann* Gutzschhahn) and *Kradschützen-Bataillon 7* (*Hauptmann* von Schütz) fought in the area just south of Isjum in the Kamenka-Mal and Kamyschewacha-Ssemenowka sectors. Deployed along a wide frontage, the battle group took heavy casualties, but it also turned back numerous enemy attacks along the still-frozen Donez.

During the morning of 10 March, the right wing of the battle group at Kamenka was attacked by especially strong forces. All of the landlines were cut by the enemy's artillery fires and also the continuous employment of aircraft. The enemy succeeded in overrunning a portion of the *I./Panzergrenadier-Regiment 7*. In three days of heavy fighting, von Steinkeller's forces, augmented by support from *Oberstleutnant* Adalbert Schulz's *Panzer-Regiment 25*, drove the enemy back across the river.

On 13 April, *Major* Grünert was killed by shrapnel. In a moving regimental order-of-the-day, *Oberst* Steinkeller provided an apt eulogy to his long-time commander and comrade-in-arms. This exemplary officer was buried at the military cemetery at Brashowka.

The division was then moved to the area south of Kharkov, where it underwent a battlefield reconstitution and prepared for its participation in the upcoming Operation "Zitadelle." Despite local success, von Steinkeller and his men could not change the overall outcome of the battle, which forced the Germans to withdraw. In the course of the following months, more names would be entered on the battle roster of the regiment: Achtyrka; Kotelwa; the Worskla River; Tschernobyl; Kiev, Shitomir; southwest of Korosten (in the vicinity of the Teterew and Irscha Rivers).

In August 1943, *Generalleutnant* von Funck, who had received the Oak Leaves to the Knight's Cross of the Iron Cross on the 22nd of the same month, turned over the reins of command to *Generalmajor* von Manteuffel.

An idea of the severity of the fighting in 1943 can be obtained by looking at some of the combat losses of just one of its battalions. From 1 January 1943 until the end of October of the same year, the 1st Battalion suffered the loss of 20 officers killed, including four battalion commanders or acting battalion commanders (*Major* Grünert, *Hauptmann* Legler, *Oberleutnant* Opdenhoff and *Hauptmann* Mächtig). In addition, 95 noncommissioned officers had been killed as well as 395 enlisted personnel. Wounded were 33 officers, 217 noncommissioned officers and 1,141 enlisted personnel. Reported missing were 2 officers, 25 noncommissioned officers and 216 enlisted personnel. That meant that in the period of 10 months, the battalion had suffered 2,144 casualties.

On 12 December 1943, *Oberst* von Steinkeller assumed acting command of the division when von Manteuffel was called away for a short period on orders. Early on the morning of that same day, the enemy penetrated through the lines of the neighboring division by skillfully exploiting the woods. Enemy forces soon showed up unexpectedly at the command post of the *7. Panzer-Division*. That also meant that the right wing of his regiment had been enveloped. In order to get himself oriented on the situation, von Steinkeller immediately headed towards the positions of *Panzergrenadier-Regiment 7*.

At about the same time, a Soviet battalion attacked the gun positions of the artillery located behind the wing battalion on the right. Despite the bitter defense of the guns by the crews, the artillerymen had to pull back in the face of the enemy forces, which attacked in waves.

The guns fell into enemy hands. Reacting quickly, von Steinkeller had his *SPW* attack the Soviets, along with the *SPW* of the regimental adjutant, *Oberleutnant* Hohensee, and the 2-centimeter armored car of *Hauptmann* von Messling. With this "armored force" and the artillerymen, von Steinkeller succeeded in driving back the enemy and regaining the guns. Another crisis had been mastered.

Under the skillful hand of von Steinkeller, the division was able to provide the hard-fighting infantry of the *XIII. Armee-Korps* with significant relief in and around Korosten over the next few days. On 30 December, the division was able to open up the road south of Shitomir by a boldly executed surprise advance from the northeast. Following that, the division covered the southern flank of the corps in the area around Ljubar.

On 10 January 1944, von Steinkeller was reassigned from the division he had served in for four years. In parting, *Generalmajor* von Manteuffel wrote in an order-of-the-day:

> The successes of the division in the campaign in the West and against Russia are closely associated with his name, at least whenever he was not temporarily unavailable due to having been wounded 10 times. In the attack, he was one with the spearheads; in the defense, he was the soul of the resistance of his regiment or the *Kampfgruppe* led by him. His warrior spirit, frequently bordering on self-sacrifice, has preserved the division from setbacks in the defense or, in the case of unavoidable setbacks, from far worse consequences.

In an officer efficiency report from 1943, *Generalleutnant* von Funck had written this about the officer:

> An exemplary officer and warrior. Puts himself into the fighting completely and without regard for self. A cliff in the ocean.

✠

From the middle of January to March 1944, von Steinkeller attended a division command course in Hirschberg (Silesia). On 1 April, he was given acting command of the *Panzergrenadier-Division*

Feldherrnhalle, which had been formed from the redesignated remnants of the *60. Infanterie-Division (mot.).* The division had been effectively destroyed at Stalingrad. It originally came from the Danzig, Elbing and Marienburg areas. It was a good division, which also fought with such bravado during the weeks of the collapse of *Heeresgruppe Mitte* in the summer of 1944 that it even wrung high praise from the Soviet command.

The division had fought in December 1943 in the fighting around Smolensk and, later on, in the withdrawal actions around Leningrad. At the beginning of April 1944, considerably weakened, it was in position about 20 kilometers southwest of Narwa.

At the end of May, it was pulled out of the line to be reconstituted. Von Steinkeller requested that his division be moved to a training area in the homeland for the reconstitution process. The request was not granted, however, and was sent to the area around Mogilew to serve as part of the German Army's operational reserve in the East. On 1 June, von Steinkeller was promoted to *Generalmajor* and given command of the division.

Around the middle of June, the division was back up to authorized strength and equipment. The training at division level had just started, when the Soviets launched Operation Bagration on 22 June. On the very first day of the offensive, which came as a complete surprise and failure of intelligence on the part of the Germans, the division was released for immediate employment. It was initially allocated to *Generalleutnant* Martinek's *XXXIX. Panzer-Korps.*

It was given the mission of plugging a gap in the lines that had been created about 30 kilometers east of Dnjepr. The mission was not founded in reality, since the entire sector had already been caved in by the Soviets and some of their lead elements had already crossed the river. Despite that, von Steinkeller and his division prevented the Soviets from advancing from 23 to 25 June, despite their overwhelming superiority in numbers. Enveloped by the enemy to both flanks, he succeeded in getting his forces across the river during the night of 25/26 June. As he would later write, it was a question more of "luck than design."

At noon on that day, while von Steinkeller was employing his armored elements against enemy tanks advancing northwest of Mogilew, he received the following radio traffic from the field army, as relayed by the *XII. Armee-Korps*: "Forces are to break through to the west. Divisions are released [from field army command and control]."

That order caused unbelievable chaos all along the frontage of the *4. Armee.* Von Steinkeller harbored no illusions about the consequences of such an order. He decided to employ his division on both sides of the Mogilew–Minsk road to act as a sort of rearguard, fighting its way back sector by sector. The commanding general, *Generalleutnant* Martinek, who linked up with von Steinkeller that evening agreed with the divisional commander's decision. As a result, the division covered the withdrawal of the remnants of other divisions along the road to Minsk until 5 July. It was a difficult struggle, unending and full of self-sacrifice. The division continued to shrink in size, but not in spirit under the firm command of von Steinkeller. It saved thousands in sacrificing itself.

Early on the morning of 9 July, von Steinkeller and the last remaining elements of his division were taken prisoner in an unsuccessful attempt to break out south of Minsk. The general was in Soviet captivity for the next 11 years. He was interrogated by the NKVD for more than 400 hours. Von Steinkeller was eventually convicted on trumped-up charges and covered more than 18,000 kilometers in the Soviet Union, being moved from prisons, punishment facilities and work camps in places such as Moscow and Kiev, Zazakstan and Workuta, Stalingrad and the Urals. For him, the 11 years in the Soviet Union were worse than any battlefield experience he had endured in either world war. Unbroken, he returned home to Germany—one of the last—on 9 October 1955.

Friedrich-Carl von Steinkeller passed away in Hanover on 19 October 1981.

Sd.Kfz. 251 armored personnel carriers of the *16.Panzer-Division* in Russia 1944.

Issuing of new orders before the start of a new operation.

Orders conference on the morning of 8 December 1943 outside of Malin. From left to right: *Oberleutnant* Hohensee (face not visible), the battalion adjutant of *Panzergrenadier-Regiment 7*; *Generalmajor* von Manteuffel, the division commander of the *7. Panzer-Division*; *Oberst* Bleicken (partially blocked by Manteuffel), the operations officer of the *7. Panzer-Division*; *Oberst* Adalbert Schulz, the commander of *Panzer-Regiment 25*; and *Oberst* von Steinkeller (with walking stick), the commander of *Panzergrenadier-Regiment 7*.

A German machine-gun position in a snowed-over Soviet woods at -35°C (-31F°).

A Soviet T-34/76 at a German training area. The *Obergefreiter* is training in close-combat methods for employing against the Soviet tank. He has a practice *Teller* mine in his hands.

If the soldier managed to place the *Teller* mine correctly, the destruction of the enemy tank was the result. This is a still from a training film called *Men against Tanks*.

The face of a battle-weary *Landser*. Who knows what hardship and deprivation he may have seen and experienced?

An *Sd.Kfz. 251 Ausf. C* in Russia during the early stages of the campaign. The burning building is most likely a farmer's house or barn because of the, very flammable, thatched roof. The war in Russia was fought without mercy.

The following series of photographs are of *Leutnant* Helmut Mohr, *Panzergrenadier-Regiment 115, 15 Panzergrenadier-Division*. These photographs have been generously provided by Patrick Cassidy.

The *15. Panzergrenadier-Division* was formed in July 1943 from the remnants of the *15. Panzer-Division* that was destroyed in Africa. The division served in Sicily and Italy before being transferred to southern France in August 1944. It saw action in the Ardennes offensive in December 1944. The division ended the war in the Bremervörde area in northwest Germany.

Helmut Mohr was born 10 August 1924 and entered military service on 16 February 1943. He served in Italy, near Monte Cassino; Salerno and the Western Front. Helmut Mohr was promoted to *Leutnant* on 1 August 1944. In the spring of 1945, he was severely wounded in the lung. In this formal portrait, he is wearing the peaked field cap.

On leave wearing the field gray over-seas cap. He is wearing cut-down lace-up boots and gaiters. These items replaced the distinctive black marching boots, commonly known as "jackboots." The new footwear was issued to conserve leather and was universally despised by the frontline soldiers who referred to the gaiters as "retreat gaiters" as their issue coincided with the declining fortunes of the *Werhrmacht*.

Helmut Mohr survived the war and currently lives in Germany. This uniform was obtained directly from him in 1997. On the right, note the Wound Badge in Black worn on the left breast pocket.

A camouflaged hemet cover in the Army Splinter A pattern. The use of camouflage uniforms by the Army was far behind that of the *Waffen-SS*.

The Infantry Assault Badge (*Infanterie-Sturmabzeichen*) was awarded to Army and *Waffen-SS* personnel who had taken part in at least 3 infantry assaults, including counterattacks.

A late-war canvas magazine pouch and magazine for the *MP 38/40* machine pistol. Originally, the pouches were made of leather. The small pouch on the right holds the magazine loading tool; the magazine holds 32 9-millimeter rounds. The *MP 38/40* was widely used by *Panzergrenadiers;* over one million of these very effective weapons were produced during the war.

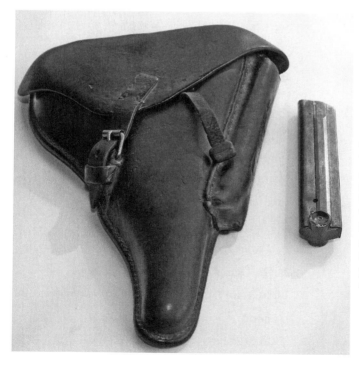

Leather holster and magazine for a *P-08 Luger.* A *Walther P-38* could also be used with this holster. The *P-38* was the standard German combat pistol in World War II, although it never totally replaced the more complicated, and prone to jam, *Luger.*

APPENDIX A

Rank Comparisons

U.S. ARMY	BRITISH ARMY	GERMAN ARMY
Enlisted Men		
Private	Private	*Schütze*
Private First Class	Private 1st Class	*Oberschütze*
Corporal	Lance Corporal	*Gefreiter*
Senior Corporal	Corporal	*Obergefreiter*
Staff Corporal		*Stabsgefreiter*
Noncommissioned Officers		
Sergeant	Sergeant	*Unteroffizier*
	Staff Sergeant	*Unterfeldwebel*
Staff Sergeant	Technical Sergeant	*Feldwebel*
Sergeant First Class	Master Sergeant	*Oberfeldwebel*
Master Sergeant	Sergeant Major	*Hauptfeldwebel*
Sergeant Major		*Stabsfeldwebel*
Officers		
Second Lieutenant	Second Lieutenant	*Leutnant*
First Lieutenant	First Lieutenant	*Oberleutnant*
Captain	Captain	*Hauptman*
Major	Major	*Major*
Lieutenant Colonel	Lieutenant Colonel	*Oberst Leutnant*
Colonel	Colonel	*Oberst*
Brigadier General	Brigadier General	*Generalmajor*
Major General	Major General	*Generalleutnant*
Lieutenant General	Lieutenant General	*General der Fallschirmjäger, etc.*
General	General	*Generaloberst*
General of the Army	Field Marshal	*Feldmarschall*

Panzergrenadier Divisions, 1939–45

Wehrmacht

3. *Panzergrenadier-Division*

Formed in June 1943 from the *3. Infanterie-Division (mot)* that was destroyed at Stalingrad.

Combat Units

Panzer-Abteilung 103

3 *Sturmgeschütz* (assault gun) batteries with 14 *StuG* per battery.

Panzergrenadier-Regiment 8

Consisted of: 3 Battalions with 4 motorized Grenadier companies.
One self-propelled heavy infantry gun company.
One *Panzerjäger* company with towed *PAK 40* and *PAK 38*.

Panzergrenadier-Regiment 29

The same organization as *Panzergrenadier-Regiment 8*.

Panzer-Aufklärungs-Abteilung 103

Consisted of: a heavy platoon; 1 light armored car company; 1 reconnaissance company (half-track); 2 heavy reconnaissance companies (half-track) and 1 heavy company with an engineer platoon, an anti-tank platoon plus a light infantry gun section (2 7.5-cm infantry guns).

Artillerie-Regiment 3

1st Battalion: 3 self-propelled *"Wespe"* batteries each with 4 fully tracked 10.5-cm *leFH*.

2nd Battalion: 3 batteries of 4 *(motZ)*[1] 10.5-cm *leFH*[2].
3rd Battalion: 2 batteries of 4 *(motZ)* 15-cm *sFH* and 1 battery with 4 10-cm *K18*.

Heeres-Flakartillerie-Abteilung (mot) 312
Two heavy anti-aircraft batteries with 4 8.8-cm *Flak,* 2 20mm *Flak* and 3 light machine guns each.

Pionier-Battailon 3
3 motorized engineer companies; 1 motorized bridging column and 1 light engineer column.

10. Panzergrenadier-Division
Formed in June 1943 from the *10. Infanterie-Division (mot)*.

Combat Units:
Panzer-Abteilung 7
Staff battery with 3 *StuG*.
3 *Sturmgeschütz* (assault gun) batteries with 14 *StuG* per battery.
Tank maintenance platoon.

Panzergrenadier-Regiment 20
Consisted of: 3 Battalions each with 3 motorized Grenadier companies; a machine-gun company with 2 machine-gun platoons with 6 heavy machine-guns each.
One motorized infantry gun company with 2 15-cm *sIG* and 6 7.5-cm *leIG*.

Panzergrenadier-Regiment 41
The same organization as *Panzergrenadier-Regiment 20*.

Panzer-Aufklärungs-Abteilung 110
1 light armored car company; 3 motorcycle companies; 1 heavy reconnaissance company (motorized) and 1 heavy company with an engi-

---

1. *(motZ)* refers to units towed by half-track vehicles, *(mot)* refers to wheeled towing vehicles - usually trucks..
2. *leFH* = light field gun/howitzer; *sFH* = heavy field gun/howitzer; *leIG* = light infantry gun; *sIG* = heavy infantry gun; *PAK* = anti-tank gun.

neer platoon, 2 anti-tank platoons plus a light infantry gun section (2 7.5-cm infantry guns).

Artillerie-Regiment 10
1st Battalion: 3 motorized *(motZ)* batteries each with 3 10.5-cm *leFH.*
2nd Battalion: as per the first battalion.
3rd Battalion: 2 batteries of 3 towed *(motZ)* 15-cm *sFH* and 1 battery with 3 10-cm *K18.*

Panzerjäger-Abteilung 10
3 self-propelled tank-hunter companies each with 14 7.5-cm *PAK 40.*
1 self-propelled anti-aircraft company with 12 2.0-cm *Flak.*

Heeres-Flakartillerie-Abteilung 275

Pionier-Battailon 10
3 motorized engineer companies and 1 light engineer column.

15. Panzergrenadier-Division
Formed in July 1943 from *Panzergrenadier-Division "Sizilien,"* a unit that consisted of various "march" units awaiting shipment to Tunisia.

Combat Units: - January 1944 establishment.
Panzer-Abteilung 115
Staff company with 1 *Panzer III,* 1 *Panzer IV* and 2 self-proelled 2-cm guns.
3 *Panzer* companies each with 13 Panzer IV.
Tank maintenance company.
Tank supply company motorized.

Panzerjäger-Abteilung
1 tank-hunter platoon (3 fully-tracked vehicles), 2 tank-hunter companies with 8 and 10 fully-tracked vehicles respectively (possibly *Jagdpanther*), 1 *Sturmgeschütz* platoon (5 *StuG*). 1 motorized anti-tank company with 8 7.5-cm *PAK 40.*

Panzergrenadier-Regiment 115
Redesignated from the 129th Regiment.

Consisted of: 3 Battalions each with 3 motorized Grenadier companies One motorized heavy company with 3 12-cm and 2 8-cm mortars. The 3rd battalion included a *(motZ)* infantry gun company with 4 15-cm *sIG* and 8 7.5-cm *leIG* and a motorized engineer company

Panzergrenadier-Regiment 104
A similar organization to *Panzergrenadier-Regiment 115*.

Panzer-Aufklärungs-Abteilung 33
1 armored car platoon; 3 reconnaissance companies (motorized); 1 heavy reconnaissance company (motorized) and 1 heavy company with an engineer platoon, 1 infantry gun platoon plus a mortar platoon.

Artillerie-Regiment 33
1st Battalion: 3 *(motZ)* batteries each with 6 10.5-cm *leFH*.
2nd Battalion: as per the first battalion.
3rd Battalion: 3 batteries of 4 *(motZ)* 15-cm *sFH*.

Heeres-Flakartillerie-Abteilung 315
3 batteries with 8 8.8-cm *Flak*, 3 2-cm *Flak* and 2 self-propelled 2-cm *Flak*.

Pionier-Battailon 33
3 motorized engineer companies and 1 light engineer column.

16. Panzergrenadier-Division
Formed in June 1943 from *16. Infanterie-Division (mot)*.

Combat Units
Panzer-Abteilung 116
Staff company with 3 *StuG*.
1 medium *Panzer* company
2 light *Panzer* companies
Tank maintenance company.
Tank supply company - motorized.

Panzerjäger-Abteilung 228
2 or 3 self-propelled tank-hunter companies.

Panzergrenadier-Regiment 60
3 Battalions each with 3 motorized Grenadier companies.
1 motorized machine-gun company.
1 *(motZ)* infantry gun company, 2 15-cm *sIG* and 6 7.5-cm *leIG* 1 self-propelled *Flak* company

Panzergrenadier-Regiment 156
A similar organization to *Panzergrenadier-Regiment 60.*

Panzer-Aufklärungs-Abteilung 116
1 light armored car company; 3 reconnaissance companies (motorized); 1 heavy reconnaissance company (motorized) and 1 heavy company with an engineer platoon, 1 infantry gun platoon plus a mortar platoon.

Artillerie-Regiment 146
1st Battalion: 3 *(motZ)* batteries each with 3 10.5-cm *leFH.*
2nd Battalion: as per the first battalion.
3rd Battalion: 2 batteries of 3 *(motZ)* 15-cm *sFH* and 1 battery of 3 10-cm *K18.*

Heeres-Flakartillerie-Abteilung 281
2 batteries with *(motZ)* 4 8.8-cm *Flak* and 3 2-cm *Flak.*

Pionier-Battailon 675
3 motorized engineer companies and 1 light engineer column.

18. Panzergrenadier-Division
Formed in June 1943 from *18. Infanterie-Division (mot).*

Combat Units
Panzer-Abteilung 118
Staff company with 3 *StuG.*
Flak platoon with 3 self-propelled quad 2.0-cm.
3 Assault gun batteries each with 14 *StuG.*
Tank maintenance platoon.

Panzerjäger-Abteilung 118
2 or 3 self-propelled tank-hunter companies with 7.5-cm *PAK 40.*

Panzergrenadier-Regiment 30
3 Battalions each with 3 motorized Grenadier companies.
1 motorized machine-gun company.
1 *(motZ)* infantry gun company, 2 15-cm *sIG* and 6 7.5-cm *leIG*, 1 self-propelled *Flak* company

Panzergrenadier-Regiment 51
A similar organization to *Panzergrenadier-Regiment 60*.

Panzer-Aufklärungs-Abteilung 118
1 light armored car company; 3 motorcycle companies; 1 heavy reconnaissance company (motorized) and 1 heavy company with an engineer platoon, 2 *Panzerjäger* platoons plus a light infantry gun section.

Artillerie-Regiment 18
1st Battalion: 3 *(motZ)* batteries each with 3 10.5-cm *leFH* and 1 *(motZ)* battery of 15.2-cm Russian howitzers.
2nd Battalion: 3 *(motZ)* batteries each with 3 10.5-cm *leFH*.
3rd Battalion: 2 *(motZ)* batteries of 3 15-cm *sFH*, 1 *(motZ)* battery of 3 10-cm *K18*, 1 battery of 15.5-cm French howitzers.

Pionier-Battailon 18
3 motorized engineer companies and 1 light engineer column *(mot.)*.

20. Panzergrenadier-Division
Formed in July 1943 from *20. Infanterie-Division (mot)*.

Combat Units
Panzer-Abteilung 5
Staff company with 3 *StuG*.
Flak platoon with 3 self-propelled quad 2.0-cm.
3 Assault gun batteries each with 14 *StuG*.
Tank maintenance platoon.

Panzerjäger-Abteilung 20
3 self-propelled tank-hunter companies with 38 7.5-cm *PAK 40*.
1 self-propelled *Flak* company.

Panzergrenadier-Regiment 76
3 Battalions each with 3 motorized Grenadier companies.
1 motorized machine-gun company.
1 *(motZ)* infantry gun company, 2 15-cm *sIG* and 6 7.5-cm *leIG*.

Panzergrenadier-Regiment 90
A similar organization to *Panzergrenadier-Regiment 76*.

Panzer-Aufklärungs-Abteilung 120
1 light armored car company; 3 motorcycle companies; 1 heavy reconnaissance company (motorized) and 1 heavy company with an engineer platoon, 2 *Panzerjäger* platoons plus a light infantry gun section.

Artillerie-Regiment 20
1st Battalion: 3 *(motZ)* batteries each with 3 10.5-cm *leFH*.
2nd Battalion: as per 1st battalion.
3rd Battalion: 2 *(motZ)* batteries of 3 15-cm *sFH*, 1 *(motZ))*battery of 3 10-cm *K18*.

Pionier-Battailon 20
3 motorized engineer companies and 1 light engineer column (*mot.*).

25. Panzergrenadier-Division
Formed in June 1943 from *25. Infanterie-Division (mot)*.

Combat Units
Panzer-Abteilung 8
Staff company with 3 *StuG*.
Flak platoon with 3 self-propelled quad 2.0-cm.
3 Assault gun batteries each with 14 *StuG*.
Tank maintenance platoon.

Panzerjäger-Abteilung 125
3 self-propelled tank-hunter companies with 36 7.5-cm *PAK 40*.
1 self-propelled *Flak* company with 12 2-cm *Flak*.

Panzergrenadier-Regiment 35

3 Battalions each with 3 motorized Grenadier companies.

1 motorized machine-gun company.

1 *(motZ)* infantry gun company, 2 15-cm *sIG* and 6 7.5-cm *leIG*.

Panzergrenadier-Regiment 119

A similar organization to *Panzergrenadier-Regiment 35*.

Panzer-Aufklärungs-Abteilung 125

1 light armored car company; 3 motorcycle companies; 1 heavy reconnaissance company (motorized) and 1 heavy company with an engineer platoon, 2 *Panzerjäger* platoons plus a light infantry gun section.

Artillerie-Regiment 25

1st Battalion: 2 *(motZ)* batteries each with 3 10.5-cm Czech howitzers, 1 *(motZ)* battery each with 3 8.8-cm *PAK 43/41*.

2nd Battalion: as per 1st battalion.

3rd Battalion: 2 *(motZ)* batteries of 3 15-cm *sFH*, 1 *(motZ)* battery of 3 10-cm *K18* and 1 *(motZ)* battery of 2 22-cm and 1 10.5-cm French howitzers.

Pionier-Battailon 25

3 motorized engineer companies and 1 light engineer column (*mot*).

29. Panzergrenadier-Division

Formed in June 1943 from *29. Infanterie-Division (mot)*.

Combat Units
Panzer-Abteilung 129

Staff company with 3 *StuG*.

Flak platoon with 3 self-propelled quad 2.0-cm.

3 Assault gun batteries each with 14 *StuG*.

Tank maintenance platoon.

Panzergrenadier-Regiment 15

3 Battalions each with 4 Grenadier companies (*mot*).

1 motorized machine-gun company.

1 self-propelled heavy infantry gun company with 6 15-cm *sIG*.

1 *(motZ) Panzerjäger* company with 3 7.5-cm *PAK 40* and 6 5-cm *PAK 38*.

Panzergrenadier-Regiment 71
A similar organization to *Panzergrenadier-Regiment 35.*

Panzer-Aufklärungs-Abteilung 129
1 heavy platoon;1 light armored car company; 1 reconnaissance company *(motZ)* 2 heavy reconnaissance companies *(motZ)* and 1 heavy company with an engineer platoon, 1 *Panzerjäger* platoon plus a light infantry gun section.

Artillerie-Regiment 29
1st Battalion: 3 self-propelled batteries each with 3 10.5-cm *Wespe.*
2nd Battalion: 3 *(motZ)*.batteries of 4 10.5-cm *leFH*
3rd Battalion: 2 *(motZ)* batteries of 3 15-cm *sFH,* 1 *(motZ)* battery of 4 10-cm *K18.*

Pionier-Battailon 29
3 motorized engineer companies, 1 bridging column *(mot)* and 1 light engineer column *(mot).*

Heeres-Flakartillerie-Abteilung 313
2 batteries with *(motZ)* 4 8.8-cm *Flak* and 3 2-cm *Flak.*
1 battery with *(motZ)* 9 2-cm *Flak* and 2 quad 2-cm *Flak.*

90. Panzergrenadier-Division
Formed in July 1943 from *90. Leichte Afrika-Division.*

Combat Units
Panzer-Abteilung 190
2 *Panzer* companies with *Panzer IV*
Tank maintenance platoon.

Heeres-Sturmgeschütz-Abteilung 242
3 Sturmgeschütz batteries.

Panzergrenadier-Regiment 155
2 Battalions each with 4 Grenadier companies *(mot).*
1 motorized machine-gun company.
1 *(motZ)* infantry gun company.

Panzergrenadier-Regiment 200
A similar organization to *Panzergrenadier-Regiment 155*.

Panzergrenadier-Regiment 361
A similar organization to *Panzergrenadier-Regiment 155*.

Artillerie-Regiment 29
1st Battalion: 3 self-propelled batteries each with 3 10.5-cm *leFH*.
2nd Battalion: 1 (*motZ*).battery of 10-cm *K18*, 2 batteries15-cm *sFH*.
3rd Battalion: 2 self-propelled batteries of 6 10.5-cm *Wespe*, 1 self-propelled battery of 6 15-cm *Hummel*.

Pionier-Battailon 29
3 motorized engineer companies.

2/5 Luftwaffe-Flakartillerie-Regiment
3 heavy batteries with (*motZ*) 8.8-cm *Flak*.
2 light batteries with 2-cm *Flak* and quad 2-cm *Flak*.

Panzergrenadier-Division "Brandenburg"
Formed in September1944 from the *Brandenburg-Division*.

Combat Units
Panzer-Regiment "Brandenburg"
1st Battalion: 4 *Panzer* companies with 17 *Pz.Kpfw. V Panther* each. 1 self propelled armored[3] *Flak* company with 3 quad 2-cm.
2nd Battalion: 4 *Panzer* companies with 17 *Pz.Kpfw. IV* each.
1 self propelled armored *Flak* company with 3 quad 2-cm.

Panzerjäger-Abteilung "Brandenburg"
2 *Sturmgeschütz* companies with 14 *StuG* each.
1 (*motZ*) tank-hunter company with 12 8.8-cm *PAK*.

Jager-Regiment 1
1 armored and 1 motorized *Panzergrenadier* battalions each with 3 mechanized/motorized *Grenadier* companies.

---

3. The designation armored (*gep=gepanzert*) refers to fully armored half-tracks such as the *Sd.Kfz. 250* and *251*.

1 heavy *Panzergrenadier* company that includes 4 12-cm mortars and 6 7.5-cm light infantry guns.
1 self-propelled heavy infantry gun company with 8 15-cm *sIG*.

Jager-Regiment 2
1 armored and 1 motorized *Panzergrenadier* battalions each with 3 mechanized/motorized *Grenadier* companies.
1 heavy *Panzergrenadier* company with6 2-cm *Flak*, 4 12-cm mortars and 8 8-cm mortars.
1 self-propelled heavy infantry gun company with 8 15-cm *sIG*.
An engineer company with 18 flamethrowers.

Aufklärungs-Abteilung "Brandenburg"
1 armored car company; 3 armored reconnaissance companies with infantry guns, *Flak* and mortars.

Artillerie-Regiment "Brandenburg"
1st Battalion: 1 self-propelled *Flak* platoon, 2 *Wespe* batteries (10.5-cm) and 1 *Hummel* battery (15-cm).
2nd Battalion: 2 *(motZ)* batteries each with 6 10.5-cm *leFH*.
3rd Battalion: 3 *(motZ)* batteries of 6 15-cm *sFH*.

Pionier-Battailon "Brandenburg"
1 armored engineer company, 2 motorized engineer companies.

Heeres-Flakartillerie-Abteilung "Brandenburg"
2 batteries with *(motZ)* 6 8.8-cm *Flak* and 3 2-cm *Flak*.
1 light battery with 9 3.7-cm *Flak* .

Panzergrenadier-Division "Feldherrnhalle"
Formed in June1943 from the *60. Infanterie-Division (mot)*.

Combat Units
Panzer-Regiment "FHH"
3 *Sturmgeschütz* batteries with 14 *StuG* each.

Panzerjäger-Abteilung "Brandenburg"

Added in 1944 with 2 *Sturmgeschütz* batteries 14 *StuG* each and a *(motZ)* *Panzerjäger* company with 12 heavy anti-tank guns.

Fusilier-Regiment "FHH"

3 *Fusilier* battalions each with 4 motorized *Fusilier* companies.
1 self-propelled heavy infantry gun company with 6 15-cm *sIG*.
1 *(motZ)* *Panzerjäger* company with 9 *PAK*.

Grenadier-Regiment "FHH"

3 *Grenadier* battalions each with 4 motorized *Fusilier* companies.
1 self-propelled heavy infantry gun company with 6 15-cm *sIG*.
1 *(motZ)* *Panzerjäger* company with 9 *PAK*.

Aufklärungs-Abteilung "FHH"

1 armored car company; 3 armored reconnaissance companies with infantry guns, *Flak* and mortars.

Artillerie-Regiment "FHH"

1st Battalion: 1 self-propelled *Flak* platoon, 2 *Wespe* batteries (10.5-cm) and 1 *Hummel* battery (15-cm).
2nd Battalion: 3 *(motZ)* batteries each with 4 10.5-cm *leFH*.
3rd Battalion: 2 *(motZ)* batteries of 4 15-cm *sFH* each and 1 *(motZ)* battery of 4 10-cm *K18*.

Pionier-Battailon "FHH"

3 motorized engineer companies.
1 bridging column "K".

Flakartillerie-Abteilung "FHH"

2 batteries with *(motZ)* 4 8.8-cm *Flak* and 3 2-cm *Flak*.
1 light battery with *(motZ)* 12 2-cm *Flak*.

Panzergrenadier-Division "Grossdeutschland"

Formed in June1943 from *Infanterie-Division "Grossdeutschland" (mot)*. *GD* was a powerful and elite unit that went through many organizational changes.

Combat Units

Panzer-Regiment "Grossdeutschland"

1st Battalion:4 *Panther* platoons.

2nd Battalion: 4 *Panzer IV* platoons.

3rd Battalion: 3 *Pz.Kpfw. VI Tiger* platoons.

Panzerjäger-Abteilung "Grossdeutschland"

1 self-propelled heavy *Panzerjäger* company with 9 *PAK 40.*

2 *(motZ)* heavy *Panzerjäger* company with 9 *PAK 40.*

Sturmgeschütz-Abteilung "Grossdeutschland"

3 *Sturmgeschütz* batteries with 11 *StuG* each.

Grenadier/Fusilier-Regimenter "Grossdeutschland"

1 armored battalion with 3 *Panzergrenadier* companies and a heavy *Panzergrenadier* company.

2 motorized battalions with 3 *Panzergrenadier* companies each.

1 self-propelled heavy battalion. with a light *Flak* company (12 2-cm-*Flak*), infantry gun company (8 15-cm) and heavy *Panzerjäger* company (9 *PAK 40*).

Aufklärungs-Abteilung "Grossdeutschland"

1 armored car company; 1 armored reconnaissance company, 1 heavy armored reconnaissance company with an engineer platoon, medium anti-tank gun platoon (*PAK 38*) and a *Panzerjäger* platoon with 6 *Sd.Kfz. 251/22* mounting 7.5-cm *PAK 40.*

Artillerie-Regiment "Grossdeutschland"

1st Battalion: 2 *(motZ)* batteries each with 4 10.5-cm *leFH.* 1 battery *(motZ)* of 4 15-cm *sFH*

2nd Battalion: 2 *Wespe* batteries (10.5-cm) and 1 *Hummel* battery (15-cm).

3rd Battalion: 1 *(motZ)* battery with 4 10.5-cm *leFH,* 1 *(motZ)* battery of 4 15-cm *sFH* each and 1 *(motZ)* battery of 4 10-cm *K18.*

4th Battalion: 2 *(motZ)* batteries with 4 10.5-cm *leFH,* 1 *(motZ)* battery of 6 *Nebelwerfer* (rocket artillery).

Pionier-Battailon "Grossdeutschland"
1 motorized engineer reconnaissance company.
3 motorized engineer companies.
1 armored engineer company with 6 flamethrowers.
1 bridging column "K".

Heeres-Flakartillerie-Abteilung "Grossdeutschland"
3 heavy batteries with *(motZ)* 4 8.8-cm *Flak* and 3 2-cm self-propelled *Flak*.
2 self-propelled medium batteries with 9 3.7-cm *Flak*.
1 light battery with *(mot)* 3 quad 2-cm *Flak*.

Fallschirm-Panzergrenadier-Division "Hermann Göring"
Formed in the Summer of 1944 and combined with *Fallschirm-Panzer-Division "Hermann Göring"* in October 1944.

Primary units consisted of the following: a *Panzerjäger* battalion with 2 *StuG* batteries of 14 *StuG* each; 2 *Grenadier* regiments with 2 battalions each; a *Flak* battalion; an engineer battalion; an artillery regiment with 3 battalions.

Panzergrenadier-Division "Kurmark"
This formation never exceeded brigade strength and consisted of a *Panzer-Abteilung* with 3 *Panzer* companies (32 *StuG* and 10 *Panzer IV*), a *Panzergrenadier* regiment of 2 battalions, a reconnaissance regiment (1 company), a tank-hunter battalion (12 7.5-cm *PAK 40*) and an artillery regiment with one battalion – 3 *(motZ)* batteries each with 4 10.5-cm *leFH*.

Waffen SS

4. SS-Polizei-Panzergrenadier-Division
Formed in January 1943 from the *SS-Polizei-Division*.

Combat Units
SS-Panzergrenadier-Regiment 7
1st Battalion: 3 *Panzergrenadier* Companies, 1 heavy *Panzergrenadier* company, 1 mortar platoon (6 8-cm mortars), 1 tank-hunter platoon (3 7.5-cm *PAK*), 1 support platoon (4 7.5-cm *leIG*).

2nd and 3rd Battalions as per the 1st Battalion.

1 (*motZ*) heavy infantry gun company – 6 15-cm *sIG*.

1 (*motZ*) *Flak* company – 12 2-cm.

1 (*mot*) engineer company with 18 flamethrowers and 2 8-cm mortars.

SS-Panzergrenadier-Regiment 8

The same organization as *SS-Panzergrenadier-Regiment 7*.

SS-Panzerjäger-Abteilung 4

2 *Jagdpanzer* companies with 14 *Jagdpanzer IV* each.

1 (*motZ*) *Panzerjäger* company with 12 7.5-cm *PAK 40*.

1 armored *Flak* company with 12 self-propelled 2-cm *Flak*.

SS-Flak-Abteilung 4

3 heavy batteries with (*motZ*) 4 8.8-cm *Flak* and 3 2-cm self-propelled *Flak*.

2 (*motZ*) medium batteries with 9 3.7-cm *Flak*.

SS-Aufklärungs-Abteilung 4

1 armored car company; 1 motorized reconnaissance company; 1 heavy company with 1 engineer platoon, 1 tank-hunter platoon (3 7.5-cm *PAK 40)* and 1 light infantry gun section with 2 7.5-cm *leIG*.

SS-Artillery-Regiment 4

1st Battalion: 2 (*motZ*) batteries each with 6 10.5-cm *leFH*. 1

2nd Battalion: as per 1st battalion.

3rd Battalion: as per 1st battalion.

4th Battalion: 2 (*motZ*) batteries with 6 15-cm *sFH*, 1 (*motZ*) battery of 6 10.5-cm *sK18/40*.

SS-Pionier-Abteilung 4

3 motorized engineer companies.

11. SS-Freiwilligen-Panzergrenadier-Division "Nordland"

Formed in July 1943.

Combat Units

SS-Panzergrenadier-Regiment 23 "Norge"

1st Battalion: 3 *Panzergrenadier* Companies, 1 mortar platoon (4 12-cm mortars), 1 tank-hunter platoon (3 7.5-cm *PAK*), 1 infantry gun section (2 7.5-cm *leIG*).

2nd and 3rd Battalions as per the 1st Battalion.

1 self-propelled heavy infantry gun company - 6 15-cm *sIG*.

1 self-propelled *Flak* company - 12 2-cm.

1 (*mot*) engineer company with 6 flamethrowers and 2 8-cm mortars.

SS-Panzergrenadier-Regiment 24 "Danmark"

The same organization as *SS-Panzergrenadier-Regiment 23 "Norge"*.

SS-Panzerjäger-Abteilung 11

1 mechanized company with 12 7.5-cm *PAK 40*.

1 (*motZ*) *Panzerjäger* company with 12 7.5-cm *PAK 40*.

1 armored *Flak* company with 12 self-propelled 2-cm *Flak*.

SS-Sturmgeschütz-Abteilung 11

3 *Sturmgeschütz* batteries with 10 *StuG* in each.

SS-Flak-Abteilung 11

3 heavy batteries with (*motZ*) 4 8.8-cm *Flak* and 3 2-cm self-propelled *Flak*.

2 (*motZ*) medium batteries with 9 3.7-cm *Flak*.

SS-Aufklärungs-Abteilung 11

1 light armored car company; 3 motorized reconnaissance companies; 1 reconnaissance company with 1 engineer platoon, 1 tank-hunter platoon (3 7.5-cm *PAK 40)* and 1 light infantry gun section with 2 7.5-cm *leIG*.

SS-Artillery-Regiment 11

1st Battalion: 2 (*motZ*) batteries each with 6 10.5-cm *leFH*. 1

2nd Battalion: as per 1st battalion.

3rd Battalion: as per 1st battalion.

4th Battalion: 2 (*motZ*) batteries with 6 15-cm *sFH*, 1 (*motZ*) battery of 6 10.5-cm *sK18/40*.

SS-Flakartillerie-Abteilung 11
3 heavy batteries with *(motZ)* 4 8.8-cm *Flak* and 3 2-cm self-propelled *Flak*.
2 (*motZ*) medium batteries with 9 3.7-cm *Flak*.

SS-Pionier-Abteilung 11
3 motorized engineer companies with 2 8-cm mortars and 6 flamethowers.

16. SS-Panzergrenadier-Division "Reichsführer SS"
Formed in March 1943 from *Sturmbrigade "Reichsführer SS"*.

Combat Units
SS-Panzer-Abteilung 16
Staff *Panzer* platoon with 8 *Panzer IV*.
4 *Panzer* companies with 17 *Panzer IV* each.

SS-Panzergrenadier-Regiment 35 (mot)
1st Battalion: 3 *Panzergrenadier* Companies, 1 mortar platoon (4 12-cm mortars), 1 tank-hunter platoon (3 7.5-cm *PAK*), 1 infantry gun section (2 7.5-cm *leIG*).
2nd and 3rd Battalions as per the 1st Battalion.
1 (*motZ*) heavy infantry gun company - 6 15-cm *sIG*.
1 self-propelled *Flak* company - 12 2-cm.
1 (*mot*) engineer company with 6 flamethrowers and 2 8-cm mortars.

SS-Panzergrenadier-Regiment 36 (mot)
The same organization as *SS-Panzergrenadier-Regiment 35*.

SS-Panzerjäger-Abteilung 16
1 mechanized company with 14 7.5-cm *PAK 40*.
1 (*motZ*) *Panzerjäger* company with 12 7.5-cm *PAK 40*.
1 self-propelled *Flak* company with 12 self-propelled 2-cm *Flak*.

SS-Flak-Abteilung 16
3 heavy batteries with *(motZ)* 4 8.8-cm *Flak* and 3 2-cm self-propelled *Flak*.

2 (*motZ*) medium batteries with 9 3.7-cm *Flak.*

SS-Aufklärungs-Abteilung 16
1 armored car company; 3 mechanized reconnaissance companies; 1 reconnaissance company with 1 engineer platoon, 1 tank-hunter pla toon (3 7.5-cm *PAK 40*) and 1 light infantry gun section with 2 7.5-cm *leIG.*

SS-Artillery-Regiment 16
1 mechanized *Flak* battery - 4 quad 2-cm.
1st Battalion: 2 (*motZ*) batteries each with 6 10.5-cm *leFH.* 1
2nd Battalion: as per 1st battalion.
3rd Battalion: as per 1st battalion.
4th Battalion: 2 (*motZ*) batteries with 6 15-cm *sFH*, 1 (*motZ*) battery of 6 10.5-cm *sK18/40.*

SS-Flakartillerie-Abteilung 16
3 heavy batteries with (*motZ*) 4 8.8-cm *Flak* and 3 2-cm self-propelled *Flak.*
2 (*motZ*) medium batteries with 9 3.7-cm *Flak.*
1 searchlight platoon.

SS-Pionier-Abteilung 16
3 motorized engineer companies with 2 8-cm mortars and 6 flamethowers.

17. SS-Panzergrenadier-Division "Götz von Berlichingen"
Formed in March 1943 from parts of *10. SS-Panzer-Division.*

Combat Units
SS-Panzer-Abteilung 17
Staff *Panzer* platoon with 8 *Panzer IV.*
4 *Panzer* companies with 17 *Panzer IV* each.

SS-Panzergrenadier-Regiment (mot) 37
1st Battalion: 3 *Panzergrenadier* Companies, 1 mortar platoon (4 12-cm mortars), 1 tank-hunter platoon (3 7.5-cm *PAK*), 1 infantry gun sec tion (2 7.5-cm *leIG*).

2nd and 3rd Battalions as per the 1st Battalion.
1 self-propelled (*motZ*) heavy infantry gun company – 6 15-cm *sIG*.
1 self-propelled *Flak* company – 12 2-cm.
1 (*mot*) engineer company with 6 flamethrowers and 2 8-cm mortars.

SS-Panzergrenadier-Regiment 38
The same organization as *SS-Panzergrenadier-Regiment 37*.

SS-Panzerjäger-Abteilung 17
1 mechanized company with 14 7.5-cm *PAK 40*.
1 (*motZ*) *Panzerjäger* company with 12 7.5-cm *PAK 40*.
1 *Flak* company with 12 self-propelled 2-cm *Flak*.

SS-Flak-Abteilung 17
3 heavy batteries with (*motZ*) 4 8.8-cm *Flak* and 3 2-cm self-propelled *Flak*.
2 (*motZ*) medium batteries with 9 3.7-cm *Flak*.
1 searchlight platoon.

SS-Aufklärungs-Abteilung 17
1 armored car company; 3 mechanized reconnaissance companies; 1 mechanized reconnaissance company with 1 engineer platoon, 1 tank-hunter platoon (3 7.5-cm *PAK 40)* and 1 light infantry gun section with 2 7.5-cm *leIG*.

SS-Artillery-Regiment 17
1st Battalion: 2 (*motZ*) batteries each with 6 10.5-cm *leFH*. 1
2nd Battalion: as per 1st battalion.
3rd Battalion: as per 1st battalion.
4th Battalion: 2 (*motZ*) batteries with 6 15-cm *sFH*, 1 (*motZ*) battery of 6 10.5-cm *sK18/40*.
1mechanized *Flak* battery with 4 quad 2-cm *Flak*.

SS-Flakartillerie-Abteilung 17
3 heavy batteries with (*motZ*) 4 8.8-cm *Flak* and 3 2-cm self-propelled *Flak*.
2 (*motZ*) medium batteries with 9 3.7-cm *Flak*.

SS-Pionier-Abteilung 17
3 motorized engineer companies with 2 8-cm mortars and 6 flamethowers.
1 *(motZ)* medium battery with 9 3.7-cm *Flak.*
1 armored light bridging section.

18. SS-Freiwilligen-Panzergrenadier-Division "Horst Wessel"
Formed in January 1944 from the *1. SS-Brigade (mot).*

Combat Units
SS-Sturmgeschütz-Abteilung 16
Staff *Sturmgeschütz* platoon with *StuG.*
4 *Sturmgeschütz* companies with 10 *StuG* each.
1 *Flak* battery with 3 quad 2-cm

SS-Panzergrenadier-Regiment (mot) 39
1st Battalion: 3 *Panzergrenadier* Companies, 1 mortar platoon (4 12-cm mortars), 1 tank-hunter platoon (3 7.5-cm *PAK*), 2 infantry gun sections (2 7.5-cm *leIG*).
2nd and 3rd Battalions as per the 1st Battalion.
1 self-propelled *(motZ)* heavy infantry gun company – 6 15-cm *sIG.*
1 self-propelled *Flak* company – 12 2-cm.
1 *(mot)* engineer company with 6 flamethrowers and 2 8-cm mortars.

SS-Panzergrenadier-Regiment 40
The same organization as *SS-Panzergrenadier-Regiment 39.*

SS-Panzerjäger-Abteilung 18
1 mechanized company with 14 7.5-cm *PAK 40.*
1 *(motZ) Panzerjäger* company with 12 7.5-cm *PAK 40.*
1 *Flak* company with 12 self-propelled 2-cm *Flak.*

SS-Flak-Abteilung 18
3 heavy batteries with *(motZ)* 4 8.8-cm *Flak* and 3 2-cm self-propelled *Flak.*
2 *(motZ)* medium batteries with 9 3.7-cm *Flak.*
1 searchlight platoon.

SS-Aufklärungs-Abteilung 18

1 armored car company; 3 mechanized reconnaissance companies; 1 mechanized reconnaissance company with 1 engineer platoon, 1 tank-hunter platoon (3 7.5-cm *PAK 40)* and 1 light infantry gun section with 2 7.5-cm *leIG.*

SS-Artillery-Regiment 18

1st Battalion: 2 *(motZ)* batteries each with 6 10.5-cm *leFH.* 1
2nd Battalion: as per 1st battalion.
3rd Battalion: as per 1st battalion.
4th Battalion: 2 *(motZ)* batteries with 6 15-cm *sFH,* 1 *(motZ)* battery of 6 10.5-cm *sK18/40.*
1 mechanized *Flak* battery with 4 quad 2-cm *Flak.*

SS-Flakartillerie-Abteilung 18

3 heavy batteries with *(motZ)* 4 8.8-cm *Flak* and 3 2-cm self-propelled *Flak.*
2 (*motZ*) medium batteries with 9 3.7-cm *Flak.*
1 searchlight platoon *(mot).*

SS-Pionier-Abteilung 18

3 motorized engineer companies with 2 8-cm mortars and 6 flamethowers.
1 bridging section "K".

23. SS-Freiwilligen-Panzergrenadier-Division "Nederland"

This division was ordered to be constituted in February 1945 but was never fully organized and equipped. It was to consist of 2 *Panzergrenadier* regiments; a *Panzer* regiment with 4 *Panzer* companies; a *Panzerjäger* battalion; reconnaissance battalion; a *Flak* battalion and an artillery regiment.

APPENDIX C

The *mittlerer Schützenpanzerwagen Sd.Kfz. 251*

The vehicles most associated with the *Panzergrenadiere* are the armored halftracks, *Schützenpanzerwagen,* that carried them into battle. The *Sd.Kfz. 251* was the most produced German armored vehicle of the war with a total of 15,200 being manufactured.

Weight: 8.5 metric tons.
Armor: 14.5 mm front of hull, 8 mm hull sides and 5.5 mm belly and top of superstructure. The armor was intended to be proof against 7.92 mm armor-piercing bullets.
Maximum speed on the road: 52 kilometers per hour (limited to 30 kn/hr). Cross country speed: 10 km/hr.
Range cross country: 150 kilometers.
Engine: Maybach 42 TUKRM 6 cylinder of 4.17 liters developing 100 bhp at 2800 rpm.
Transmission: 4 forward gears and 1 reverse gear operating through a 2 speed transfer case, effectively giving 8 forward and 2 reverse gears.

The *Sd.Kfz. 251* was produced in numerous variants.
Sd.Kfz. 251/1–standard armored personnel carrier.
Sd.Kfz. 251/2–8-cm mortar carrier.
Sd.Kfz. 251/3–radio vehicle.
Sd.Kfz. 251/4–ammunition carrier.
Sd.Kfz. 251/5,7–engineer vehicle.
Sd.Kfz. 251/6–command vehicle.
Sd.Kfz. 251/8–ambulance.
Sd.Kfz. 251/9–7.5-cm L/24 close support vehicle.
Sd.Kfz. 251/10–Platoon leader's vehicle with 3.7-cm *PAK*.
Sd.Kfz. 251/11,19–field telephone communication vehicle.
Sd.Kfz. 251/12-15,17–artillery, ranging, survey and spotting vehicle.
Sd.Kfz. 251/16–flame thrower vehicle.
Sd.Kfz. 251/17–2-cm anti-aircraft vehicle.
Sd.Kfz. 251/20–infra-red searchlight carrier.
Sd.Kfz. 251/21 "Drilling"–1.5-cm/2-cm anti-aircraft vehicle.
Sd.Kfz. 251/22–tank destroyer vehicle with 7.5-cm *PAK*.

APPENDIX D

The *leichter Schützenpanzerwagen Sd.Kfz. 250*

The *Sd.Kfz. 250* was developed on the *le.Zgkw.1* artillery tractor chassis. Its role was to support the *Panzer* and *Panzergrenadier* divisions undertaking various roles as a more economic alternative to the larger *Sd.Kfz 251*. The smaller vehicle was very well recieved by the combat units. As with the *Sd.Kfz. 251* the *Sd.Kfz. 250* was produced in numerous variants.

Weight: 5.8 metric tons.

Armor: 14.5 mm front of hull, 10 mm rear, 8 mm hull sides and 5.5 mm belly and top of superstructure. The armor was intended to be proof against 7.92 mm armor-piercing bullets.

Maximum speed on the road: 65 kilometers per hour (limited to 45 kn/hr). Cross country speed: 10/15 km/hr.

Range cross country: 200 kilometers.

Engine: Maybach 42 TKRM of 4.17 liters developing 100 bhp at 2800 rpm.

Transmission: Maybach Varioex 120 128 with 7 forward gears and 3 reverse gears.

Sd.Kfz. 250/1–standard armored personnel carrier.
Sd.Kfz. 250/2–field telephone communication vehicle.
Sd.Kfz. 250/3–radio vehicle.
Sd.Kfz. 250/4–artillery observation vehicle.
Sd.Kfz. 250/5–reconnaissance vehicle.
Sd.Kfz. 250/6–ammunition carrier.
Sd.Kfz. 250/7–mortar carrier.
Sd.Kfz. 250/8–7.5-cm K 51 close support vehicle.
Sd.Kfz. 250/9–semi-tracked armored car with *2-cm* 360 degree turret.
Sd.Kfz. 250/10–Platoon leader's vehicle with 3.7-cm *PAK*.
Sd.Kfz. 250/11–Platoon leader's vehicle with 2.8-cm *Pz 41*.
Sd.Kfz. 250/12–artillery ranging survey vehicle.

Select Bibliography

PRIMARY SOURCES

Bergmann, S. *Mein Regimentskommandeur, Adalbert Schulz*. Unpublished manuscript: ?

Beukemann, *Helmuth, Handstreich auf Lemnos*. Unpublished manuscript: ?

————. *Einsatz in Griechenland*. Unpublished manuscript: ?

Brasche, Rudolf. *Lebenslauf*. Unpublished manuscript: ?

————. *Einsatzschilderungen*. Unpublished manuscript: ?

————. *Als MG-Schütze am Mius*. Unpublished manuscript: ?

Brux, Albert. Combat reports. ?

Eberbach, Heinrich. *4. Panzer-Division im Ostfeldzug*. Unpublished manuscript: ?

Edelsheim, Reichsgraf, Maximilian von. *Schützen-Regiment 26 im Vorstoß auf Woronesch*. Unpublished manuscript: ?

————. *Schörner, General und Feldmarschall*. Unpublished manuscript: ?

German Army General Staff. *Das Buch der Sturmartillerie*. Berlin: 1943.

Grimminger, Hans. Diaries. ?

Grimminger, Robert. Memorial notes concerning the fallen sons of the Grimminger family. ?

Jüttner, Arthur. *Mit der 62. Volks-Grenadier-Division in den Ardennen*. Unpublished manuscript: ?

Karczewski, Bruno. *Mit der Teufels-Division im Einsatz*. Unpublished manuscript: ?

Kahler, Joachim. *Curriculum vitae*. ?

Manteuffel, Hasso von. *Vor Moskau-Jachroma*. Unpublished manuscript: ?

————. *Kurzfassung der Geschichten der 7. Panzer-Division und der Panzergrenadier-Division "Großdeutschland."* Unpublished manuscript: ?

Michael, Georg. Diaries. ?

Oberkommando der Wehrmacht. Reports, 1939–1945.

————. *"Deutschland im Kampf."* 1939–1944.

Remmert, Heinz. Combat reports of *Grenadier-Regiment 464*. ?

Sachse, Ulrich. *Streiflichter—Kriegseinsatz des Kradschützen-Bataillons 34*. Unpublished manuscript: ?

Schaub, Milla. *Mein Mann, Oskar Schaub*. Unpublished manuscript: ?

Schneider, Josef. *Curriculum vitae*. ?

————. Firsthand accounts. ?

Schrijnen, Remy. Firsthand accounts. ?

Schönleber, ? *Durchbruch mit Hurra—Grenadier-Regiment 521 im Einsatze*. Unpublished manuscript: ?

Sevenich, Friedrich. *Die 296. Infanterie-Division (in Dokumenten, Berichten und Befehlen)*. Unpublished manuscript: ?

Steglich, Martin. *Curriculum vitae*. ?

Steinkeller, Friedrich-Carl. *Fester Platz Sslawjansk*. Unpublished manuscript: ?

Wenck, Walther. *Überblick über die Endkämpfe zwischen Oder und Elbe im April/Mai 1945*. Unpublished manuscript: ?

Zeller, Konrad. After-action reports. ?

———. Essays. ?

SECONDARY SOURCES

Alman, Karl. *Panzer vor*. Rastatt: 1966.

———. *Sprung in die Hölle*. Rastatt: 1964.

Bauer, Eddy. *Der Panzerkrieg*. Bonn: 1965.

Baumann, Hans. *35. Infanterie-Division, 1939–1945*. Linz: 1955.

Benary, Albert. *Die Berliner Bären-Division, Geschichte der 257. Infanterie-Division, 1939-1945*. Bad Nauheim: 1955.

Beyersdorff, Ernst. *Geschichte der 110. Infanterie-Division*. Bad Nauheim: 1965.

Borchert, Hubert. *Panzerkampf im Westen*. Berlin: 1940.

Bourret, Viktor. *La Tragédie de l'Armee Francaise*. Paris: 1947.

Brehem, Werner. *Mein Kriegstagebuch*. Kassel: 1953.

Breithaupt, Hans. *Geschichte der 30. Infanterie-Division, 1939–1945*. Bad Nauheim: 1955.

Buchner, Alex. *Der Deutsche Griechenland-Feldzug*. Heidelberg: 1957.

Buxa, Werner. *Weg und Schicksal der 11. Infanterie-Division*. Kiel: 1952.

Carell, Paul. *Unternehmen Barbarossa*. Frankfurt a.M.: 1963.

———. *Verbrannte Erde*. Frankfurt a.M.: 1966.

Cassidy, Henry. *Moskau, 1941–1943*. Zürich: 1944.

Carius, Otto. *Tiger im Schlamm*. Neckargemünd: 1960.

Charles de Beaulieu, W. *Der Vorstoß der Panzergruppe 4 auf Leningrad, 1941*. Neckargemünd: 1961.

Conze, Werner. *Geschichte der 291. Infanterie-Division*. Bad Nauheim: 1953.

Dahms, Helmuth G. *Geschichte des zweiten Weltkriegs*. Tübingen: 1965.

Dieckhoff, Gerhard. *3. Panzergrenadier-Division*. Göttingen: 1960.

Dieckert, Kurt and Horst Grossmann. *Der Kampf um Ostpreußen*. Munich: 1960.

Doerr, Hans. *Der Feldzug nach Stalingrad*. Darmstadt: 1955.

Dotti, Stefano. *Ritirata in Russia, 1942–1943*. Bologna: 1956.

Dwinger, Edwin Erich. *Panzerführer*. Jena: 1941.

Eremenko, A.I. *Tage der Bewährung*. East Berlin: 1961.

———. *Stalingrad, Notes du Commandant en chef*. Paris: 1963.

Erickson, John. *The Soviet High Command*. London: 1962.

Ettighoffer, P. C. *44 Tage und Nächte*. Stuttgart: 1953.

Fey, Willy. *Panzer im Brennpunkt der Fronten*. Munich: 1959.

Fretter-Pico, Maximilian. *Mißbrauchte Infanterie*. Frankfurt a.M.: 1957.

Frießner, Hans. *Verratene Schlachten*. Hamburg: 1956.

Fuller, J.F. *Der Zweite Weltkrieg*. Vienna: 1952.

Gackenholz, Hermann. *Zusammenbruch der Heeresgruppe Mitte, 1944*. Frankfurt a.M.: 1957.

Galkin, Fedor I. *Tanki vozvrascajutsa v boj*. Moscow: 1964.

Gareis, Martin. *Kampf und Untergang der 98. Infanterie-Division*. Tegernsee: 1965.

Görliz, Walter. *Der Zweite Weltkrieg*. Stuttgart: 1952.

———. Paulus: *Ich stehe hier auf Befehl*. Frankfurt a.M.: 1960.

Grams, Rolf. *14. Panzer-Division*. Bad Nauheim: 1957.

Graser, Gerhard. *Zwischen Kattegatt und Kaukasus, Weg und Kämpfe der 198. Infanterie-Division*. Tübingen: 1963.

Greelen, Lothar von. *Verkauft und verraten*. Munich: 1963.

Greiner, Helmuth. *Die oberste Wehrmachtsführung*. Wiesbaden: 1951.

Großmann, Horst. Rshew, *Eckpfeiler der Ostfront*. Bad Nauheim: 1962.

Grote, Hans-Henning von. *Unvergleichliche deutsche Infanterie*. Hamburg: 1938.

Guderian, Heinz. *Erinnerungen eines Soldaten*. Heidelberg: 1951.

———. *Panzer—marsch!* Munich: 1956.

Haupt, Werner. *Kiew—die größte Kesselschlacht der Geschichte*. Bad Nauheim: 1964.

———. *Baltikum, 1941*. Neckargemünd: 1963.

———. *Berlin—Hitlers letzte Schlacht*. Rastatt: 1964.

Halder, Franz. *Kriegstagebuch*. Stuttgart: 1964.

Hayn, Friedrich. *Die Invasion*. Heidelberg: 1954.

Hausser, Paul. *Waffen-SS im Einsatz*. Göttingen: 1953.

———. *Soldaten wie andere auch*. Osnabrück: 1966.

Heidkämper, Otto. *Witebsk*. Heidelberg: 1954.

Heymann, Ludwig. *Geschichte des Grenadier-Regiments 992*. Celle: 1959.

Hofmann, Rudolf. *Die Schlacht um Moskau*. Frankfurt a.M.: 1960.

Hoppe, Harry. *Die 278. Infanterie-Division in Italien*. Bad Nauheim: 1953.

Hossbach, Friedrich. *Infanterie im Ostfeldzug*. Osterode: 1951.

Hoth, Hermann. *Panzer-Operationen*. Heidelberg: 1956.

Hubatsch, Walther. *61. Infanterie-Division*. Bad Nauheim: 1961.

Hubatsch, Hillgruber und Schramm (editors), *Das Kriegstagebuch des Oberkommandos der Wehrmacht*. Frankfurt: 1963.

Hess, Wilhelm. *Eismeerfront, 1941*. Heidelberg: 1956.

Hoelter, Hermann. *Armee in der Arktis*. Bad Nauheim: 1953.

Hossbach, Friedrich. *Die Schlacht um Ostpreußen*. Überlingen: 1951.

Jacobsen, Dr. H.A. *Der zweiten Weltkrieg in Chroniken und Dokumenten*. Darmstadt: 1959.

——— and Dr. J. Rohwer. *Entscheidungsschlachten des zweiten Weltkriegs*. Frankfurt a.M.: 1960.

Jenner, Martin. *216. Infanterie-Division / 272. Infanterie-Division*. Bad Nauheim: 1964.

Kalinov, Kyrill D. *Sowjetmarschälle haben das Wort*. Munich: 1950.

Karov, D. *Die Partisanenbewegung in der Sowjetunion*. Munich: 1954.

Keilig, Wolf. *Das deutsche Heer, 1939–1945*. Bad Nauheim: 1955.

———. *Rangliste des deutschen Heeres*. Bad Nauheim: 1955.

Kern, Erich. *Der große Rausch*. Göttingen: 1961.

Kesselring, Albert. *Soldat bis zum letzten Tag*. Bonn: 1953.

Kissel, Hans. *Die Panzerschlachten in der Puszta*. Neckargemünd: 1958

————. *Angriff einer Infanterie-Division.* Neckargemünd: 1960.

Kjellberg, Sven H. *Rußland im Krieg, 1920–1945.* Zürich: 1945.

Klatt, Paul. *3. Gebirgs-Division.* Bad Nauheim: 1958.

Knobelsdorff, Otto von. *Geschichte der 19. Panzer-Division.* Bad Nauheim: 1958.

Konrad, Rudolf. *Kampf um den Kaukausus.* Munich: 1955.

Kardel, Hennecke. *Geschichte der 170. Infanterie-Division.* Bad Nauheim: 1953.

Kneppers, F.W. *Taten und Schicksal der 197. Infanterie-Division.* Wiesbaden: ?

Klietmann, Kurt Gerhard. *Die Waffen-SS.* Osnabrück: 1965.

Krätschmer, E.G. *Die Ritterkreuzträger der Waffen-SS.* Göttingen: 1955.

Kurowski, Franz. *Die Panzer-Lehr-Division.* Bad Nauheim: 1964.

————. *Von den Ardennen zum Ruhrkessel.* Herford: 1965.

————. *Die Abwehr- und Rückzugskämpfe auf Sizilien.* Neckargemünd: 1966.

————. *Armee Wenck.* Neckargemünd: 1967.

————. *Deutsche Offiziere in Staat, Wirtschaft und Wissenschaft.* Herford: 1967.

Lange, Wolfgang. *Korpsabteilung C.* Neckargemünd: 1961.

Lasch, Otto. *So fiel Königsberg.* Munich: 1958.

Lohse, Gerhart. *Geschichte der 126. Infanterie-Division.* Bad Nauheim: 1957.

Lubs, Gerhard. *Geschichte des Panzergrenadier-Regiments 5.* Bochum: 1965.

Mackensen, Eberhard von. *Vom Bug zum Kaukasus.* Neckargemünd: 1967.

Manstein, Erich von. *Verlorene Siege.* Bonn: 1955.

Melzer, Erich. *Geschichte der 252. Infanterie-Division.* Bad Nauheim: 1960.

Memminger, Fritz. *Geschichte der Windhund-Division.* Bochum: 1962.

Merker, Ludwig. *Das Buch der 78. Sturmdivision.* Tübingen: 1956.

Metzsch, F. August. *Geschichte der 22. Infanterie-Division.* Kiel: 1952.

Meyer, Kurt. *Grenadiere.* Munich: 1956.

Manteuffel, Hasso von. *Die Schlacht in den Ardennen.* Frankfurt a.M.: 1960.

————. *Die 7. Panzer-Division im zweiten Weltkrieg.* Uerdingen: 1965.

Meyer-Detring, Wilhelm. *Die 137. Infanterie-Division im Mittelabschnitt der Ostfront.* Petzenkirchen: 1962.

Mellinthin, F.W. von. *Panzer-Schlachten.* Neckargemünd: 1963.

Middeldorf, Eike. *Taktik im Rußlandfeldzug.* Berlin: 1956.

Morozov, V.P. *Westlich von Woronesch.* East Berlin: 1959.

Montgomery, Bernard Law. *Von der Normandie zur Ostsee.* Hamburg: 1949.

Möller-Witten, Hans. *Männer und Taten.* Munich: 1959.

————. *Mit dem Eichenlaub zum Ritterkreuz.* Rastatt: 1962.

Moorehead, Alan. *Afrikanische Trilogie.* Braunschweig: 1948.

Muck, Richard. *Kampfgruppe Scherer.* Oldenburg: 1943.

Müller, Dr. W. *Die Sturmartillerie.* Berlin: ?

Munzel, Oskar. *Panzertaktik.* Neckargemünd: 1959.

————. *Gepanzerte Truppen.* Herford: 1965.

Murawski, Dr. Erich (Editor). *Der deutsche Wehrmachtsbericht, 1939–1944.* Boppard: ?

Payk, Ernst. *Geschichte der 206. Infanterie-Division.* Bad Nauheim: 1952.

Philippi, Alfred and Ferdinand Heim. *Der Feldzug gegen Sowjetrußland, 1941-1945.* Stuttgart: 1962.

Pickert, Wolfgang. *Vom Kuban-Brückenkopf bis Sewastopol.* Heidelberg: 1955.

Ploetz, A.G. *Geschichte des zweiten Weltkriegs.* Wurzburg: 1960.

Podzun, Hans-Henning. *Das deutsche Heer 1939.* Bad Nauheim: 1953.

―――. *Weg und Schicksal der 21. Infanterie-Division.* Bad Nauheim: 1951.

Pohlmann, Hartwig. *Geschichte der 96. Infanterie-Division.* Bad Nauheim: 1959.

―――. *Wolchow.* Bad Nauheim: 1962.

Popjel, Nikolaj K. *Panzer greifen an.* East Berlin: 1964.

Pottgiesser, Hans. *Die Reichsbahn im Ostfeldzug.* Neckargemünd: 1960.

Rathke, Artur. *Ewige Infanterie.* Berlin: 1942.

Redelis, Walter. *Partisanenkrieg.* Heidelberg: 1958.

Rehm, Walter. *Jassy.* Neckargemünd: 1959.

Rudel, Hans-Ulrich. *Aus Krieg und Frieden.* Göttingen: 1954.

Samsonov, Aleksandr M. *Die große Schlacht vor Moskau, 1941–1942.* East Berlin: 1959.

Scheibert, Horst. *Nach Stalingrad—48 Kilometer.* Heidelberg: 1956

―――. *Zwischen Don und Donez.* Neckargemünd: 1961.

Schelm, Walter. *Von den Kämpfen der 215. Infanterie-Division.* Stuttgart: 1955.

Schmidt, August. *Geschichte der 10. Infanterie-Division—10. Panzergrenadier-Division.* Bad Nauheim: 1963.

Schroeder, Jürgen. *Geschichte der 32. Infanterie-Division.* Bad Nauheim: 1956.

Schaub, Oskar. *Geschichte des Panzergrenadier-Regiments 12.* Bergisch Gladbach: 1957.

Schuler, Emil. *Infanterie im Kampf.* Darmstadt: 1963.

Senger und Etterlin, Frido von. *Krieg in Europa.* Cologne: 1960.

―――. *Die deutschen Panzer.* Munich: 1959.

―――. *24. Panzer-Division.* Neckargemünd: 1959.

―――. *1. Kavallerie-Division.* Neckargemünd: 1962.

Seemen, Gerhard von. *Die Ritterkreuzträger, 1939–1945.* Bad Nauheim: 1955.

Sevenich, Friedrich. *Geschichte des Infanterie-Regiments 521.* ?

Spaeter, Helmuth. *Geschichte des Panzer-Korps "Großdeutschland".* Duisburg: 1959.

Steets, Hans. *Gebirgsjäger zwischen Dnjepr und Don.* Heidelberg: ?

―――. *Gebirgsjäger in der Nogaiischen Steppe.* Heidelberg: ?

―――. *Gebirgsjäger bei Uman.* Heidelberg: ?

Stoves. Rolf O. *Die 1. Panzer-Division, 1935–1945.* ?

Strutz, Dr. Georg. *Die Tankschlacht bei Cambrai.* Berlin: 1929.

Teske, Hermann. *Bewegungskrieg.* Heidelberg: 1955.

―――. *Die silbernen Spiegel.* ?: 1952.

Thorwald, Jürgen. *Es begann an der Weichsel.* Stuttgart: 1949.

―――. *Das Ende an der Elbe.* Stuttgart: 1950.

―――. *Wen sie verderben wollen.* Stuttgart: 1952.

Tippelskirch, Kurt von. *Geschichte des zweiten Weltkriegs.* Bonn: 1951.

Toland, John. *Ardennenschlacht.* Bern: 1960.

Tornau, Gottfried and Franz Kurowski. *Sturmartillerie—Fels in der Brandung.* Herford: 1965.

Telpuchowski, S. *Die sowjetische Geschichte des großen Vaterländischen Krieges.* Frankfurt a.M.: 1961.

Trevor-Roper, H.R. *Hitlers letzte Tage.* Hamburg: 1947.

Vormann, Nikolaus von. *Tscherkassy.* Heidelberg: 1954).

Warlimont, Walter. *Im Hauptquartier der deutschen Wehrmacht.* Frankfurt a.M.: 1962.

Werth, Alexander. *Rußland im Krieg.* Munich: 1965.

Wilmot, Chester. *Der Kampf am Europa.* Frankfurt a.M.: 1954.

Westphal, Siegfried. *Heer in Fesseln.* Bonn: 1950.

Zimmermann, Hermann. *Der Griff ins Ungewisse.* Neckargemünd: 1964.

PERIODICALS

Barth, Hans G. *"Nonstop-Angriff auf Kiew."* 1941.

Bannert, Josef. *"Geschichte der 62. Volks-Grenadier-Division."* ?

Feig, Georg. *"Tauroggen—der erste Tag in Rußland."* ?

———. *"Nur noch zwei Tage, Beloy, Ende 1942."* ?

———. *"Kampf und Vorstoß auf Kalinin."* ?

———. *"Einsatz bei Mjednoje."* ?

———. *"Der Kampf um Gniletz."* ?

Kissel, Hans. *"Der deutsche Volkssturm."* ?

Kollatz, Karl. *"Sturm auf Woronesch."* ?

———. *"Feldwebel Rudolf Brasche."* ?

———. *"General der Panzertruppen von Manteuffel."* ?

———. *"Generalmajor Horst Niemack."* ?

———. *"Generalfeldmarschall Walter Model."* ?

———. *"Der Sturm der stählernen Kolosse."* ?

———. *"Eupatoria."* ?

———. *"Der Kampf um den Totendeich."* ?

———. *"Generalleutnant Martin Unrein."* ?

———. *"Generalleutnant von Wietersheim."* ?

———. *"Oberstleutnant Hogrebe."* ?

———. *"Obergefreiter Arndt."* ?

———. *"Nächte am Mius."* ?

Kügelgen, Dr. Helmut von. *"Die Nüchternen handeln."* ?

Nearing, Walther K. *"Der wandernde Kessel"* in Deutscher Soldatenkalender. ?

———. *"Das Ende der 1. Panzer-Armee"* in Deutscher Soldatenkalender. ?

———. *"18. Panzer-Division, 1941"* in Deutscher Soldatenkalender. ?

Polar, Dr. Hans. *"Panzerführer Eberbach."* ?

Reinhardt, Hans. *"Der Vorstoß des XXXXI. Armee-Korps (mot.) im Sommer 1941."* ?

Stilicho, Martin. *"Krisengefecht im Rahmen eider Kompanie."* ?

———. *"Krisengefecht im Rahmen seines Bataillons."* ?

———. *"Das seltsame Ski-Bataillon."* ?

———. *"Ohne Blumen—ein einfaches Grab."* ?

Wegener, Carl. *"Der Ausbruch der 1. Panzer-Armee aus dem Kessel von Kamenez-Podolsk."* ?

Index

Page numbers in italics indicate photographs

Stackpole Military History Series

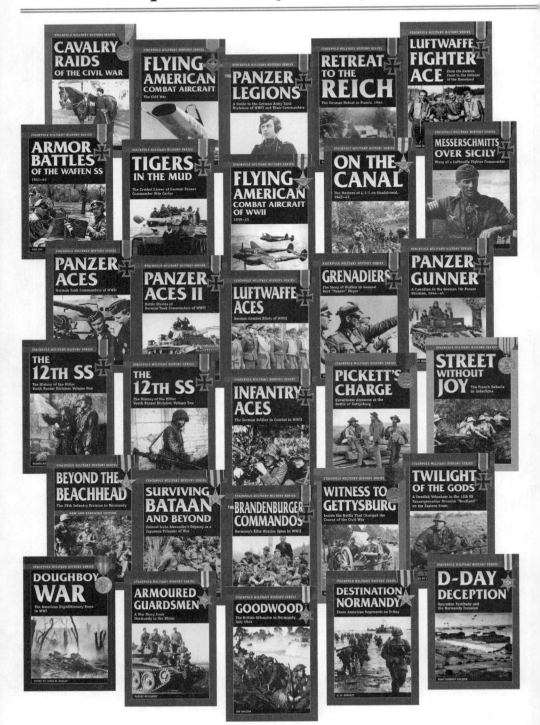

Real battles. Real soldiers. Real stories.

Stackpole Military History Series

Real battles. Real soldiers. Real stories.

Stackpole Military History Series

PANZER ACES III
STACKPOLE MILITARY HISTORY SERIES
German Tank Commanders in Combat in WWII
FRANZ

THE EARLY BATTLES OF EIGHTH ARMY
STACKPOLE MILITARY HISTORY SERIES
Crusader to the Alamein Line, 1941–42

PANZER-GRENADIER ACES
STACKPOLE MILITARY HISTORY SERIES
German Mechanized Infantrymen in WWII

BODEN-PLATTE
STACKPOLE MILITARY HISTORY SERIES
The Luftwaffe's Last Hope
JOHN MANRHO AND RON PUTZ

MIGS OVER NORTH VIETNAM
STACKPOLE MILITARY HISTORY SERIES
The Vietnam People's Air Force in Combat, 1965–75
ROGER BONIFACE

LUFTWAFFE FIGHTER-BOMBERS OVER BRITAIN
STACKPOLE MILITARY HISTORY SERIES
The Tip and Run Campaign, 1942–43
CHRIS G

THE RHODESIAN WAR
STACKPOLE MILITARY HISTORY SERIES
A Military History
ER MCLAUGHLIN

NEW for Fall 2010

CONDOR
STACKPOLE MILITARY HISTORY SERIES
The Luftwaffe in Spain
PATRICK LAUREAU

BLOSSOMING SILK AGAINST THE RISING SUN
STACKPOLE MILITARY HISTORY SERIES
U.S. and Japanese Paratroopers at War in the Pacific in WWII
GENE ERIC SALECKER

BLITZKRIEG UNLEASHED
STACKPOLE MILITARY HISTORY SERIES
The German Invasion of Poland, 1939
RICHARD HARGREAVES

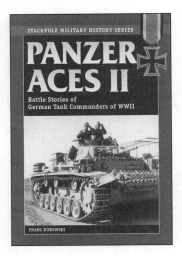

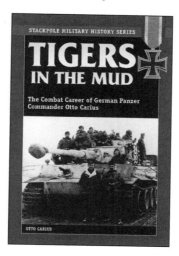

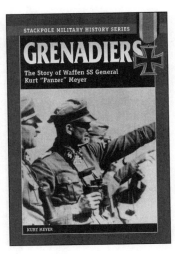

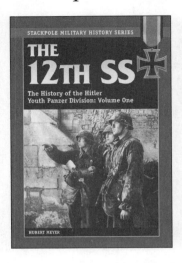
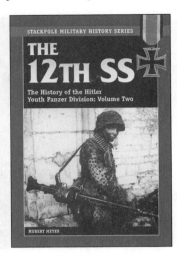

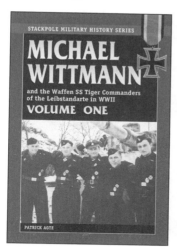
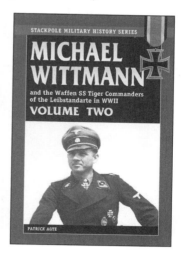

Stackpole Military History Series

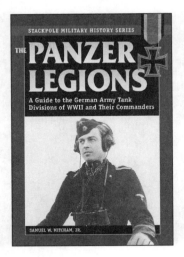

THE PANZER LEGIONS
A GUIDE TO THE GERMAN ARMY TANK DIVISIONS
OF WWII AND THEIR COMMANDERS
Samuel W. Mitcham, Jr.

Drawing on years of research and covering all of the
German Army's panzer divisions from their creation
through their destruction or surrender, Samuel Mitcham
chronicles the combat histories of the tank units that
formed the backbone of the Nazi war machine. He also
details the careers of the divisions' commanders, men like
Erwin Rommel and Heinz Guderian who revolutionized
modern warfare. In-depth and comprehensive, this is an
essential resource on German armor in World War II.

$19.95 • Paperback • 6 x 9 • 352 pages • 30 b/w photos • 8 maps

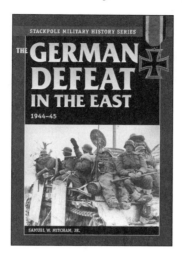

Stackpole Military History Series

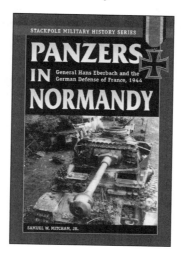

PANZERS IN NORMANDY
GENERAL HANS EBERBACH AND THE
GERMAN DEFENSE OF FRANCE, 1944
Samuel W. Mitcham, Jr.

In July 1944, after fighting in Poland, the invasion of France, and Russia and then serving as Heinz Guderian's troubleshooter, General of Panzer Troops Heinrich "Hans" Eberbach took command of Panzer Group West near the vital city of Caen in Normandy. During the next two months, Eberbach led German tank units in an ultimately vain attempt to stop the Allied breakthrough into France's interior. One of Germany's best panzer commanders, even Eberbach could not overcome supply shortages, flagging morale, and murderous Allied fighter-bombers. The British captured him at the end of August.

$18.95 • Paperback • 6 x 9 • 224 pages • 47 b/w photos, 14 maps

WWW.STACKPOLEBOOKS.COM
1-800-732-3669

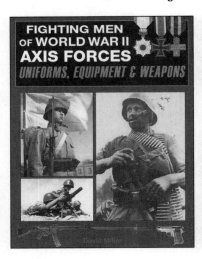
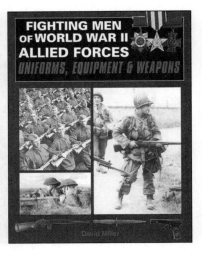